Portraits by Graham Sutherland

Cover
Max Egon, Prince von Fürstenberg, 1959 (No. 70)

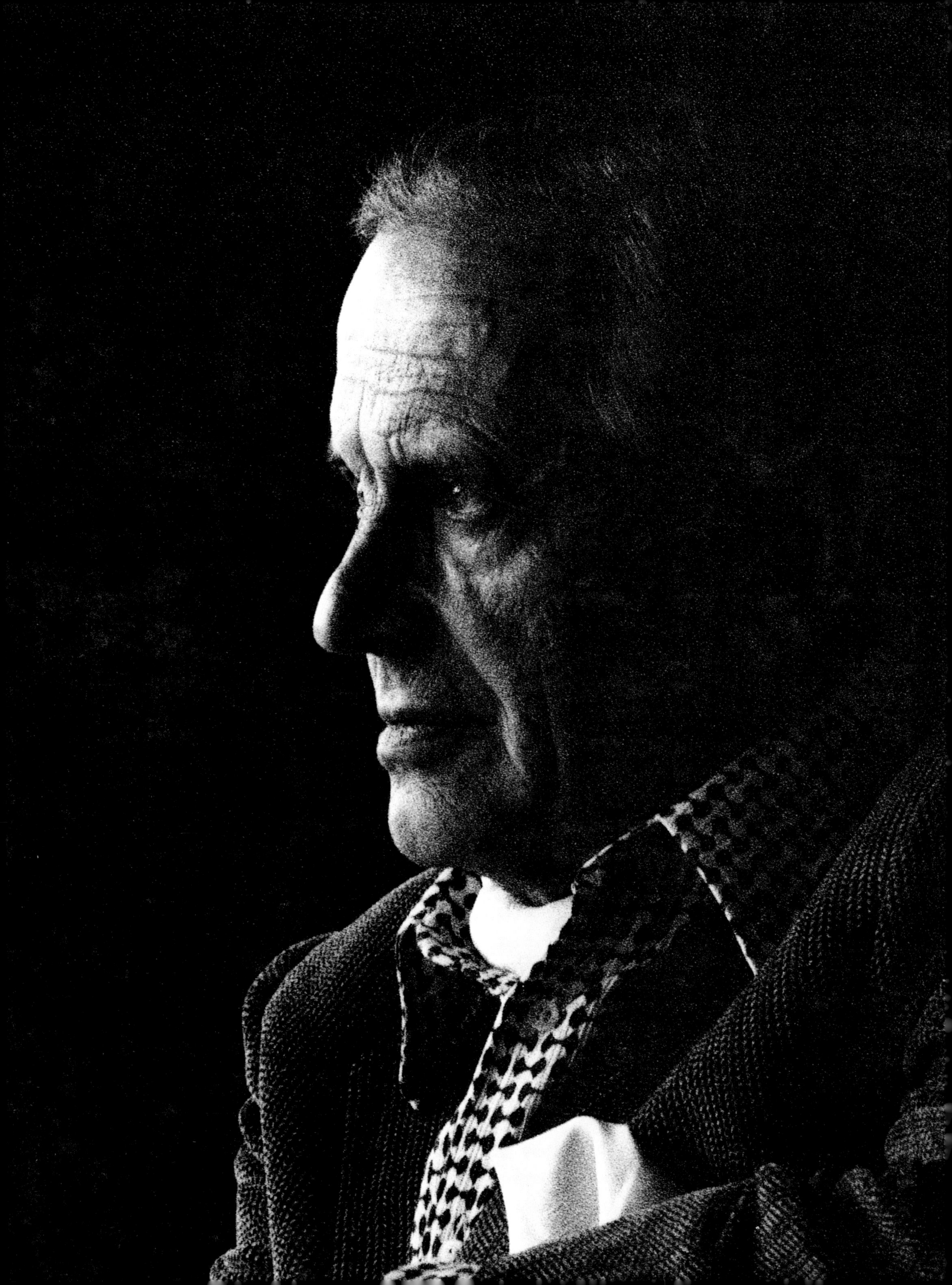

John Hayes

PORTRAITS BY GRAHAM SUTHERLAND

Frontispiece
Graham Sutherland, 1975
(Photograph: Romano Vada)

National Portrait Gallery

Contents

Published for the exhibition held at the
National Portrait Gallery from 24 June to 16 October 1977

Exhibition designed by Caroline Brown

ISBN 0 904017 18 4
Published by the National Portrait Gallery, London WC2H 0HE
Catalogue designed by Roger Huggett/Sinc
Printed by Westerham Press

Preface

Graham Sutherland stands in the front rank of the great British portrait painters of all time. In spite of his pre-eminence, however, and in spite of the fact that he has been active as a portraitist for nearly thirty years, no exhibition devoted solely to his portraiture has previously been held, and very few of his portraits are generally known. It is a rare thing for the National Portrait Gallery to be able to hold an exhibition of the work of a great living painter, and the Trustees are especially privileged and delighted that, during the summer of this Silver Jubilee year – twenty-five years, too, since Graham Sutherland undertook his greatest commission, the Coventry tapestry – their exhibition galleries at 15 Carlton House Terrace should be devoted to a retrospective of Mr Sutherland's portraits, a project first envisaged by my predecessor, Dr Roy Strong.

Such an exhibition could never have been contemplated without the enthusiastic and whole-hearted support of Mr Sutherland himself, and of his wife, Katharine, and my first debt is to Lady Hartwell, who introduced us, and in whose house the venture was originally discussed. We agreed that the exhibition must be restricted in scope and that the selection should be undertaken jointly; sadly, since the choice had to be limited, not every picture we would like to have shown could be included in our final list, though well over half of Sutherland's sitters are represented. Mr Sutherland has most generously allowed many of his surviving preparatory sketches and studies to be included – most generously because it is material which he regards as notational and normally destroys: these exhibits will be of inestimable value not only in illuminating his 'absorbent' and searching methods of work but for the full appreciation of the finished pictures themselves. Both Graham and Katharine Sutherland have been exceptionally patient with me during the period of preparation, and I am happy to place on record my immense gratitude to them for the hours of helpful and revealing conversation, the information they have provided from their own papers, the constant and ready help they have given over innumerable matters of detail and, not least, their encouragement and their generous hospitality. Graham Sutherland kindly recorded an interview, which is printed in the catalogue, and in this he has been at particular pains to make statements about his work which will supplement what he has already said elsewhere. He has also read the drafts of my introduction and catalogue entries (in the preparation of which my primary debt has been to Douglas Cooper's fine monograph), providing extra information at this stage and saving me from various errors of fact; the errors that may remain are my responsibility.

For some of the catalogue entries I have written detailed analytical notes. No doubt I shall be accused of being prolix; but the revelation of human personality in a portrait springs from the whole artistic conception and my excuse is that portraits are rarely discussed in these terms in exhibition catalogues. I have tried, throughout the text, to use the artist's own words as much as possible and all quotations are his, unless otherwise stated.

The universal esteem in which Mr Sutherland is held has been amply attested by the warmth of the replies to our requests for loans. Hardly anyone we approached has felt unable to lend, and many owners and curators have given additional help, notably in connection with photography. The Trustees are deeply appreciative, the more so because they recognize that private owners in particular have readily agreed, for the sake of the exhibition, to deprive themselves of works which have a very personal significance. I also wish to thank Mr Alfred Hecht, who has framed several pictures specially for the exhibition, Mr James Kirkman, Mr Gilbert Lloyd and Marlborough Fine Art Ltd, and the staffs of the libraries I have consulted, for kind assistance; and, far from least, Mr Felix H. Man for his characteristic courtesy in placing at my disposal his uniquely important photographs of Mr Sutherland at work.

John Hayes
Director
National Portrait Gallery
April 1977

Short bibliography

Graham Sutherland's principal writings on art and 'statements' about his own work

Graham Sutherland, 'A Trend in English Draughtsmanship', *Signature*, July 1936, pp. 7–13. An essay, profoundly revealing of his own creative processes, which is concerned with the approach to their subject-matter characteristic of 'subjective', as opposed to 'objective', artists, and illustrated by reference to Blake (chiefly), Palmer, Turner, Paul Nash and Henry Moore.

Henry Moore on Sculpture, edited by Philip James, London, 1966 (available in paperback), pp. 76–83. Includes the transcript of part of a radio discussion entitled *The Living Image: Art and Life* between V. S. (now Sir Victor) Pritchett, Sir Kenneth (now Lord) Clark, Henry Moore and Graham Sutherland, as printed in *The Listener*, 13 November 1941.

Graham Sutherland, 'Welsh Sketch Book', *Horizon*, April 1942, pp. 225–35 (reprinted in *Sutherland in Wales*, the Picton Castle Trust and the National Museum of Wales, London, 1976, pp. 11–15). An incisive, exact and deeply-felt description of the Pembrokeshire countryside which made him a painter. If Sutherland had not been an artist one feels that he might have chosen to be a poet. No admirer should fail to read this open letter to Sir Colin Anderson.

'Modern Art Explained by Modern Artists: Part I', *The Artist*, March 1944, pp. 17–18. Sutherland in conversation with R. Myerscough-Walker.

Letter to H. P. Juda, dated Trottiscliffe, 10 August 1950, printed in Melville, 1950 (see below).

Graham Sutherland, 'Thoughts on Painting', *The Listener*, 6 September 1951, pp. 376–8. Includes the artist's first remarks on portraiture, brief but important.

Statement dated 4 December 1951, printed in *Eight European Artists*, photographed and edited by Felix H. Man, London, n.d. (= 1954).

Sutherland: Christ in Glory in the Tetramorph, edited by Andrew Révai, London, 1964, pp. 26–83. A detailed discussion between Sutherland and Révai which explores every aspect of the genesis of the great tapestry for Coventry Cathedral.

Noel Barber, *Conversations with Painters*, London, 1964, pp. 43–53. The most extended, most autobiographical and most valuable of Sutherland's general statements, including a short account of his approach to portraiture and his methods as a portraitist.

The most important books on Sutherland's painting

Edward Sackville-West, *Graham Sutherland* (The Penguin Modern Painters), London, 1943 (revised edn. 1955). A deeply sensitive critique by one of Sutherland's close friends.

Robert Melville, *The Imagery of Graham Sutherland*, introduction to volume edited by H. P. Juda, London, 1950. An exceptionally revealing essay, written with the precision of poetry, which describes the workings of Sutherland's imagination.

Douglas Cooper, *The Work of Graham Sutherland*, London, 1961. A fully-documented, accurate and penetrating study, written with the full cooperation of the artist. Includes a long section on the portraits, 1949–60. This authoritative and masterly account is by far the best introduction to Sutherland's work, style and development. There are about 400 illustrations (15 in colour).

Francesco Arcangeli, *Graham Sutherland*, Milan, 1973 (English edition, New York, 1975). The author, though deeply moved by Sutherland's religious outlook, moral sense and personal anguish at a tormented world, concentrates on the artist's 'nature' painting. The text seeks to reveal the depths of Sutherland's imaginative processes but is not entirely easy either to understand or to interpret. The book is invaluable for its 222 (230) illustrations (about half of which are of works executed subsequent to the appearance of Douglas Cooper's book), and especially for its 113 (117) colour plates. None of the portraits is reproduced in the original Italian publication, but 8 have been added to the plates for the English edition.

Some of the principal events in Graham Sutherland's life

1903	Born on 24 August
1914–18	Went to school at Epsom College
1919–20	Apprentice at the Midland Railway works in Derby
1921–6	Studied at Goldsmiths' College of Art
1925	Elected an Associate of the Royal Society of Painter-Etchers and Engravers First one-man exhibition of drawings and engravings, at the XXI Gallery
1926	Converted to Roman Catholicism
1927	Married Kathleen Barry on 29 December
1928–39	Taught at Chelsea School of Art (engraving until 1932, then composition and book-illustration)
1931	Began to paint, following the decline of the market for etchings and engravings
1934	First visit to Pembrokeshire, which he revisited every summer until the War
1938	First one-man exhibition of paintings, at the Rosenberg and Helft Gallery
1940–5	Served as an official war artist
1944	First visit to Paris
1945	Bought the White House at Trottiscliffe, in Kent
1946	First one-man exhibition in New York, at Curt Valentin's Buchholz Gallery
1947	First visit to the South of France; began to work there for several months every year. First met Picasso and Matisse
1948	First portrait commission, from Somerset Maugham Appointed Trustee of the Tate Gallery
1952	Retrospective exhibition in the British Pavilion at the Venice Biennale. An enlarged version was subsequently shown at the Musée d'Art Moderne, Paris Commissioned to design the great tapestry for Coventry Cathedral
1953	Retrospective exhibitions in Amsterdam and Zürich, and at the Tate Gallery
1954	Resigned as Trustee of the Tate Gallery Painted the portrait of Sir Winston Churchill
1954–5	Retrospective exhibition circulated in Austria and Germany
1955	Bought a house at Menton, *La Villa Blanche*
1960	Awarded the Order of Merit
1962	Received Honorary Degree of Doctor of Literature in the University of Oxford
1965	Retrospective exhibition at the Galleria Civica d'Arte Moderna, Turin
1966	Retrospective exhibition at the Kunsthalle, Basel
1967	Retrospective exhibition circulated in Germany and Holland Revisited Pembrokeshire, where he has returned every year since
1972	Elected Honorary Fellow of the American Academy of Arts and Letters
1973	Appointed Commandeur des Arts et des Lettres, France, and Honorary Fellow of the Accademia di San Luca, Rome
1973–6	Engaged on work for the Picton Castle Trust (Graham Sutherland Foundation)
1974	Awarded the Shakespeare Prize, Hamburg (the first artist to be so honoured)
1976	Opening of the Graham Sutherland Gallery at Picton Castle in Pembrokeshire

Introduction

Sutherland's emergence as a portrait painter in his mid-forties was partly fortuitous. He had become acquainted with Somerset Maugham at St Jean Cap Ferrat, and casually remarked to a mutual friend that, had he been a portrait rather than a landscape painter, Maugham's remarkable head and personality were of precisely the kind that would have excited his pictorial imagination. Shortly afterwards, Maugham took up this oblique challenge and invited him to paint his portrait: Sutherland replied that 'if it can be regarded purely as an experiment I would very much like to try'. On the other hand, one must remember that portraits were nothing new for Sutherland – he had done them as a student, and his drawings of tin-miners made during his visit to Cornwall as a war artist in 1942 (Nos. 10–11) are not only accomplished but deeply moving; while, in a profound sense, 'portraiture', the exact description of isolated forms in nature, was the very essence of his study of landscape from the beginning of his career as a painter in the early 1930s. When Robert Melville was writing about one of his best-known early works, the *Gorse on Sea Wall* of 1939, he almost instinctively described it as a 'grave and noble portrait'.

On his first visit to Pembrokeshire in 1934 (and Pembrokeshire has continued to be the place to which he returns to nourish his imagination) Sutherland learnt that 'landscape was not necessarily scenic, but that its parts have an individual figurative detachment . . . the spaces and concentrations of this clearly constructed land were stuff for storing in the mind'. The particular, and the structure and convolutions of the particular, were what especially fascinated him. Out of the hundreds of shapes that came under his scrutiny during his daily walks, certain forms would dominate others, 'as if in response to some internal need of the nerves' – 'rare and hidden forms' which were the configurations that really started him off, things that might engage his attention one day and be totally lost to him when he passed the same way on the next.

Such configurations, and other more obviously 'picturesque' material, were the subjects of his sketches: hollow tree trunks, the branches and roots of trees, gorse, plants, rocks, some unusual 'juxtaposition of forms at a roadside' – the lineaments and shapes of which were suggestive of the mystery of organic growth. From this storehouse of sketches, gradually, sometimes after years of gestation, he developed images in his mind – metamorphoses of these natural forms, metamorphoses frequently involving a total loss of identity – that welled up from the subconscious and became the subjects of landscape compositions. These compositions nearly always remained as anthropomorphic in character as his original studies, and the relationships between shapes inspired by the study of inanimate nature and human or animal forms were often overt, as in such wholly different pictures as his *Red Monolith* of 1938 or his *Green Tree Form* of 1940. For Sutherland, landscape, and all its elements, bears the impress of the divine creation, of which he seeks to catch a reflection. 'It is a question of bringing out the anonymous personality of these things; at the same time they must bear the mould of their ancestry'.

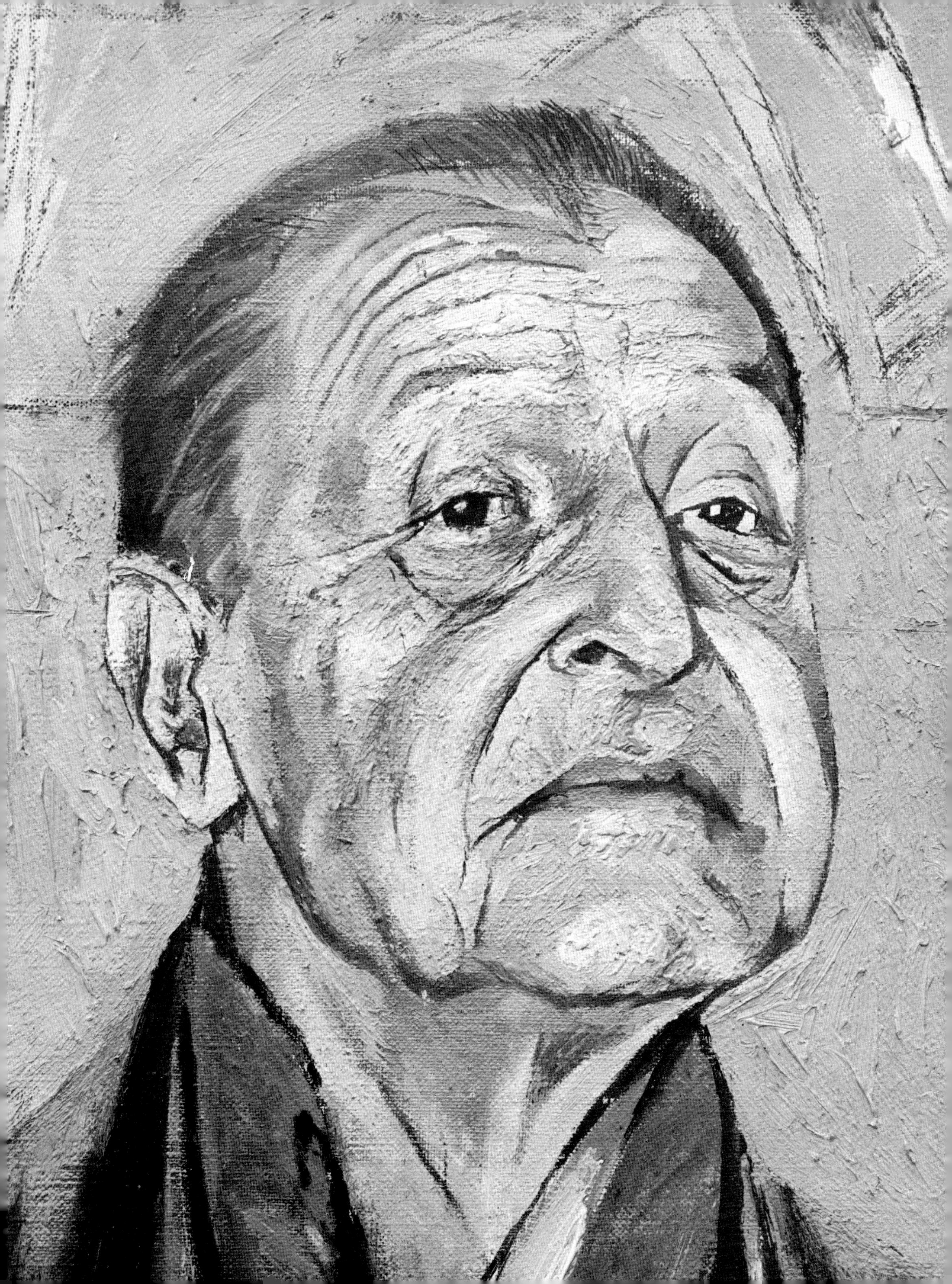

Maugham's invitation of 1948 awakened a specific interest that had been part of Sutherland's general world of ideas for twenty years or more; but it also raised questions of method and technique that were fundamentally at variance with his practice in landscape. There, as Robert Melville has put it perfectly, 'his draughtsmanship has a faltering, anxious quality, and, like Cézanne, he has had to be on guard against his talents and the pride of hand that could so easily make firm, precise, plausible inventions. Instead, he turns, with all his nerves exposed, to watch living substance'. Transmutation, what the artist calls 'paraphrase', was essential to his nature work; and Sutherland is instinctively a 'subjective' artist, whose 'experience of physical things . . . become[s] absorbed in the reservoir of the subconscious mind out of which emerge the reconstructed and re-created images'. For portraiture, however, accuracy and precision of draughtsmanship are obviously prerequisites. Here lay a dilemma which had to be resolved. Francis Bacon has pertinently enquired: 'Who today has been able to record anything that comes across to us as a fact without causing deep injury to the image?' And, as Sutherland later wrote: 'Skill . . . can be a dangerous thing to come by, and so easily destroy understanding and the will and ability to understand'.

But skill was in Sutherland's bones. His great-grandfather was an engineer and was involved, amongst other enterprises, with the construction of the great market hall in Derby, built in 1864. In 1919 he himself became an engineer, joining his uncle at the Midland Railway works in the same town, where he spent a year as an apprentice. Decades later, when he spoke of the thorn trees and bushes which inspired his 'thorn pictures' (No. 2), it was a simile from those early years – from his love of geometry – that naturally occurred to him: 'they were like dividers', he wrote, 'pricking out the points in space in all directions'. When he went to art school, it was the craft and technical problems involved in printmaking that most attracted him, and, under the guidance, first of Osborne and Anderson, then of F. L. Griggs, as an engraver and etcher that he made his reputation. Sutherland's delight in techniques, in craftsmanship for its own sake, in precision – whether in art, thought or speech – has endured from that day to this. The perfect drawing, an exact phrase, a beautifully constructed machine: all these things matter to him.

Thus likeness has always been the essential ingredient in Sutherland's portraiture: not, of course, what people loosely call a 'speaking likeness', but 'the result of an attempt to fuse all the characteristic directions, movements, and tensions of the head and body into terms of paint'. Such close observation and analysis of externals – every, apparently surface, aspect and idiosyncratic movement of an individual – Sutherland regards as vital to representation on the deepest level. For 'in falsifying physical truth', he writes, 'you falsify psychological truth'. Accordingly, with each commission, he draws incessantly from the life, filling whole sketchbooks with notations of the face, its proportions, lineaments and complexion, seen from different positions and under different conditions of light, of features and conjunctions of features – notations that become gradually more immaculate as he gets to know the sitter better. Characteristic expressions, movements, gestures are marked down, accurately and remorselessly. 'I have to be as absorbent as blotting-paper and as patient and watchful as a cat . . . It is a matter of accepting rather than imposing. It is also an art of letting the subject gradually reveal himself unconsciously so that by his voice and gaze as well as by his solid flesh your memory and emotions are stirred and assaulted, as with other forms of nature'. Douglas Cooper summed up this process with his customary succinctness: 'Sutherland's practice amounts to waiting while the sitter reveals himself and

Figure 1
W. Somerset Maugham
Detail from No. 27

composes his own portrait'.

It is this assimilative procedure, not so far removed, after all, from the way in which his ideas for landscapes matured in the recesses of his mind, that accounts for the extraordinary originality of Sutherland's portraits. When the portrait of Somerset Maugham (No. 27) was exhibited, it caused the kind of shock to the public imagination that must have been encountered by artistic circles in Rome during the early 1570s when El Greco's portraits emerged from his studio in Palazzo Farnese. The accepted conventions of portrait painting no longer possessed substance, though they lingered on.

Sutherland had been deeply affected by the work of Picasso in the early post-war years, and greatly admires Picasso's portraits for their strong likenesses, 'psychological truth' achieved 'by unlikely means': he recalls, for example, his instant recognition, at the Café de Flore, of Dora Maar, whom he had never seen before, from Picasso's penetrating likeness in his distorted portraits of her. Examples of their occasional influence on his work can be found as late as his *Head against Leaves* of 1963. It might have been expected, therefore, that his first portraits, of around 1950, at a time when he was feeling his way, would have shown signs of this admiration, perhaps even followed Picasso's 'way of thinking'. They did not. In portraiture he felt no such urge. 'Painters are affected by things which come to them from all over the place; from many kinds of painting and from many things. One absorbs what one needs at a given time', and, one may add, for a given purpose. In fact, Sutherland, like most great artists, and no doubt especially because he was a teacher for a number of years, has a profound knowledge of the history of art. As far as portraiture is concerned, he is an admirer, on the one hand, of the great draughtsmen, Holbein and Ingres, on the other, of Titian and Tintoretto and the leading painters of the Spanish school: El Greco, Velazquez and, above all, Goya. Most of these artists have contributed to his style at some point and in some measure, though rarely specifically; but, from the outset, his approach was governed by his own work in other fields.

Both in his religious works and in his paintings of thorn trees and pergolas of the late 1940s Sutherland had been moving steadily towards a monolithic concept of design, in which his subjects became self-contained organisms; this development reached a logical conclusion in his many paintings of *Standing Forms* (No. 5), which span the years 1949–53. 'Perhaps one of the reasons why I have recently tried to do portraits', he wrote in 1951, 'is that it is possible that I feel the need to narrow the gap between my 'stand in' monuments and the real human animal. I cannot say for certain. It is difficult to say where the things with which one is involved at the moment are likely to lead one'. Certainly his 'monumental' images might spring from an initial study of the human form. In the process of working out his ideas for the massive *Christ in Glory* for Coventry Cathedral, he started by drawing from the life, gradually bringing to these sketches a more hieratic and superhuman quality (Nos. 16–17).

At all events, there can be do doubt that Sutherland's concept of portraiture was deeply influenced by the strength, grandeur and sense of organic unity with which he imbued his *Standing Forms*. Three of his early portraits – of Somerset Maugham (No. 27), Lord Beaverbrook and Edward Sackville-West (No. 51), though showing the figure seated (his only full-length with the figure standing is that of Lord Bath), are not only equally self-contained in conception and substantially without background, but executed, most unusually for full-length portraits, on canvases of the exceptionally narrow width characteristic of his single *Standing*

Form compositions. Moreover, Sutherland has continued to think in these terms, though with more flexibility. His portrait of *Lord Rayne* (No. 85), painted in 1968–9, is a striking example of his prediliction towards the monolithic, grander than any of his early portraits save the *Churchill*. One may remark also his strong dislike both of casualness in design and of cutting the figure: the compositions of *Prince von Fürstenberg* (No. 70), *Lord Rayne* (No. 85), *Baron Elie de Rothschild* (No. 86), *Adolf Jann* (Figure 11) and *Giorgio Soavi* (No. 93) literally spring from the sitters' shoes, as if from a generator which sets the rhythms of their pictorial invention in motion. Even where, for various reasons, aesthetic or practical, the figure is truncated – as in the case of the portraits of Lord Beaverbrook, Helena Rubinstein (No. 63), Maja Sacher and the second version of Adolf Jann (No. 92), the compositions are no less bold and broadly conceived. The casualness which seemed to him appropriate for the *pose* in one of his most recent portraits, that of Pierre Schlumberger (No. 99), is counterbalanced by an emphatic design based on interlocking horizontal, vertical and diagonal forms of some weight. His approach is exactly the opposite to an artist such as Degas.

Weight, and the purely physical attributes of the body, have always been of consequence to Sutherland. He has sketched the human form all his life, often as a form of relaxation in the evenings, and, like his great contemporary, Henry Moore, he is incapable of sketching without at the same time describing the precise relationship of the body to the 'pull' of its surroundings, whether it be a chair in which a girl is happily slumped (No. 12) or the Cross upon which Christ has been impaled, as in his studies for the Northampton *Crucifixion*. A feeling for weight, monolithic form, which is almost synonymous with what he calls 'great *contained* vitality', and background colour carefully determined in relation to the tonality of the head – not always, therefore, bright and 'Post-Impressionist' in hue – have gone hand in hand in his portraits.

There are, of course, differences between the earlier and the later portraits, but largely in technique and finesse rather than in intention. Even the technical differences, however, are more a matter of changing emphasis than anything and, as one would expect from Sutherland's approach to his sitters – 'accepting rather than imposing' – the technique tends to vary in individual portraits more than it does over a period of time. Though certain developments can be distinguished, one should hesitate 'to oversimplify – to label, and to pigeonhole'.

In the case of the *Somerset Maugham* the sketches from life were followed by elaborate drawings of the head done in the studio (Nos. 20–21), drawings which accentuated the 'picturesque' folds, pouches and wrinkles of Maugham's countenance and were, in Douglas Cooper's words, 'the same sort of expression of the process of growth and struggle as he found in the rugged surfaces and irregular contours of a boulder or a range of hills'. It is symptomatic of Sutherland's specific preoccupations in his work on Maugham's head that he should have traced it onto the canvas, the first and last time he adopted this procedure. A similar, linear, approach to his subject is apparent in the multiplicity of folds and creases in the clothes in the finished canvas, a tendency towards the 'picturesque' also evident in Sutherland's second portrait, that of Lord Beaverbrook, but which was subsequently eradicated from his style; the *Beaverbrook*, one may add, is the only portrait which was conceived with the kind of curtained background traditional in European portraiture, vestigial though this is. No colour notes were made for the *Maugham* because Sutherland has an exceptionally good memory for colour – 'the "baby" translucence of Churchill's skin or the parchment of Maugham was easy to remember' – and considered his overall conception as the most important element to keep clear in his mind, a point of view which also explains why he painted the finished portrait in the studio, away from his sitter – a practice from which he has never deviated. 'Form is more difficult [than colour or atmosphere] . . . I find it distracting to have somebody in front of me . . . You know how the idea of a person forms itself in your mind, generally quite clearly? And then, when you look again, you find so many other features that the original conception is obliterated'. Some element of 'paraphrase' is thus bound to occur in a portrait by Sutherland, but the degree of generalisation or personal emphasis is controlled by the interpretation at which he has already arrived after constant watchfulness before the sitter.

In his later portraits Sutherland has usually employed a system of squaring-up for the transference of his drawings from the life to the finished work; close inspection will show the pencilled grid visible beneath the paint. He has also customarily done oil sketches in front of the sitter, because he has come to regard exactness of tone and colour, of a greater degree of subtlety than he can retain in his memory, as of prime importance, not only for its own sake in marking down truth, but for determining the whole colour scheme of a portrait. Most of these sketches, in common with his drawings and first notations (and countless 'finished' works with which he was dissatisfied), Sutherland has usually destroyed. We are especially fortunate, therefore, in the present exhibition, that the accident of preservation has enabled us to study almost every stage in his work on the *Maugham* and the *Churchill*, and, in the case of the Adolf Jann, a sequence of composition studies (Nos. 88, 89 and 91) which demonstrate his gradual refinement of the conception in his mind. *La vérité est dans une nuance*. Careful comparison of these rough preparatory sketches for the pose in the *Jann* illuminates that 'hair's breadth' between the possible answer to an artistic problem and the solution which seems afterwards to have been inevitable, the 'hair's breadth' which distinguishes a great work of art from a mediocre. As regards the head itself Sutherland is only too aware that 'the look of a face can be so easily due to the tiniest difference in proportion or the slightest extra touch and this sometimes merely because one has put a spot of paint in the wrong place . . . One can make a face very sentimental or quite the reverse just by a touch'.

The brushwork in Sutherland's portraits has also altered with the development of an interest in tone which is complementary to, and sometimes more important than, his linear description. Line now assumes an additional function, and becomes an agency of highlight or movement, as in the *Rayne* (No. 85), the *Mark Longman* (No. 94) or the *Jann* (No. 92) (where it suggests the swing of the swivel chair). Thus, where the application of paint in the *Maugham* was rough and vigorous, but followed the demarcation of forms and planes, in the later portraits it is less sweeping and serves to create form. The head and hands in the *Sackville-West* (No. 51) are modelled richly, but tonally. Even in the *Adenauer* (No. 79), where line remains crucial to the portrayal, it is the modulation of tints, arbitrary if considered as local colour, that effectively shapes the structure of the head; in such a portrait as the *Paul Sacher* (No. 58) the touch is the essential instrument of modelling. Colour is also used to add vibrancy, as with the scatter of flickering red highlights in the *Elie de Rothschild* (No. 86). What is most generally true of the later portraits is that nothing either in Sutherland's conception or his handling is wasted; nothing is merely 'picturesque', everything has its purpose and is subordinate to the interpretation of character.

Figure 2 (opposite)
Dr Paul Sacher
Detail from No. 58

The revelation of personality has not always come easily. With a sitter like

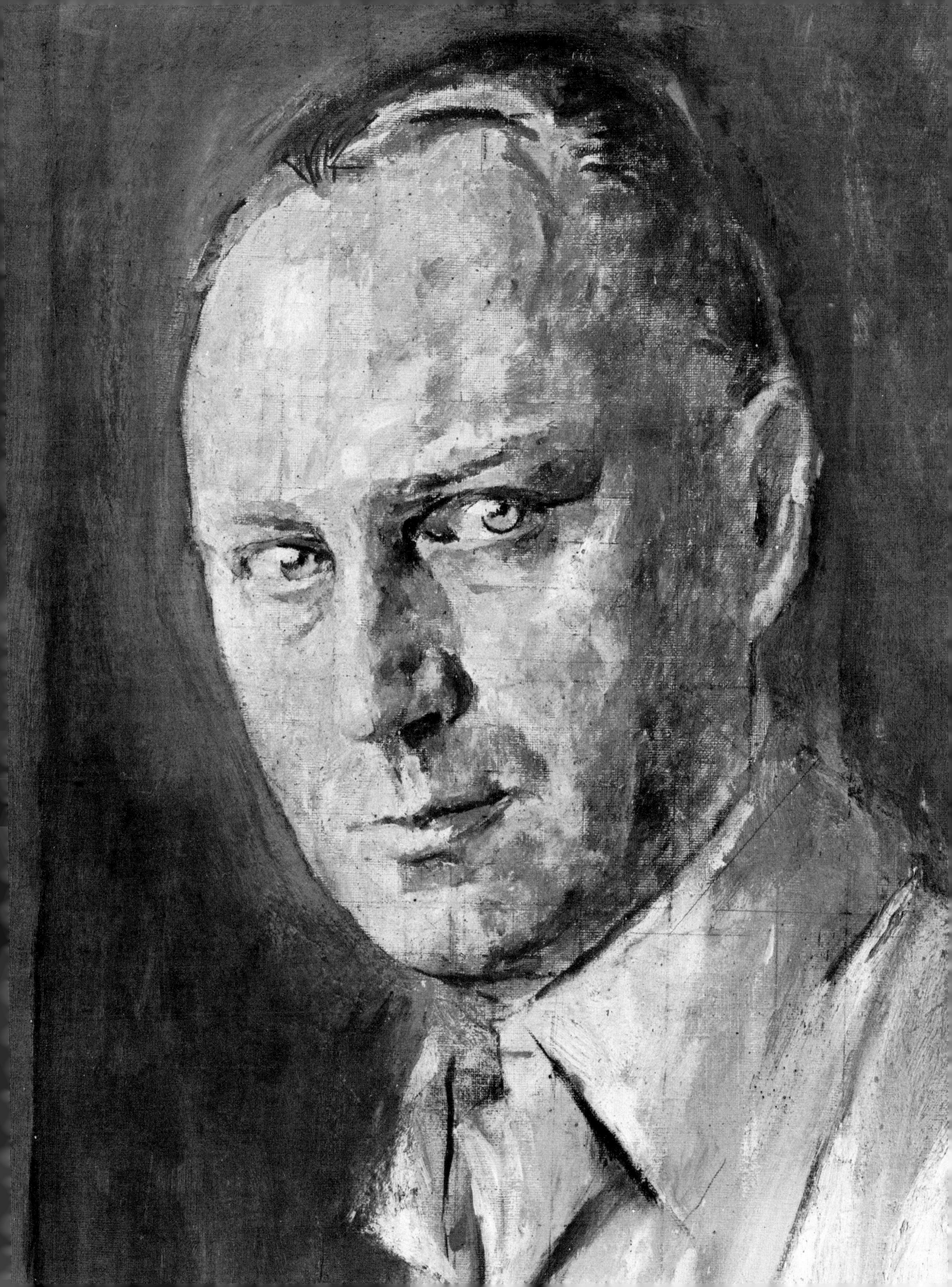

Sackville-West there was no problem; the complexities of his character were familiar from a long friendship. But some sitters, as every portraitist discovers, have sought to disguise their true nature. Others may seem impenetrable: in the case of Dr Adenauer, Sutherland only felt he had touched the nerve when he accompanied the former Chancellor on a trip across a lake to watch a firework display, and suddenly saw him as if for the first time, solitary and aloof, in the bows of the boat. Sutherland does not take on many commissions. He has painted fewer than forty sitters in the course of nearly thirty years. All of them have either been creative persons or people who have wielded some degree of power or responsibility: statesmen, churchmen, industrialists, financiers, lawyers, patrons of the arts, publishers, writers, musicians. Only certain kinds of personality and certain kinds of face appeal to him; it is the physical element that is of first importance, and the particular conjunctions of features in an individual which may happen to attract him visually are like the 'rare and hidden forms' in nature at the root of his landscape invention. His resulting physical descriptions are as exact – and can be unbearably so to the vanity of the sitter (one portrait, but one only, has been rejected by the client) – as his scrutiny of landscape.

Landscape slowly brought Sutherland to portraiture; portraiture, in its turn, has improved his memory for the structure of landscape forms. Both are contibutory to his ultimate purpose as a painter, the ever-continuing evolution of an imagery which reflects not only his passionate feelings and love of colour but his even deeper sense of the organic unity of all created things, his belief in a natural order, his increasing feeling for symmetry and control and his human compassion, values derived in part from his Roman Catholic faith and in part from the long-enduring happiness of his marriage, the twin sources of his equanimity in face of a troubled world, the weakness of the 'human animal', and his own conscience.

Conversation with Graham Sutherland

JH Your Standing Forms *more or less coincide with the beginnings of your engagement with portrait painting and – as you wrote at the time yourself – it looks very much as though they may have been related in some distinct way to this new preoccupation. If this is so, what were the reasons which made you feel it necessary to experiment with these substitutions for the human figure?*

GS The standing forms stemmed from seeing figures in gardens – half hidden in shade. At the time, I wanted to try and do forms in such a setting which were not figures but parallel to figures – figures once removed. When I started to do portraits, they were – and have in some ways remained – experiments – studies akin to the studies I would make in front of any object; and my chief preoccupation was to analyse the forms in front of my eyes and get as near to the person as I could. All else was crowded out.

JH You have come to portraiture after years of the most patient and loving scrutiny of landscape, in which you have concentrated upon the delineation – indeed the isolation – of very specific shapes and forms which have excited your curiosity. Do you find that it is the structure of the head, perhaps even particular conjunctions of features and not the head as a whole, that really stimulates and absorbs you in a certain individual and makes you wish to portray him?

GS This is a complicated question. There are certain conjunctions of form and shape which for one's personality seem right. Why this is so – why one is astonished by these particular relationships, while others do not touch one, is a mystery. When they do they announce themselves immediately.

JH Do you find that these conjunctions of features – and the folds and lines and wrinkles which gradually develop into the contours of an unmistakably individual human face – in fact intimately reveal the character of the person you are portraying?

GS I think essentially they do. They are some indication of the way a face has been used. But although they underline this usage, and sometimes emphasise the contours, they are only one indication. It is not generally realised how drastic the gradually formed changes are from youth to age. Of course, a few people scarcely change. But one has only to look at a sequence of photographs to see what I mean.

JH Does this mean that you would normally prefer to paint older people, rather than young people in whose faces the lines are necessarily less marked?

GS Not necessarily: but older people are more patient as subjects. Children are restless – the middle-aged, especially women, are always consciously or unconsciously 'arranging' their faces. But a child often has the built-in characteristics of what it will become: discontented – arch – or angelic. And a perfection of form is, of course, literally a perfection of form: there are lines in a young child's face which are not only very revealing but very beautiful. But I must agree that the last state of man holds for me the greatest interest. He has faced the responsibilities and temptations of life.

JH What exactly do you mean by what you call the 'atmosphere' of a person?

GS Everyone has their own aura – their particular mark – their unique individuality – their way of talking – their movement – their 'smell'. People may hide their timidities by a display of forcefulness. Layer upon layer of wrappings cover their real personality.

JH Do you usually manage to discover what it is that people are hiding? This must be exceedingly important for the success of the portrait in absolute terms.

GS To try to discover what people are hiding is not – deliberately and consciously, at least – the business of the painter. If one *sees* acutely enough the evidence is automatically there. Therefore my concern is primarily with the physical evidence. If I understand enough of the forms I see, the rest follows. That is not to say that one does not develop one's private speculations. Evidence such as the sound of a person's laugh – or speech – rests in one's memory too, and can be immensely important, when recalled in tranquillity, in assessing one's work. One looks at one's work and thinks: 'Could this person I have painted really talk and laugh in the way I have heard?' But how can one really – deeply – know another person? Again, therefore, one returns to the facts before one's eyes.

JH How important is it to you to have known a sitter well beforehand, as you did with Edward Sackville-West?

GS It is a help to have known a person. Conversation is easier; the atmosphere is more relaxed. The inevitable wall between oneself and the subject is thinner. With a person one has only just met one is talking and at the same time trying to mark down on paper the essential series of expressions that form on his face.

JH Is the camera of any help to you in marking down these essential series of expressions from which your final interpretation of personality is derived?

GS The camera is only sometimes of real use to me. The subject tends to freeze more under its lens than before the human eye. (The latter case is bad enough!) It is highly useful in making an inventory of positions from which to choose quickly, and it can be a guide to proportion. Only very rarely can it lead me directly to the real person.

JH Do you often find that what a sitter thinks is a characteristic position is not so to you?

GS Yes. What *is* sitting well? The subject does not usually know. For me it is when the subject composes himself in such a way that the forms, while full of diversity, complexity and variety, yet have a rhythm which holds them all together

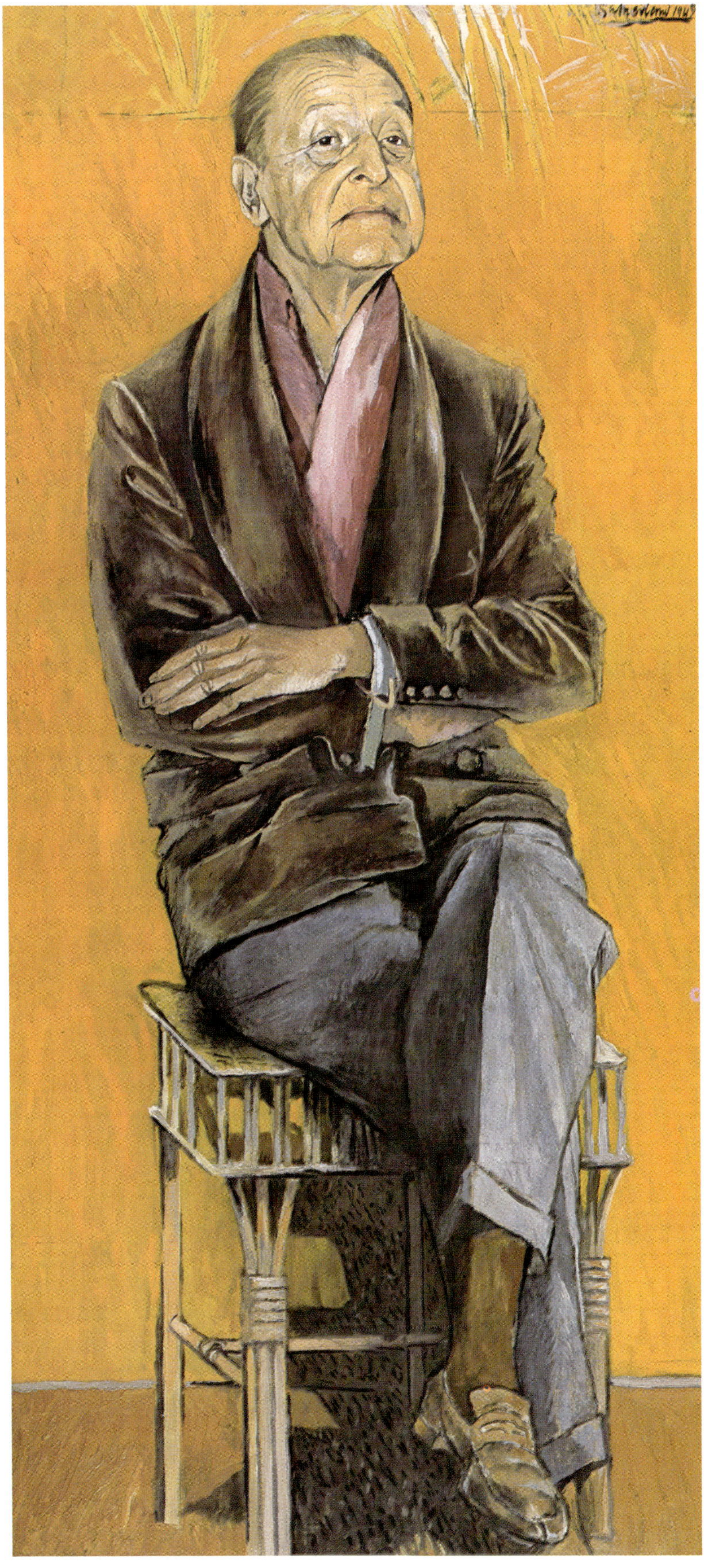

Colour plate 1
W. Somerset Maugham,
1949 (No. 27)

– where the movements and gestures coalesce as in a piece of music, where the complexities are so dovetailed as to form a single – inevitable – movement. If a subject so arranges himself in a way outside such a solution – in a way which does not 'work' – one is up against it. And it is no good trying to impose a position. Each person has his own way of sitting down, crossing his legs, moving his hands – a whole series of actions – the important thing is to contain these actions within a single rhythm, the maximum action in repose.

JH You say that everyone has their own individual way of moving their bodies. I wonder if there are also historical changes to be observed in the way people move.

GS Movements – positions – modes of walking – change drastically over periods of years. It would be interesting to make a comparative vocabulary of the changes of movements. In the history of portrait painting poses were imposed, as fashion dictated: heroic – noble – 'a class apart' – godlike – intimate – sentimentally downtrodden and defeated. It is only a painter such as Rembrandt who is really apart and natural and above such artificialities.

JH After you have finished the process of 'stalking' your sitter, what about the composition of the actual portrait? Does this suggest itself almost inevitably?

GS Naturally there are many ways of laying out the composition. But in a portrait – unlike any other figure composition – one can only work from the given facts. To obviate desperately unfortunate, awkward movements: what can one do? Accept them in the belief that the very awkwardness itself is interesting is one solution – or suppress them? Sometimes I would like to use a great deal more shadow to obscure certain elements which I don't like or which do not seem to me very interesting. Rembrandt's use of chiaroscuro was surely not simply a means of obtaining mystery: it was as much to isolate the areas of acute interest and to suppress the elements of lesser interest. Thus parts of the figure were all but obscured.

JH You have spoken of your dislike of 'cutting' the figures in your compositions, of informality. Is this something to do with your whole conception of portraiture, or is it a more practical problem?

GS These things are really connected. It is true that I like the whole movement of a composition to be contained within the canvas, as though in a vacuum. But sometimes one has to cut because of particular circumstances: for example, I may be working on a smaller canvas and not wish to reduce the size of the figure. The tyranny of the edge of the canvas, where to end the movement, is always a great problem with any kind of painting. Ingres had this problem in many of his portraits, and he was very successful in solving it. In the case of a female portrait, it is not so difficult, because a dress presents fewer problems. But trousers are very uncompromising, and not very elegant. Where to make the cut between the knee and the foot is not easy. In the case of my portrait of Dr Adenauer, the transitions were less abrupt because the tone was dark and the edge of the canvas was 'lost'.

JH How do you reconcile your feeling for precision of drawing, of definition of form, with any attempt at 'paraphrase'? Clearly the two are not contradictory, as might seem to be the case, superficially, and the decision to incline in one or other direction must, I suppose, vary constantly according to the kind of 'truth' you are trying to reveal, whether in landscape or in portraiture.

GS The degree of paraphrase does vary according to the kind of truth one wishes to express. In my 'nature paintings' the degree of paraphrase – or metamorphosis – is greater than in my portraits. I have said that my so-called 'nature paintings' are metaphors. With unfamiliar things, I am interested in pointing out their nature, and indeed their very presence, by a system of comparisons or parallels: reality told in a different way. In other words I am attempting to announce something that nobody looks at. But as far as people ever really look at anything, they *do* look at faces: and as the human head is interesting enough to me also I try to understand its essence by more direct means. The question of 'likeness' of course goes far beyond the question of simple physical likeness.

JH Are you almost inevitably drawn to make slight exaggerations in the delineation of certain features in order to accentuate your interpretation of a personality as a whole?

GS Of course one makes exaggerations. If one does six drawings of a subject they are bound to vary. What controls these variations is one's emotional involvement. One draws or paints in a way which one's emotions always direct. Emotion can alter the form itself, to a greater or lesser degree. One's versions vary also according to the skill, or lack of it, of one's hand.

JH To what extent does your emotion also affect the colours you use?

GS Colour is affected of course. For the 'scheme' I often use colour arbitrarily but very much with a view to the subject's own 'colour'. The face gives the clue, and one tries to arrive at an ensemble which is geared to the first statement – the head or the figure and clothes. Everything else springs from that.

JH You have used the term 'obscurity' a good deal in talking about art in general. Do you think – going beyond this whole question of 'paraphrasing' – that an element of obscurity is essential in portraiture, as in any other form of art, in order to affect the spectator on a far deeper level than his conscious mind?

GS Obscurity is generally misunderstood. It has been said that 'the heart and eye cannot express all they feel direct' – so we sometimes deflect reality. Castiglione has said: 'If the words used by a writer or poet carry with them, I will not say difficulty – but recondite wit – they give greater authority to the writing and cause the reader to be *more attentive and ponder more*' (my italics). In portrait painting – since the human head is obscure enough – I do not feel, at least for the moment, like making it more so. I do not want to put too much distance between the subject and the spectator. The face itself is an obscurity.

JH Does this belief of yours about the mystery inherent in the human face help to explain why the sitters in your portrait compositions are hardly ever surrounded by anything except perfectly placed abstract lines and shapes?

GS I am mainly interested, as I said earlier, in displaying the subject with all its diversities, as a unit. What I put in the background is usually to stabilize the movements and to help preserve an equilibrium as perfect as possible in the given circumstances: the exception being that I sometimes try to use a garden background or a hint (in some specialised cases) of an opulence of taste on the part of the subject.

JH You normally paint very thinly indeed. Is this in some sense a self-discipline? Or would you merely find it detracted from your essential purpose to build up form with the rich and complex paint layers characteristic of Rembrandt?

GS I don't really know. Some painters have painted thickly, others thinly. Personally, I like a system where the shadows are comparatively thin, with only the lights thick, but I don't always adhere to that: I try various different ways of painting a head. It could be that if I have put down a little truth in a way I want that I am afraid of losing it – I like to preserve the freshness and bite of the canvas until the last moment. If I lose the first statement I would probably start again.

JH Does this mean that you very often make two full-scale portraits of a particular sitter?

GS Occasionally more than two – sometimes five or six. I make these for two reasons. Firstly to be able to compare one statement with another and secondly to preserve freshness – in other words, to be able to go on working without losing what one has already achieved. This multiplication is also seen in my notebook drawings and for much the same reason.

JH So yours is really the opposite approach to an artist such as Constable, who would often go on and on until he had almost literally clogged a composition with excessive reworking?

GS Yes. Some painters can continue to preserve a freshness in such reworkings. I remember one painter who admired Constable very much saying that, if he could bring the canvas into a real mess, almost a muddle, he had the technical ability, once it was dry again, to use what was underneath almost as if he was emphasising and reiterating something that he was saying, so that, of course, the texture of the paint was often a fascinating texture for that reason. Freshness is often a matter of luck.

JH But you don't believe positively in luck, do you, in the way that Francis Bacon does, for example?

GS I believe a great deal in luck. The *whole thing* is a matter of luck: of inspiration – controlled by knowledge. When a statement is a lucky statement one should seize it with both hands and make all subsequent statements spring from this. A lot depends on how one is feeling. If you make twenty studies, of any subject you like, one – maybe – is the lucky one.

JH Has your actual procedure, the kind of sketches and studies you make, altered very much in the course of the twenty-five years or so in which you have been painting portraits?

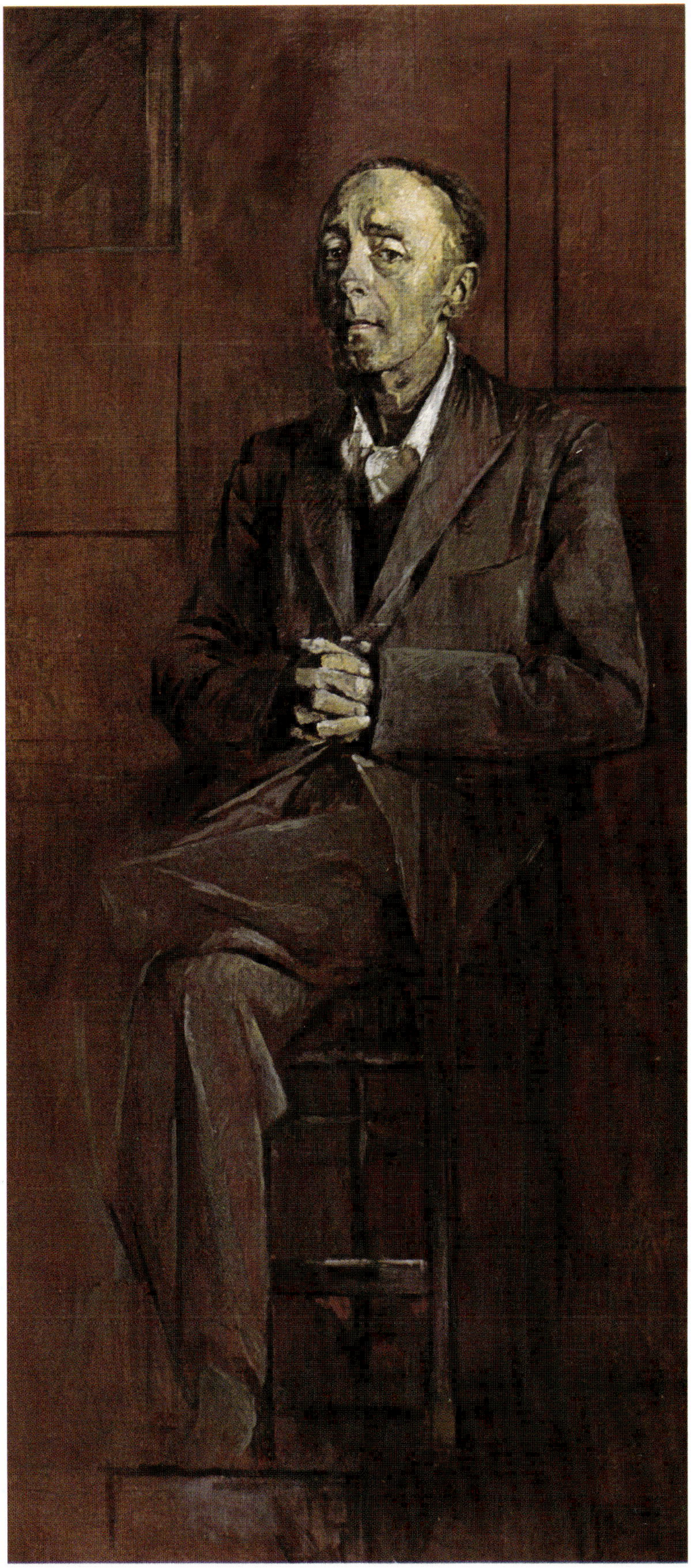

Colour plate 2
Edward Sackville-West,
1954 (No. 51)

GS Yes – of course, it has altered, and continues to alter. But one's technical approach really varies with the sitter, and with the finish required in a particular portrait.

JH You are particularly fascinated by people who wield some degree of power or responsibility. In what way are the features of such people likely to be more interesting to you – purely as a painter – than those of people who have suffered the ordinary (and perhaps they may be extra-ordinary) trials or privations of life, let us say, the type of beggar portrayed by Velazquez?

GS I have touched on this question earlier. Those who have wielded power are bound to be interesting to study. That is not to say that the beggar is not. He is normally in any case more 'picturesque'. But I do find it immensely fascinating (though not exclusively so) to deal with people who have had pressures put upon them or who have had the character necessary to direct great enterprises. There are psychological overtones in such people which it is absorbing to try and render.

JH Do you think your fascination is connected with a desire to see just how far the human mind and body can be stretched, just what tensions they undergo in the cause of directing some great enterprise: in the same way that you enjoy exploring the full capacities of a superbly tuned motor car?

GS Probably so. This also applies to the natural forms of landscape: the struggle of a tree to remain standing and grow, against all odds – a thorn branch, beaten down by the hooves of animals, and contorted – but still very much alive and growing.

JH Is your fascination by such people in any way connected with your own feelings about the nature of modern life? Speed and violence, for example, are obviously among the qualities to which you feel a particular attraction, perhaps also repulsion.

GS No. I have liked speed, of course. I like violence only in so far as it produces a repertoire of forms of exceptional interest in that they are opposed to each other. Any *combat* demonstrates this – not only Cain and Abel, but one insect destroying another. This opposition of forms was one element which fascinated me in bomb damage in London. Arrests by the police hold for me – certainly formally – similar fascinating formal and psychological possibilities.

JH There must sometimes be cases in which, for one reason or another, a sitter has put you off, made it almost impossible for you to concentrate.

GS If a client puts me off it is normally because I know I can't deal with that particular subject: I refuse the commission. But certain difficulties do arise: usually because of some inborn vanity in the subject which becomes insupportable – and I know the situation will become insupportable to such people when they see what I have done! The whole thing is like receiving a *very* cold welcome in a room when you go in.

JH Do you ever feel that you simply want to give up a particular portrait?

GS I do sometimes feel like giving up in such circumstances: but if I do go on – as I generally do, because I hate to be beaten – the result is usually a disaster.

JH Would your feeling for the figure as an entity make it difficult for you to contemplate painting people in relation to each other – in other words, double or group portraits – which is something you have not attempted to do so far?

GS While I find it difficult enough to cope with a single figure, I have often thought that I would like to try double or group portraits. Such an attempt would bring my portraits in line with my experiments with 'nature' forms or insects – and if one thinks that a diversity of movements can be contained and controlled in one entity one need not go much further in thinking that several separate subjects with their own movements could form either a conglomerate of diverse subjects or *subjects in opposition.*

JH Would a picture with just a couple of carefully related figures – let us say, one of Cézanne's Card Player *compositions – attract you as much as a work of the complexity of Rembrandt's* Belshazzar's Feast?

GS No, probably not. Interesting though the *Card Players* are, Rembrandt's *Belshazzar's Feast* is in a class by itself. I have always wanted to make a paraphrase of it. That might lead to my trying to do something of my own.

JH So you are now moving away in your thinking a very great deal from your Standing Forms, *which were so monolithic – like your first portrait, the Somerset Maugham?*

GS I cannot think into the future and say how ideas – new ideas – come to one: it is a mystery. One sees something – perhaps a newspaper cutting – or has an idea which may have been in one's mind unconsciously; and one is off. New directions arrive with stealth – out of the blue.

JH Do you find that the discipline of portraiture helps you with your work in landscape, and that the converse is also true?

GS I think they go hand in hand. People imagine that they are very different. But I think that the differences are not so great. What portraiture has done for me is perhaps to teach me to make rather more complete studies from nature – from natural objects – than I originally did, because I remember way back in 1937 I tended to make the paraphrases at once – my first drawing was a paraphrase of what I saw.

JH Is the constant study of all forms of organic life, daily sketching to no seemingly immediate purpose, an essential enrichment of your imagination which somehow seems to result in a perpetual renewal of your work?

GS Yes, absolutely. It sounds odd to say so in the context of doing a professional portrait – but it is a very good discipline for me. I find that now I can draw perhaps rather better than I could at one time.

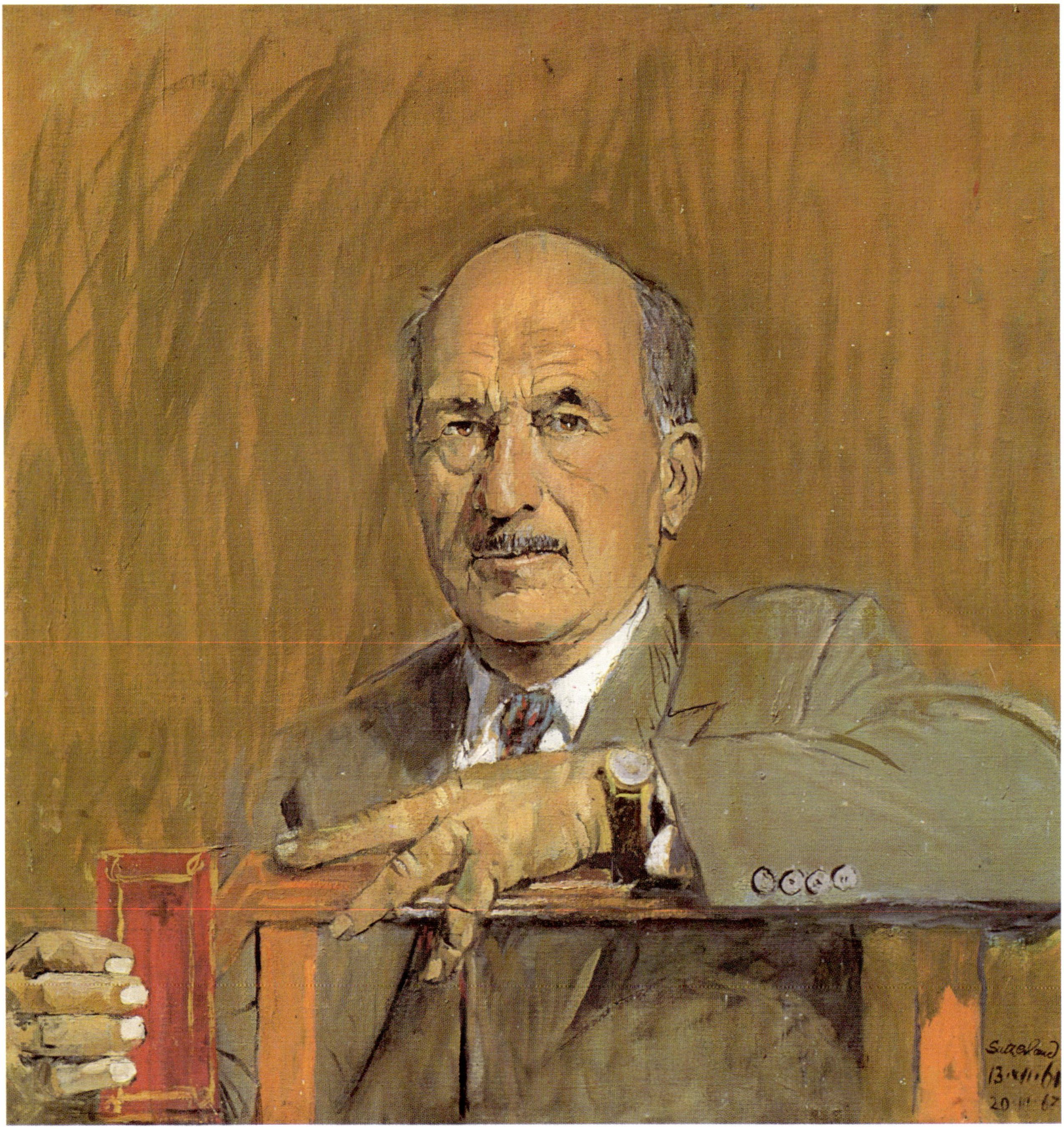

Colour plate 3
Dr Arpad Plesch, 1961–2 (No. 73)

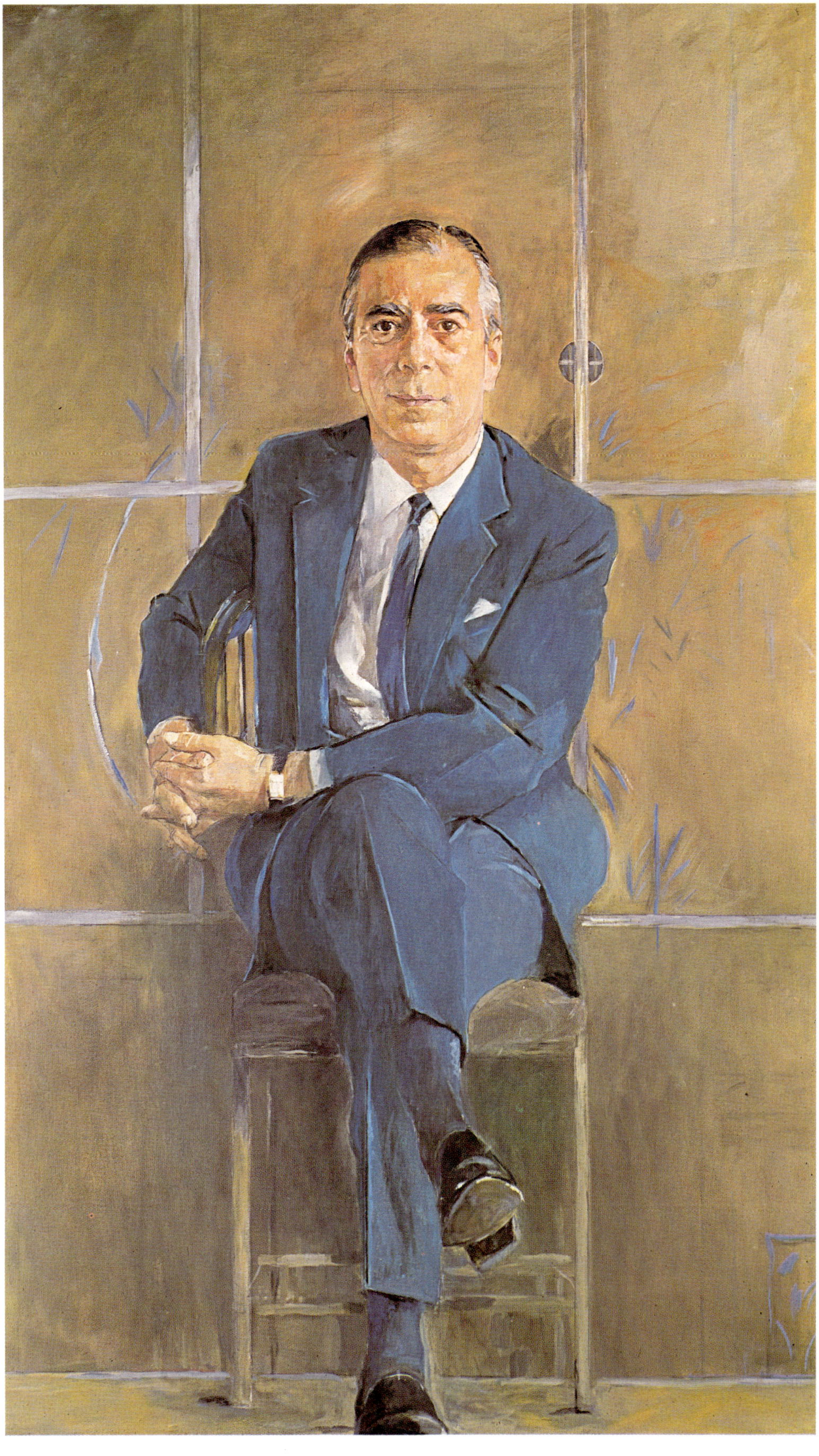

Colour plate 4
Lord Rayne, 1968–9
(No. 85)

JH In conclusion, is there anything you would like to add to what you have said already about the fundamental problem of the relationship between an artist and his sitter?

GS Portraiture – particularly 'commissioned work' – is a most difficult genre in which properly to succeed. This may always have been so – though I suspect not. Possibly because of the advent of photography people today – superficially at least – are much more aware of what they and others look like: or what they think they look like or want to look like. I think it is true that only those totally without physical vanity, educated in painting, or with exceptionally good manners, can disguise their feelings of shock or even revulsion when they are confronted for the first time with a reasonably truthful painted image of themselves: there is a quilted atmosphere of silence as when it snows. Or, on the other hand, an 'élitist' snobbery creeps in which compels them to accept a travesty of themselves if the painter is sufficiently 'different' and well-known. But for the most part it is almost possible to hear them saying: 'Do I really look like that?' It is known that Rembrandt – especially in his later periods – lost commissions to lesser but more 'polished' painters. He had failed to please his clients, and the lesser painters' style was preferred to his direct – but mysterious – truthful, penetrating and unglamorous style. But what about Goya? Surely he was almost equally frank and perhaps found himself in as difficult circumstances – perhaps more difficult – since he painted not only the people, but the royalty of his day and those of exalted 'rank'. How is it that these 'high born' clients accepted what he did? They were the very people who might have been thought likely to reject a truthful image as likely to depress them or damage their public standing. There may have been reasons for their acceptance. Was it because, as patrons, they were knowledgeable and sympathetic to the best art of their time – or had they less of a public image to bother about? At all events there were no 'media' to create it. The fact remains – or so it seems to me – that people today, inside 'society' or out (not counting the handful of people educated not only in the art of our time but of other times), do really prefer the painter to please. This sets up tensions on both sides – with the painter and his subject. Thus to 'portray' (used in the best sense) has become synonymous with 'betray'. As for myself many people have the fixed idea that my portraits are cruel. I do not aim to make them so (at the same time the word hideous does exist and one thinks of Voltaire's 'hideous smile'; even worse are the arrogant, aggressive and perfidious smiles!). But I do *look* at the person whose characteristics I try to record. I don't always succeed by any means in what I do, and from my own point of view hardly ever do so. I want neither to flatter or denigrate. Least of all do I want to soil and mortify.

Menton and London, 1976–7

Catalogue note

Measurements are given in inches and (in brackets) centimetres, height before width. Biographical information has been kept to the essential minimum. A sitter's nationality is British, unless otherwise stated.

I COMPARATIVE WORKS

1
Study for Tree Form
Pen and Indian ink
$9\frac{7}{8} \times 7\frac{3}{8}$ (25.1 × 18.7)
Drawn in 1941
Signed and dated and inscribed lower right: *Graham Sutherland/Trottiscliffe./1941*

A sketch which, like Graham Sutherland's well-known *Blasted Oak*, also drawn in 1941, reveals the fascination – strengthened by an intense feeling, derived from his religious outlook, for every manifestation of organic growth he encounters – that Sutherland has always felt for the anthropomorphic qualities suggested by natural forms: qualities which, not surprisingly, therefore, lie at the very heart of all his work in landscape. Sutherland has described the specific nature of his approach with characteristic clarity: 'It is not a question so much of a "tree like a figure" or a "root like a figure" – it is a question of bringing out the anonymous personality of these things; at the same time they must bear the mould of their ancestry'.

Lent by Mrs Graham Sutherland

2
Thorn Head
Pen and ink and gouache
$13\frac{1}{4} \times 11\frac{1}{2}$ (33.7 × 29.2)
Executed in 1946
Verso: study for the head of Christ on the Cross

PROVENANCE: Acquired from the artist.
EXHIBITED: Institute of Contemporary Arts, Boston, Houston and Palm Beach, 1953–4.
LITERATURE: Robert Melville, *Graham Sutherland*, London, 1950, plate 65; Douglas Cooper, *The Work of Graham Sutherland*, London, 1961, pp. 32 and 76, plate 83d.

In 1944 Sutherland was invited by Canon Walter Hussey to paint an *Agony in the Garden* for the church of St Matthew's, Northampton; he asked if he could paint a *Crucifixion* instead, because, perhaps owing to the searing experience of the War, he had wanted to attempt this subject for some time. Canon Hussey agreed. 'In the autumn of that year I had been thinking of the form the work was to take; in the spring of the following year the subject was still very much in my mind . . . For the first time I started to notice thorn bushes, and the structure of thorns as they pierced the air. I made some drawings, and as I made them, a curious change developed. As the thorns rearranged themselves, they became, whilst still retaining their own pricking, space-encompassing life, something else – a kind of 'stand-in' for a Crucifixion and a crucified head'. No better example could be found of the subconscious anthropomorphic workings of Sutherland's imagination. On the back of this *Thorn Head* is a study for the Northampton *Crucifixion*, showing Christ's head pierced by thorns. Sutherland's numerous *Thorn Tree* and *Thorn Head* compositions of 1945–6 were often painted against the blue, benign, background which he had wanted to use for his *Crucifixion*: 'the most tragic of all themes yet inherent in it . . . the promise of salvation'.

Lent by Mr William Roerich

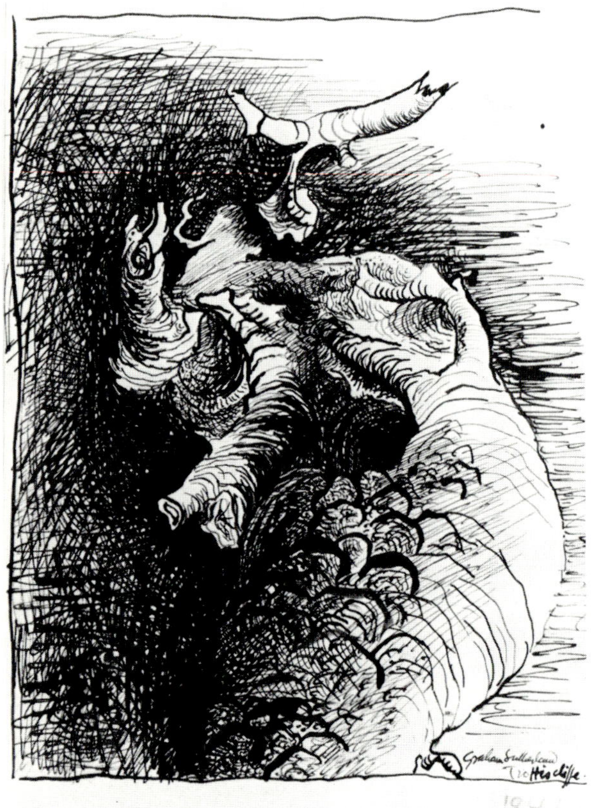
1

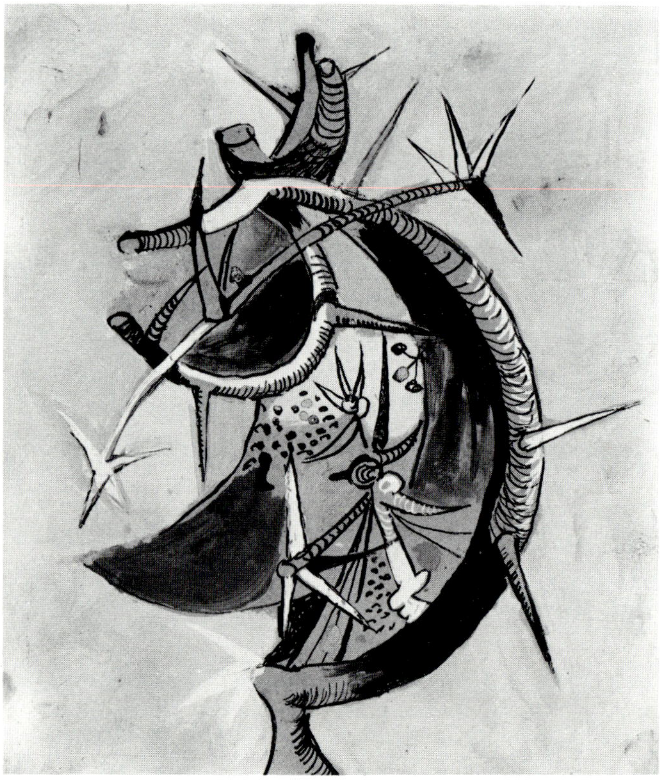
2

3
Study for a 'Thorn Head'
Pencil and black chalk
$14\frac{5}{16} \times 11\frac{1}{8}$ (36.4 × 28.3)
Drawn in 1949

EXHIBITED: *XXVI Biennale,* Venice, 1952 (44); *Graham Sutherland,* British Council, Stedelijk Museum, Amsterdam, and Kunsthaus, Zürich, January – April 1953 (42); *Drawings for Pictures,* Arts Council, 1953 (23); *Graham Sutherland: Gouaches, Watercolours and Drawings,* British Council, Akademie der Bildenden Kunste, Vienna, and Ferdinandeum, Innsbruck, 1954 (36 repr.); *Graham Sutherland,* British Council (Vienna, Innsbruck, Berlin, Cologne, Stuttgart, Mannheim and Hamburg), 1954–5 (27).
LITERATURE: Robert Melville, *Graham Sutherland,* London, 1950, plate 20; Douglas Cooper, *The Work of Graham Sutherland,* London, 1961, pp. 32 and 79, plate 111b; Francesco Arcangeli, *Graham Sutherland,* Milan, 1973, and New York, 1975, p. 36 (37), plate 81.

Sutherland's drawings of thorns set within an oval frame, and supported upon a 'metallic' base, are conscious metamorphoses of the human head and shoulders derived from the thorn trees and bushes with which he had first become obsessed in 1945–6 (compare No. 2). These inventions are the exact antithesis to his 'discovery' of human, animal or bird-like characteristics in natural forms (compare also Nos. 1 and 8). This 'reverse' process, however, developed logically from the other; and it was the prelude to his *Standing Form* compositions of 1949–53, 'stand-ins' for the human figure which strongly influenced his portraiture.

Lent by Mrs Graham Sutherland

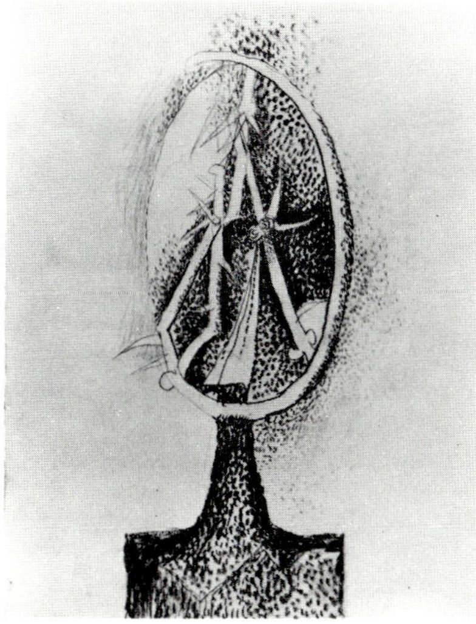

3

4
Head against Bougainvillia
Oil on canvas
24 × 20 (61 × 50.8)
Inscribed on the back: *HEAD (1951) II*

EXHIBITED: *XXVI Biennale,* Venice, 1952 (58); *Graham Sutherland,* British Council, Musée National d'Art Moderne, Paris, November–December 1952 (58); *Graham Sutherland,* British Council, Stedelijk Museum, Amsterdam, and Kunsthaus, Zürich, January–April 1953 (55); *Paintings and Drawings by Graham Sutherland,* Arts Council, Tate Gallery, May–August 1953 (63); *Graham Sutherland,* British Council (Vienna, Innsbruck, Berlin, Cologne, Stuttgart, Mannheim and Hamburg), 1954–5 (31); British Council, *IV Art International,* Japan, 1957 (12).
LITERATURE: Graham Sutherland, 'Thoughts on Painting', *The Listener,* 6 September 1951, repr. p. 377; Edward Sackville-West, *Graham Sutherland,* London, 2nd edn., 1955, p. 12, plate 27; Douglas Cooper, *The Work of Graham Sutherland,* London, 1961, p. 80, plate 117d; Francesco Arcangeli, *Graham Sutherland,* Milan, 1973, and New York, 1975, p. 36 (37), plate 84.

One of a series of skeletal heads in which Graham Sutherland seems not only to be developing the elements of the head in partly abstract, partly expressionist, terms but to be exploring the relationship between the tensions in the human head and those inherent in precision machinery.

Lent by Mrs Graham Sutherland

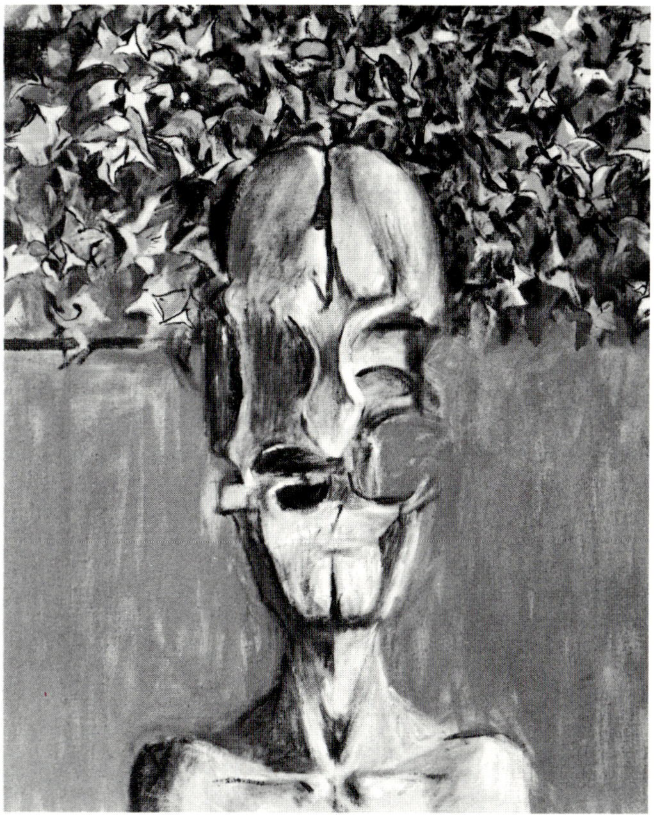

4

5

Three Standing Forms in a Garden

Oil on canvas

$52\frac{3}{8} \times 47\frac{5}{8}$ (133 × 121)

Painted in 1951. A lithograph of this subject had been made in 1950, but was not published.

EXHIBITED: *XXVI Biennale*, Venice, 1952 (56); *Graham Sutherland*, British Council, Musée National d'Art Moderne, Paris, November–December 1952 (56); *Graham Sutherland*, British Council, Stedelijk Museum, Amsterdam, and Kunsthaus, Zürich, January–April 1953 (53); *Paintings and Drawings by Graham Sutherland*, Arts Council, Tate Gallery, May–August 1953 (68, plate 13); *Graham Sutherland*, British Council (Vienna, Innsbruck, Berlin, Cologne, Stuttgart, Mannheim and Hamburg), 1954–5 (38 repr.); *Three Masters of Modern British Painting*, Arts Council (Plymouth, Sheffield, Leeds, Manchester, Cheltenham), June – October 1961 (60); *Sutherland*, Galleria Civica d'Arte Moderna, Turin, October–November 1965 (78 repr.); *Graham Sutherland*, Kunsthalle, Basel, February–March 1966 (69); *Graham Sutherland*, Munich, The Hague, Berlin and Cologne, March–November 1967 (36 repr.); *British Painting 1945–70*, British Council, Oslo and Cracow, 1972 (5).

LITERATURE: Graham Sutherland, 'Thoughts on Painting', *The Listener*, 6 September 1951, repr. p. 377; Edward Sackville-West, *Graham Sutherland*, London, 2nd edn., 1955, pp. 11 and 13, plate 30; Douglas Cooper, *The Work of Graham Sutherland*, London, 1961, p. 80, plate 121; Sir John Rothenstein, *British Art Since 1900*, London, 1962, p. 181, plate 119; Andrew Révai, *Sutherland* (The Masters Series), 1966, pp. 4 and 7, plate VII; John Rothenstein, *Modern English Painters*, Vol. 3, London, 1974, p. 64.

A group of elaborately composed parallels to the human figure, their constituent parts based upon natural, mechanical and other forms, the spiralling motifs in the 'Form' on the left, for example, deriving from the studies of burnt-out paper rolls Sutherland had drawn in the East End in 1941. The three 'Forms' in this canvas are all totally different in character, that on the right being especially hieratic and monolithic. These compositions relate directly to Graham Sutherland's conception of portraiture as first exemplified in the *Somerset Maugham* of 1949 (No. 27). An instructive comparison may also be made between the *Standing Forms* compositions of 1949–53 and earlier works which seem to lie at the root of these inventions, such as his *Red Monolith* of 1938 or the well-known *Association of Oaks*, a more delicate anthropomorphic study dating from 1940. Sutherland wrote of his *Standing Forms* at the time that they were 'based on the principles of organic growth, with which I have always been preoccupied. To me they are monuments and presences. But why use these forms instead of human figures? Because, at the moment, I find it necessary to catch the taste – the quality – the essence of the presence of the human figure: the mysterious immediacy of a figure standing in a room or against a hedge in a shadow, its awareness, its regard, as if one had never seen it before – by a *substitution* [Sutherland's italics]. I find at the moment that I can make these qualities more real to myself in this way. It happens that I find these organic forms best for my purpose'.

Lent by Mrs Graham Sutherland

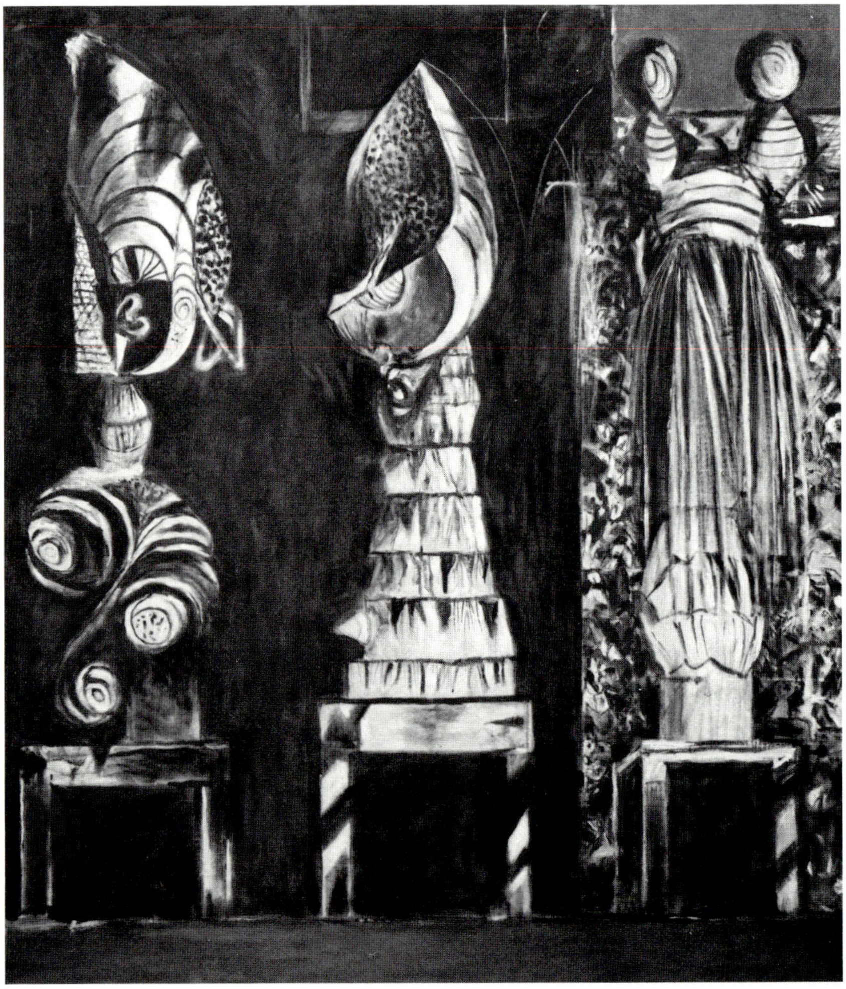

5

6
The Captive
Oil on canvas
55 × 48 (139.5 × 122)
Signed and dated lower right:
Sutherland/August 1963–Jan 1964
Signed, dated and inscribed on
the back: *THE CAPTIVE/Aug 1963 Jan 1964/G.S.*

EXHIBITED: *Sutherland*, Galleria Civica d'Arte Moderna, Turin, October – November 1965 (134 repr.).
LITERATURE: Francesco Arcangeli, *Graham Sutherland*, Milan, 1973, and New York, 1975, p. 38 (38–9), plate 142.

Sutherland was one of the first admirers of Francis Bacon, and this work shows a close affinity with the tortured images which obsess Bacon's imagination, images which he makes 'as accurately off my nervous system as I can'. But the differences are as important as the similarities. Whereas in the paintings of Bacon – to take an example, his *Inverted Crucifixion* of about the same date – the flesh almost dissolves in front of one's eyes, and the degradation is absolute, in the Sutherland there is a tension, an alertness, a defiance which suggests at least the possibility of a conquest of the flesh by the spirit. This equilibrium is fundamental to Sutherland's Christian concept of man.

Lent by the Neue Pinakothek, Munich

7
Lion's Head
Pen and Indian ink, Indian ink wash and gouache
$25\frac{7}{8} \times 19\frac{3}{4}$ (65.7 × 50.2)
Signed and dated lower right:
G.S./28.1.67
Lithographed in 1968

EXHIBITED: *Graham Sutherland A Bestiary*, Marlborough Fine Art Ltd, May – June 1968 (16 repr.).
LITERATURE: Francesco Arcangeli, *Graham Sutherland*, Milan, 1973, and New York, 1975, p. 38 (39), plate 171.

Sutherland's absorption in the organic processes of natural growth, and the visual relationships between animate and inanimate forms, has always impelled him to draw animals, birds and insects. In the mid-1960s he made a series of lithographs 'loosely linked with the idea of a Bestiary'. Though most of the illustrations were intended to be representational, some of the images derived from natural forms, some corresponded with the shapes of machines, and others were related to the human head. The *Lion's Head*, which was part of the series, is at once magnificently leonine and closely connected with Sutherland's work in portraiture at this time: compare, in particular, the drypoint of Dr Adenauer's head, also done in 1967 (No. 82).

Lent by Lord Hambleden

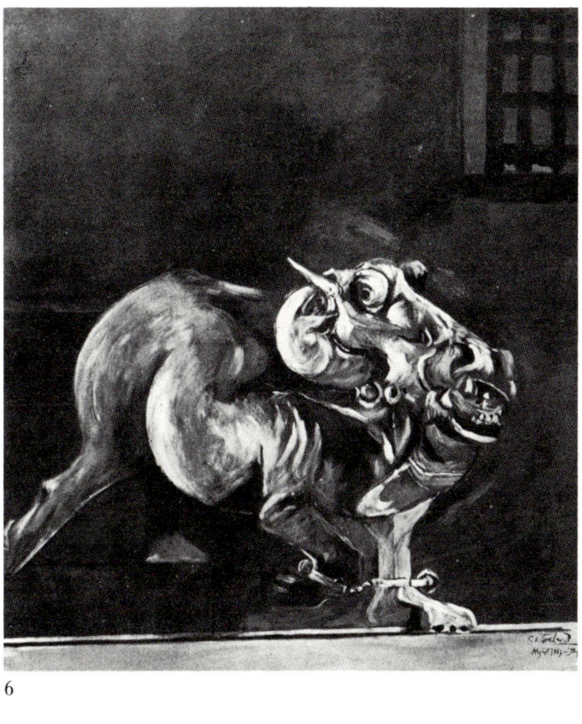
6

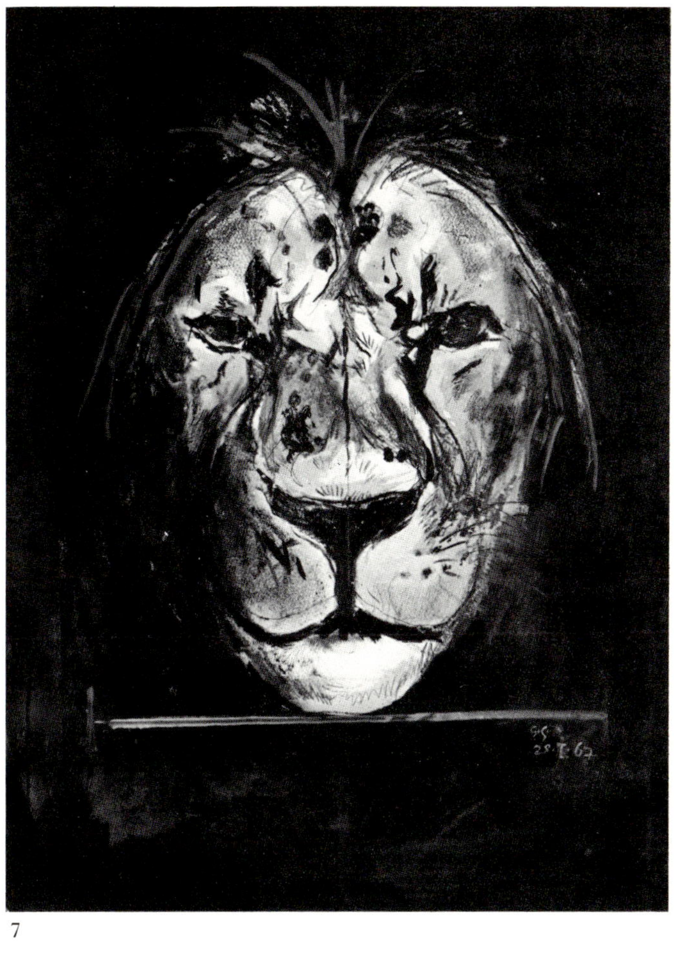
7

8

Head studies from boulders and stones

Pencil, black chalk and water-colour
$26\frac{1}{8} \times 19\frac{7}{8}$ (66.2 × 50.5)
Signed and dated lower right: *Sutherland/21.1.68.*
Lithographed in 1968

EXHIBITED: *Graham Sutherland: Druckgraphik und Zeichnungen mit dem vollständigen Bestiarium,* Kestner-Gesellschaft, Kunsthalle, Nuremberg, November 1969 – January 1970 (40 repr.).
LITERATURE: Francesco Arcangeli, *Graham Sutherland*, Milan, 1973, and New York, 1975, p. 39 (40), plate 182.

A sheet of studies, executed almost thirty years after his *Blasted Oak* and *Study for Tree Form* (No. 1), and nearly twenty years after his first portrait commission, which demonstrates Sutherland's instinctive urge to translate natural forms into images suggestive of the human head. In fact, these were the kind of forms later used as component parts in such pictures as his *Rock Fortress* of 1970 or his *Conglomerates* of the same period. It is indicative of Sutherland's concept of the universe, and of the place occupied within it by inanimate nature and by humanity, that, while some of the forms on this sheet derived from stones are semi-caricatures, he should only rarely have caricatured the human face itself, and then purely as a *jeu d'esprit*.

Lent from a Private Collection, Italy

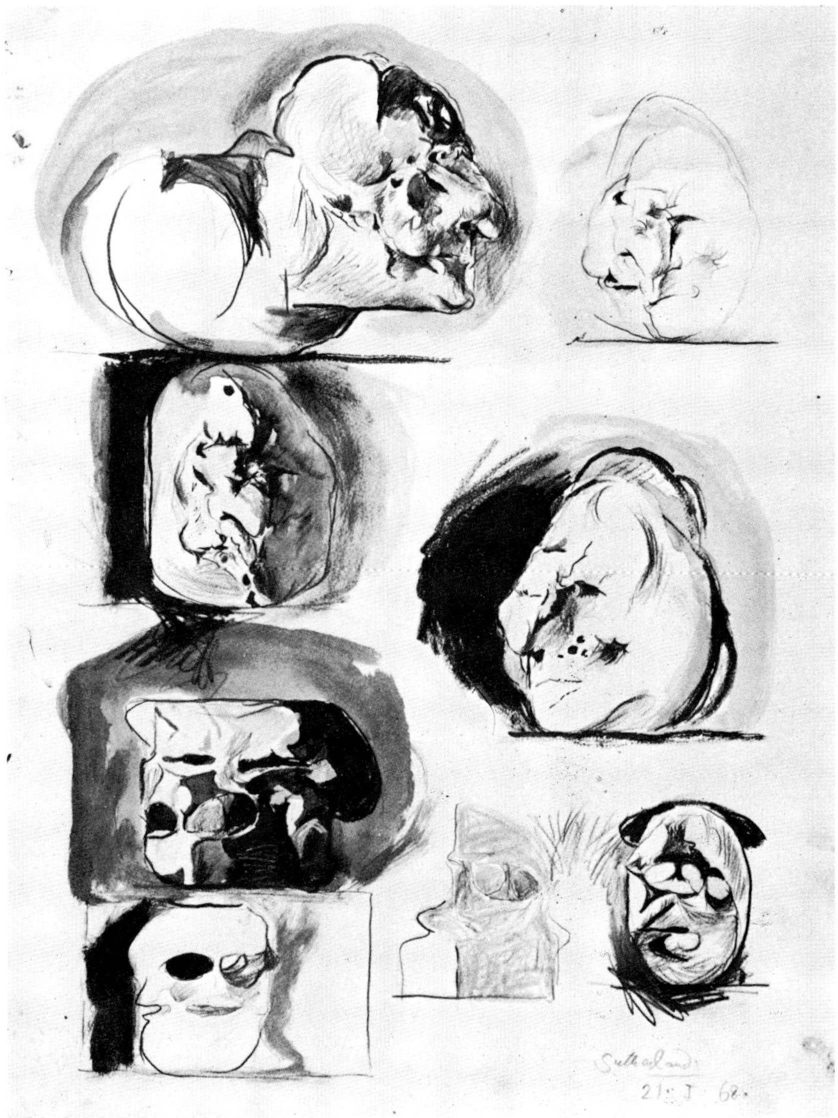

8

II PORTRAIT AND FIGURE STUDIES 1938–57

9

Study of the head of Katharine Sutherland in profile to left

Pen and ink and pencil

$4\frac{1}{2} \times 4\frac{3}{8}$ (11.4 × 11.1)

Drawn about 1938

Graham Sutherland had experimented with portraits when he was a student in a style which he referred to as 'highly finished but not academic'; all these were destroyed. This notebook sketch of his wife, Katharine, is the only surviving portrait study dating from the pre-war years, and it happily exemplifies not only Sutherland's scrupulous accuracy in observation but his brilliance of draughtsmanship: the profile, vibrant with life, is as taut and wiry in delineation as the headscarf is rough and impressionistic. Graham Sutherland met Kathleen (Katharine) Barry when they were both students at the Goldsmiths' College School of Art. They were married on 29 December 1927.

Lent by Mrs Graham Sutherland

10

Study of the head of a tin-miner in profile to right

Pencil

$9 \times 5\frac{3}{8}$ (22.9 × 13.7)

Drawn in 1942

During his years as a war artist Sutherland was given a wide range of subjects to paint; in 1942 he was asked to see what he could make of the tin mines in Cornwall. The portrait sketches he did at this time, of which this is an example, were usually made while he and the miners were waiting for the lift to take them to the surface; the idea was partly to distract them from looking at the subjects he had been drawing for the War Artists Committee and so avoid the embarrassment of their incomprehension. Sutherland greatly admired these men.

Lent by Mrs Graham Sutherland

11

Study of the head of a tin-miner in profile to right

Pencil

$9 \times 5\frac{3}{8}$ (22.9 × 13.7)

Drawn in 1942

Another sketch of the same miner (see No. 10) in a slightly different pose. The face is illuminated by the glow of the acetylene lamp, and the features are boldly drawn.

Lent by Mrs Graham Sutherland

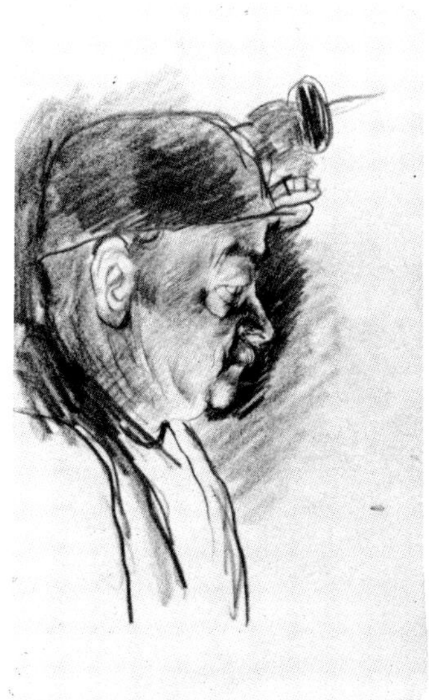

10

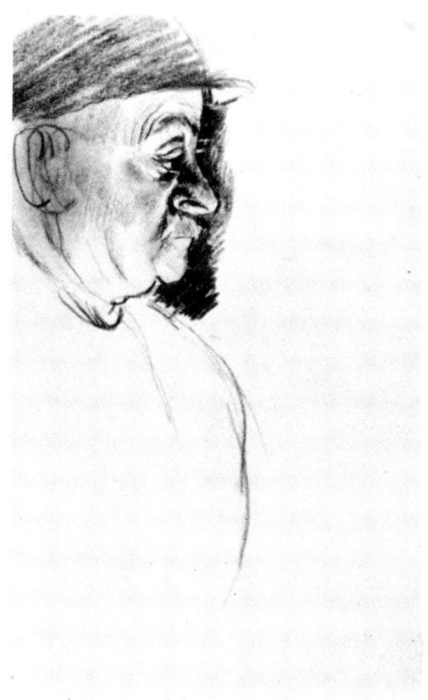

11

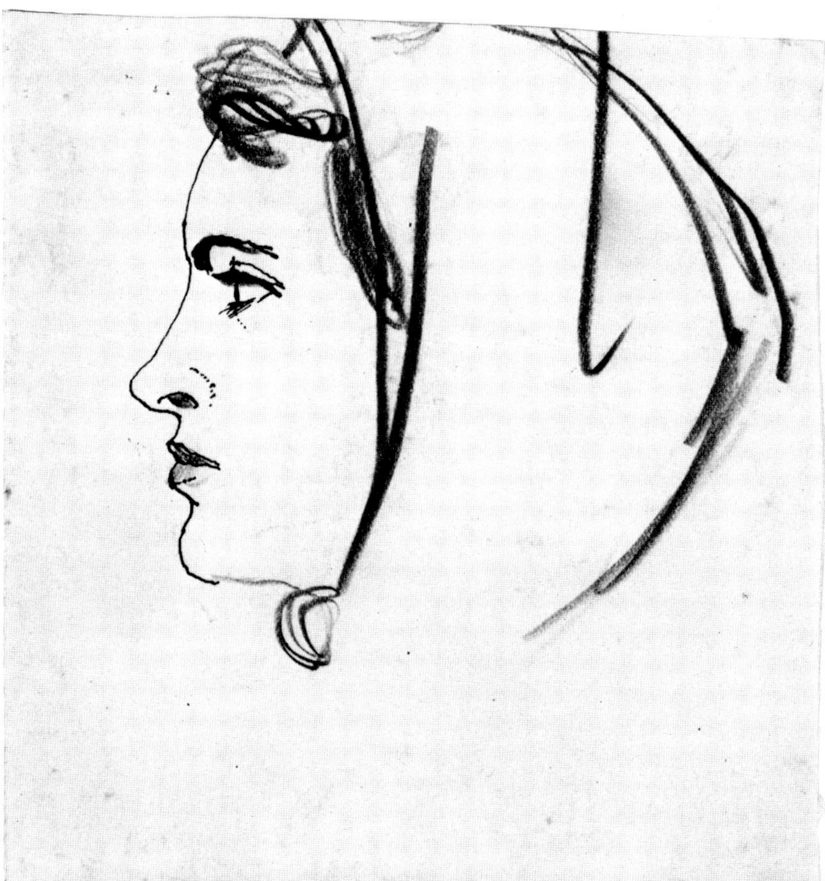

9

12
Study of Katharine Sutherland seated
Black chalk
$8\frac{1}{2} \times 4\frac{15}{16}$ (21.6 × 12.5)
Drawn about 1945–6

A rapid sketch of the artist's wife slumped in an armchair which conveys perfectly a sense of the weight of the human body in this semi-recumbent position. Sutherland's notebooks contain numerous informal sketches of this description, which demonstrate his lifelong interest in the human form and in people's expressions, movements and gestures.

Lent by Mrs Graham Sutherland

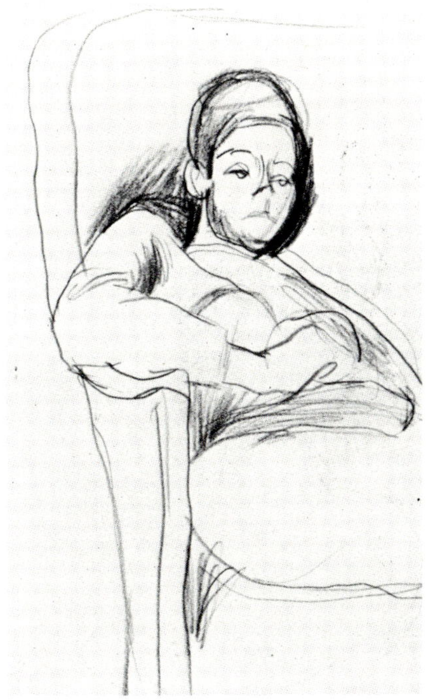

12

13
Self-portrait study
Pencil
$12\frac{3}{4} \times 8$ (32.4 × 20.3)
Drawn about 1945–6

A sketch done when the artist was in bed with mumps. The intensity of the expression is heightened by the treatment of the features in a manner which gives a hint of Sutherland's fascination, at this period, by the work of Picasso: compare the latter's portrait of Dora Maar, painted in 1942 (Wilhelm Boeck and Jaime Sabartés, *Picasso*, London, 1955, plate 410).

Lent by Mrs Graham Sutherland

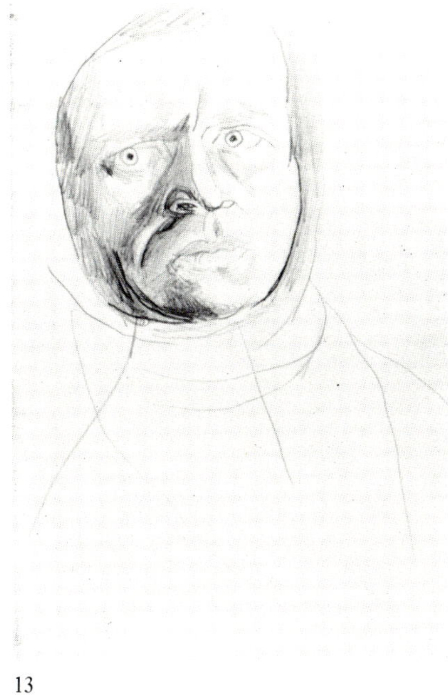

13

14
Stone head
Black chalk
$4\frac{7}{16} \times 5\frac{7}{8}$ (11.3 × 14.9)
Drawn in 1946

EXHIBITED: *Graham Sutherland*, Institute of Contemporary Arts, April–May 1951 (51); *Graham Sutherland: Gouaches, Watercolours and Drawings*, British Council, Akademie der Bildenden Kunste, Vienna, and Ferdinandeum, Innsbruck, 1954 (20); *Graham Sutherland*, British Council (Vienna, Innsbruck, Berlin, Cologne, Stuttgart, Mannheim and Hamburg), 1954–5 (15); *Graham Sutherland* Kunsthalle, Basel, February–March 1966 (32); *Graham Sutherland*, Munich, The Hague, Berlin and Cologne, March–November 1967 (135).
LITERATURE: Robert Melville, *Graham Sutherland*, London, 1950, plate 18b; Douglas Cooper, *The Work of Graham Sutherland*, London, 1961, pp. 41 and 75, plate 74a; Francesco Arcangeli, *Graham Sutherland*, Milan, 1973, and New York, 1975, p. 35 (36), plate 64.

An image inspired by Picasso's approach to portraiture, drawn in 1946, the year of Sutherland's fruitful visit to Paris. However distorted the head itself, and however exaggerated the forms, individual features, such as those of the nose and left eye, are carefully described. But the tension between the conception and such particularisation is highly disturbing, and the compulsively organic nature of this expressionistic image is quite different from the effects created by Picasso: compare, for example, the latter's portrait of his old friend Jaime Sabartés, painted in 1939 (Wilhelm Boeck and Jaime Sabartés, *Picasso*, London, 1955, plate 408).

Lent by Mrs Graham Sutherland

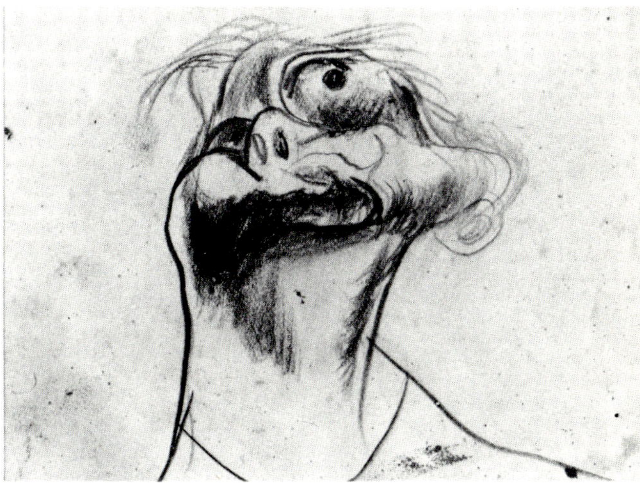

14

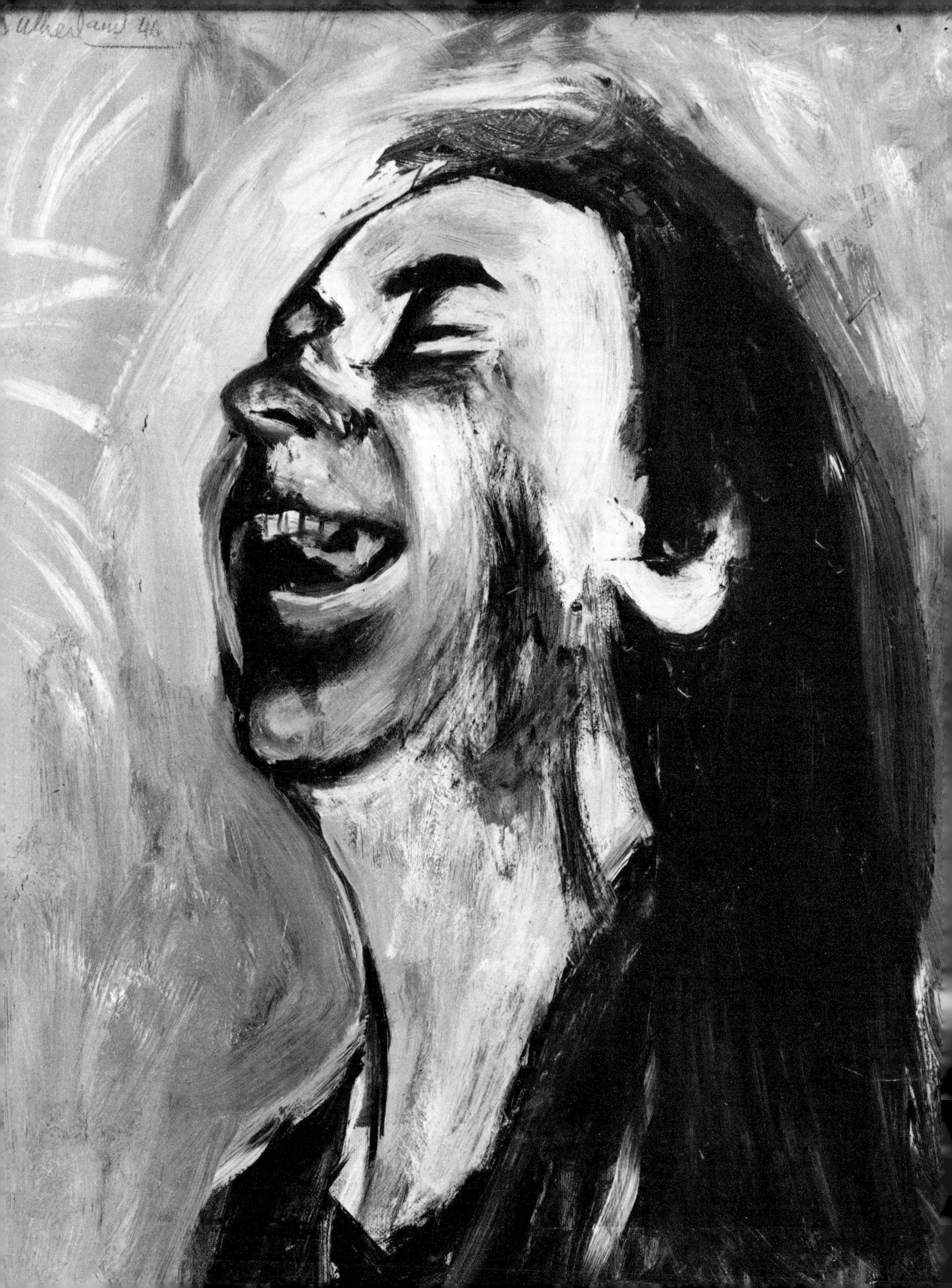
Sutherland 46

15
Study for 'The Laughing Woman'
Oil on canvas
18 × 14½ (45.7 × 36.8)
Signed and dated upper left:
Sutherland 46

PROVENANCE: With Roland, Browse & Delbanco, from whom it was purchased 1955.
EXHIBITED: *Modern British Portraits*, Arts Council (Cambridge, Newcastle, Torquay, Nottingham, Newport and Bolton), 1960–1 (33).
LITERATURE: Douglas Cooper, *The Work of Graham Sutherland*, London, 1961, pp.49–50 and 83, plate 163.

A brilliant and broadly painted study of the contortion of human features under the stress of strong emotion; the extraordinary power and violence of the image is in the tradition of such masterpieces of expressionist art as Munch's famous *Shouting* of 1895, and the arbitrary colour scheme – blues predominating in the flesh tones, deep blues and greens in the hair – suggests the direct influence of northern Expressionism. The background brushwork emphasises and supports the study of the head in a way which was later to become characteristic of the portraits. Sutherland did not pursue this vein (which he had tackled here at its most challenging) because, at the time, he felt his visual memory was inadequate to combine an accurate description of so fleeting an expression with a sufficient sense of structure; now this would present him with no difficulties. Dissatisfied with the finished work derived from this study, Sutherland destroyed it, but he returned to the theme later, and the pose was used in his *Laughing Woman* signed and dated 1952 now with Brook Street Gallery.

Lent by Mrs A. F. Kessler

16
Study of a woman seated facing frontally
Black chalk
9 × 7 (22.9 × 17.8)
Drawn about 1952

A sketch from life of a woman seated in a chair; the weight of the body is as surely suggested as in the earlier sketch of his wife (No. 12). This was one of Sutherland's first studies for his interpretation of the *Christ in Glory* for the tapestry behind the high altar of Coventry Cathedral, and it is characteristic of his approach to any subject, whether religious or secular, that he should have started off by drawing from the life.

Lent by Mrs Graham Sutherland

17
Study of a woman seated facing frontally
Black chalk
9 × 7 (22.9 × 17.8)
Drawn about 1952

A later sketch from the life for the *Christ in Glory* for Coventry Cathedral. The figure has now become much more erect and hieratic, and is a counterpart to the sculptural ideas of Henry Moore. The success of Sutherland's religious subjects has been due, at least in part, to his practice of working from the living model until the last possible moment. As natural forms have always suggested human affinities, so human forms have been contributory to his concept of the divine.

Lent by Mrs Graham Sutherland

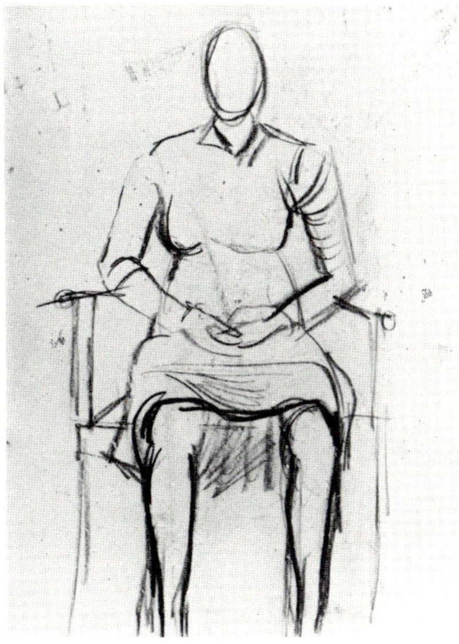
16

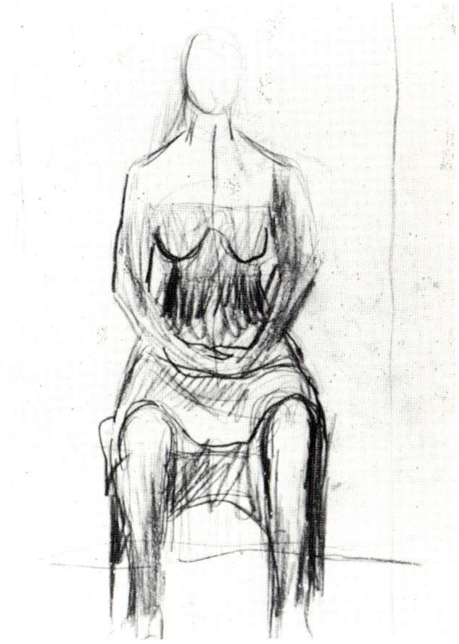
17

15

18
Study of the Head of Christ for the Coventry Cathedral 'Christ in Glory'
Gouache
9 × $4\frac{3}{4}$ (22.9 × 12.1)
Executed in 1957

EXHIBITED: *Sutherland: Christ in Glory in the Tetramorph*, Redfern Gallery, May – June 1964 (18).
LITERATURE: Andrew Révai (ed.), *Sutherland: Christ in Glory in the Tetramorph*, London, 1964, p. 103, plate 23.

The Northampton *Crucifixion* was Sutherland's first great religious painting, a deeply moving work; in the same year, 1946, he completed a *Deposition*, now in the Fitzwilliam Museum, Cambridge. His barbaric *Christ Carrying the Cross*, an image anticipating the savagery and degradation of human values of our own decade, was executed in 1953, a year after he accepted the commission for the largest tapestry ever contemplated, a work to occupy the entire east wall behind the high altar of Coventry Cathedral. Sutherland's pre-occupation with the human figure, and with human emotions expressed in terms of figure painting, in the post-war years, was to a large extent the result of his meditation on the composition of different religious themes. This gouache was a preliminary working drawing which became the basis for the three future cartoons. The schematized and hieratic representation of Christ the Saviour is comparable with the Christian images of Byzantine or Romanesque art, or Van Eyck's God the Father painted for the Ghent Altarpiece in the second quarter of the fifteenth century. But the concept is in fact timeless: 'After much thought I felt I wanted to do a large figure like a Buddha or one of the Egyptian figures in the Valley of the Kings . . . a figure of great *contained* vitality . . . which contained in it some of the quality of pent-up force which I had felt in Egyptian sculpture'.

Lent by the Civic Arts Trust, Herbert Art Gallery and Museum, Coventry

19
Sketch of the head of one of the figures in Rembrandt's 'The Night Watch'
Oil on canvas
$26\frac{5}{8}$ × $17\frac{3}{4}$ (67.6 × 45.1)
Signed and dated lower left: *G.S. 1953.*

EXHIBITED: *Paintings and Watercolours by Graham Sutherland*, Lefèvre Gallery, April – May 1975 (12a repr.).
LITERATURE: Douglas Cooper, *The Work of Graham Sutherland*, London, 1961, p. 63, plate 162.

A brilliant, impressionistic sketch based on one of the background figures in *The Night Watch*. Significantly, the 'paraphrase' is more introspective than Rembrandt's original head, which, like those of most of the other participants in the scene he had painted, is distinctly theatrical in intent. This introspective quality is linked with Sutherland's exploration, in this sketch, of the mysterious effects of shadow on the description and interpretation of features.

Lent from a Private Collection (verso of No. 40)

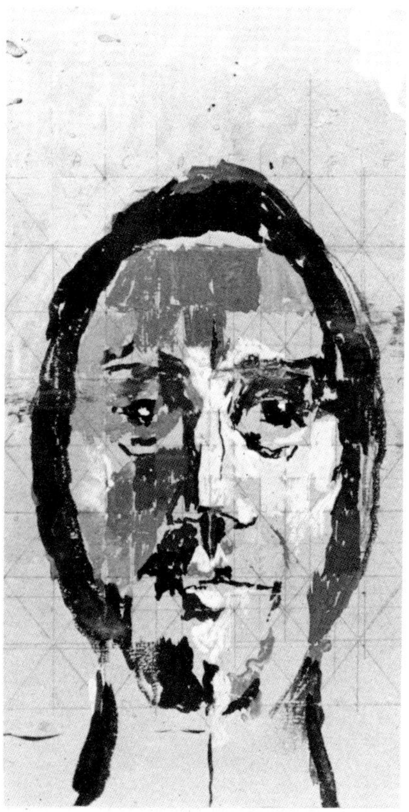

18

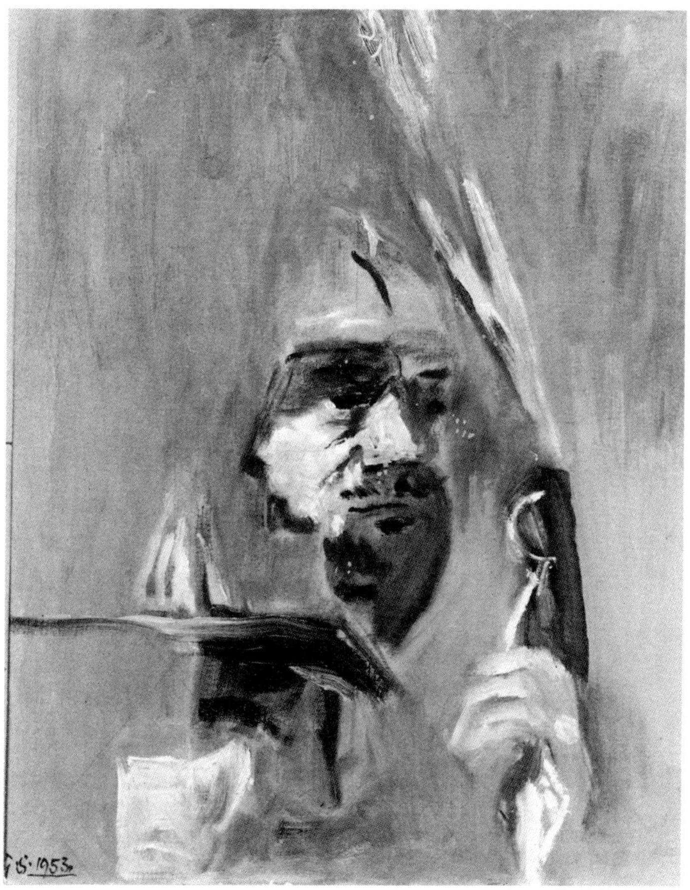

19

III THE PORTRAITS 1949–77

W. Somerset Maugham
1874–1965

Novelist, short-story writer and dramatist.

The commission was begun on 17 February 1949 and finished in June. Sutherland had about ten sittings lasting an hour each day, which took place at a rented house at St Jean Cap Ferrat. Other sketches, a small oil, and a lithograph were executed later.

20
Study of head facing half left
Pen and ink, black chalk and grey wash
12 × 10½ (30.5 × 26)
Signed and dated lower right:
Sutherland. 1949.

PROVENANCE: Hans Juda; Anon. sale, Sotheby's, 1 November 1967 Lot 111 bt. Fitzwilliam Museum.
EXHIBITED: *"In our View": Some paintings and sculpture bought by Hans and Elsbeth Juda between 1931 and 1967*, Graves Art Gallery, Sheffield, May – June 1967 (135b repr.).
LITERATURE: Douglas Cooper, *The Work of Graham Sutherland*, London, 1961, p. 58 Note.

Study for the definitive portrait, executed in the studio from notebook drawings done from the life. This pose was not adopted.

Lent by the Fitzwilliam Museum, Cambridge (PD12–1967: verso)

21
Study of head facing half right
Pen and ink, black chalk and grey wash
12 × 10½ (30.5 × 26)
Signed and dated upper left:
Sutherland. 1949

PROVENANCE: Hans Juda; Anon. sale, Sotheby's, 1 November 1967 Lot 111 bt. Fitzwilliam Museum.
EXHIBITED: *"In Our View": Some paintings and sculpture bought by Hans and Elsbeth Juda between 1931 and 1967*, Graves Art Gallery, Sheffield, May–June 1967 (135a repr.).
LITERATURE: Douglas Cooper, *The Work of Graham Sutherland*, London, 1961, pp. 58 Note and 83, plate 164; Andrew Révai, *Graham Sutherland* (The Masters Series), 1966, fig. 3.

Drawn on the other side of the sheet catalogued above (No. 20). Study for the definitive portrait, also made in the studio from notebook drawings done in front of the sitter, which shows the pose as adopted. The features are even more sharply defined than in the previous study, and Sutherland's fascination by the folds, pouches and wrinkles in Maugham's face is exactly comparable with his feeling for the structural details of natural forms demonstrated in his landscape studies.

Lent by the Fitzwilliam Museum, Cambridge (PD12–1967: recto)

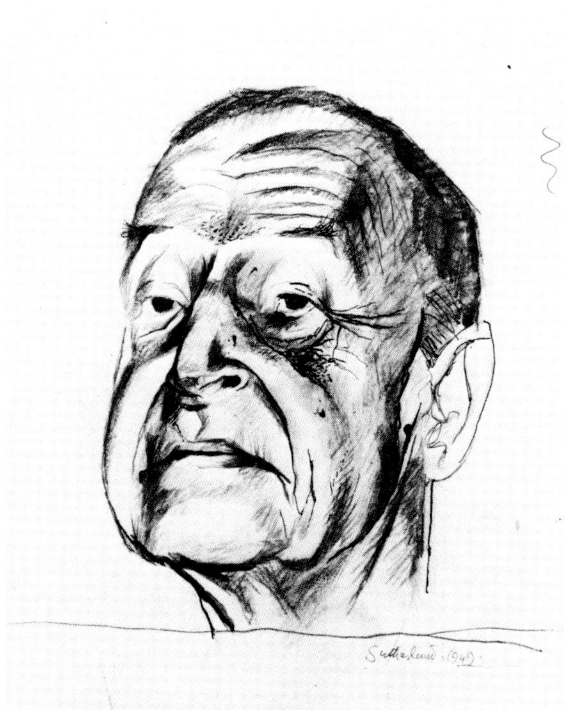

20

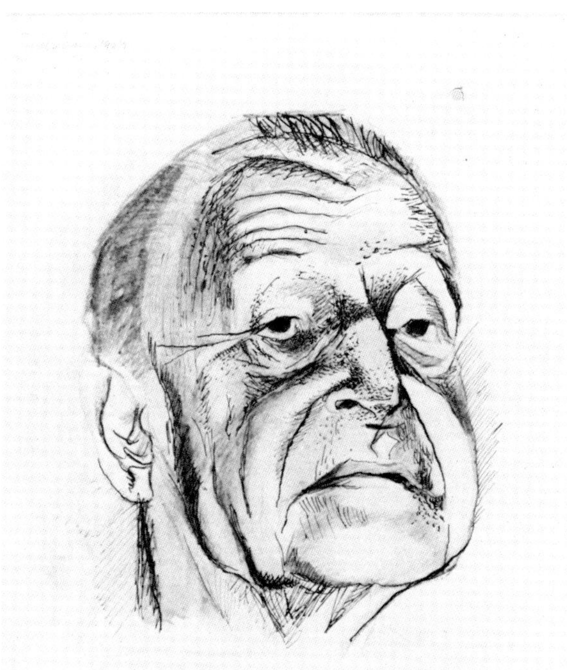

21

22
Composition study
Pencil and crayon
$8\frac{1}{2} \times 5\frac{1}{16}$ (21.6 × 12.9)
Executed in 1949

Study for the definitive portrait. One of numerous sketches for the pose, at first envisaged in the opposite direction, in which Sutherland has finally reached the formula for his ultimate solution: the sitter is still seated in a chair, however, rather than on the bamboo stool eventually adopted, and the left foot is seen frontally.

Lent by Mrs Graham Sutherland

23
Composition study
Pencil and chalk
$8\frac{7}{16} \times 5\frac{1}{8}$ (21.4 × 13)
Size of the image $4\frac{1}{2} \times 2$ (10.8 × 5.1)
Executed in 1949

Study for the definitive portrait. A cursory sketch of the final solution, in which the massiveness of the head and the erectness of the body are indicated in roughest outline. The stool and positioning of the legs and feet are as adopted. The background is roughed out in orange chalk; the choice for the finished canvas was closer to yellow.

Lent by Mrs Graham Sutherland

24
Study of the trousers and feet
Black chalk
$8\frac{1}{2} \times 5\frac{1}{16}$ (21.6 × 12.9)
Executed in 1949

Study for the definitive portrait. One of numerous sketches for the crossing of the legs and the placing of the feet, showing the pose as finally adopted.

Lent by Mrs Graham Sutherland

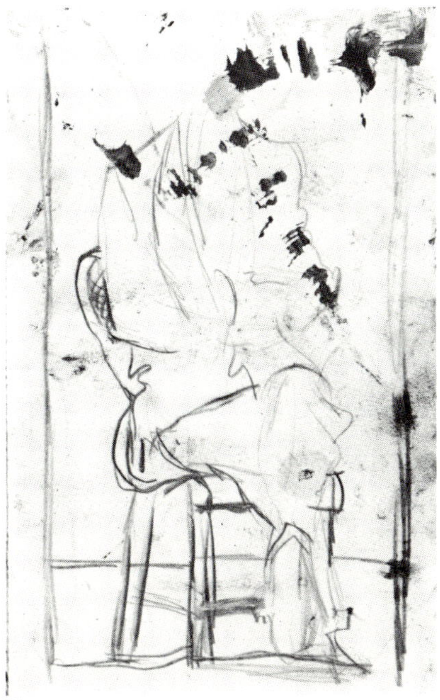

22

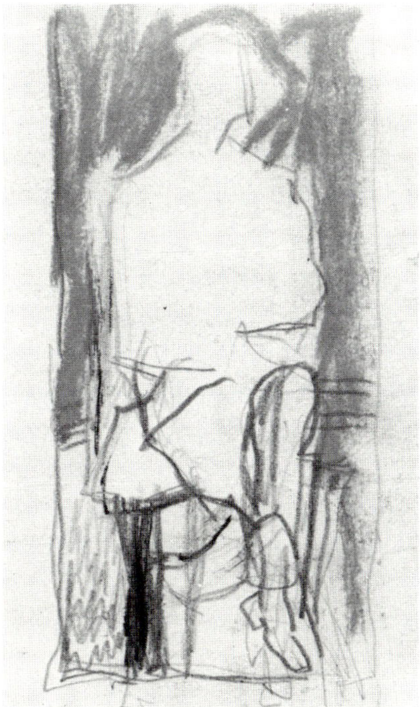

23 *detail*

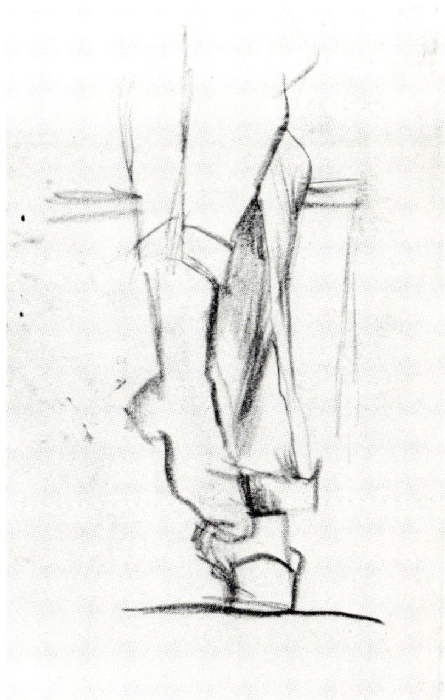

24

25

Study of right ear

Pencil on tracing paper

$3\frac{9}{16} \times 2\frac{7}{8}$ (9.1 × 7.3)

Executed in 1949

LITERATURE: Douglas Cooper, *The Work of Graham Sutherland*, London, 1961, p.58 Note.

Study for the definitive portrait. Sutherland has customarily made a number of sketches of individual features, or conjunctions of features, either before starting on a portrait or else whilst actually engaged on the finished work; only a few such preliminary sketches now survive. In this case Sutherland had asked Maugham for further sittings to make detailed drawings after he had begun work on the canvas in his studio.

Lent by Mrs Graham Sutherland

26

Study of left foot and shoe

Oil on canvas

$11\frac{1}{8} \times 10\frac{1}{2}$ (28.3 × 26.7)

Executed in 1949

PROVENANCE: Purchased by Lord Beaverbrook 1955, and presented by him.

A full-scale study for the definitive portrait, squared up for transfer to the canvas. This is almost the only occasion on which Sutherland has made a study of this kind.

Lent by the Beaverbrook Foundation, Beaverbrook Art Gallery, Fredericton, New Brunswick (59.241)

27

The definitive portrait

(Colour plate 1, page 19)

Oil on canvas

54 × 25 (137.2 × 63.5)

Signed and dated upper right: *Sutherland 1949*

PROVENANCE: Given by the sitter to his daughter, Lady John Hope (now Lady Glendevon); presented by her to the Tate Gallery, 1951.

EXHIBITED: *Graham Sutherland*, Institute of Contemporary Arts, April–May 1951 (32); XXVI Biennale, Venice, 1952 (43); *Graham Sutherland*, British Council, Musée National d'Art Moderne, Paris, November–December 1952 (42 repr.); *Graham Sutherland*, British Council, Stedelijk Museum, Amsterdam, and Kunsthaus, Zürich, January–April 1953 (41 repr.); *Paintings and Drawings by Graham Sutherland*, Arts Council, Tate Gallery, May–August 1953 (49); *Graham Sutherland*, Kunsthalle, Basel, February–March 1966 (56 repr.); *Graham*

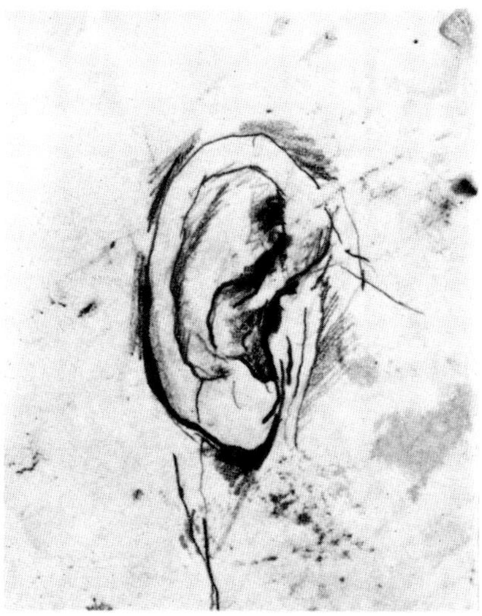

25

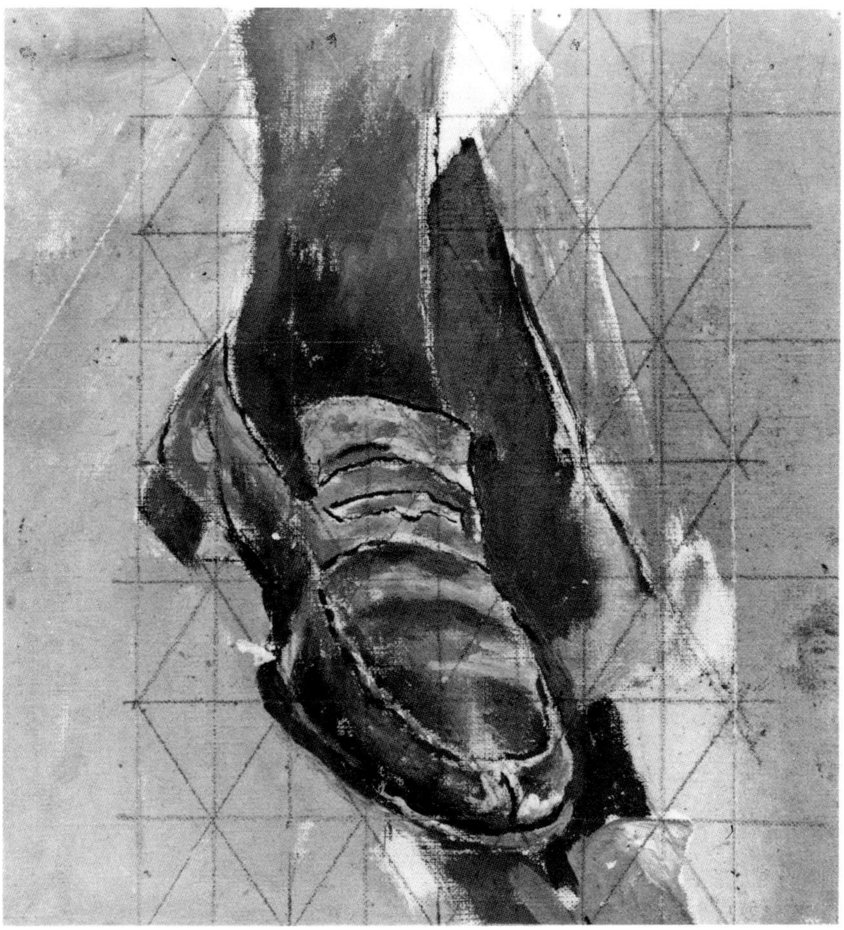

26

Sutherland, Munich, The Hague, Berlin and Cologne, March–November 1967 (27 repr.); *English Portraits*, British Council, Bucharest (repr. p. 56) and Budapest (53 repr.), November 1972–March 1973.
LITERATURE: Robert Melville, *Graham Sutherland*, London, 1950, plate 64; Douglas Cooper, *The Work of Graham Sutherland*, London, 1961, pp.39, 56–8 and 83, plate 165; *The modern British paintings, drawings and sculpture*, Vol. II, Tate Gallery, 1964, p.708, plate 44; Andrew Révai, *Graham Sutherland* (The Masters Series), London, 1966, pp.2 and 6; John Rothenstein, *Modern English Painters*, Vol. 3, London, 1974, pp. 66–7; Francesco Arcangeli, *Graham Sutherland*, New York, 1975, p.5; John Sunderland, *Painting in Britain 1525 to 1975*, London, 1976, p.245.

The immense power of this image – which is unexpectedly small in scale – derives largely from Sutherland's interpretation of the head and from the precision of drawing. The set of the jaw, the erect pose, the unusual narrowness of the canvas, and the plain, though broken and thickly impasted, background – apricot to yellow-green in colour, with a few palm fronds at the top – all contribute to the monolithic quality which was Sutherland's aim. This is Maugham the inscrutable, sardonic observer of, and commentator upon, the problems of mortal men. Difficulties in the management of the legs, the subject of numerous trial sketches (compare No. 24), are masked by the incisive line of the trouser crease: Sutherland encountered similar difficulties in his second commission, that of Lord Beaverbrook, which were due chiefly to the shortness of the sitter's legs. The familiarity of the *Somerset Maugham* (indeed it is perhaps the most familiar of all Sutherland's portraits) has tended to obscure the fact that it is not only Sutherland's first – brilliantly successful – incursion into portraiture, arguably the most difficult of all branches of painting, but also a work of total originality: one may comb the history of art for antecedents, but there are no antecedents (the closest affinity, and then only in certain respects, is with Van Gogh).

Lent by the Trustees of the Tate Gallery (6034)

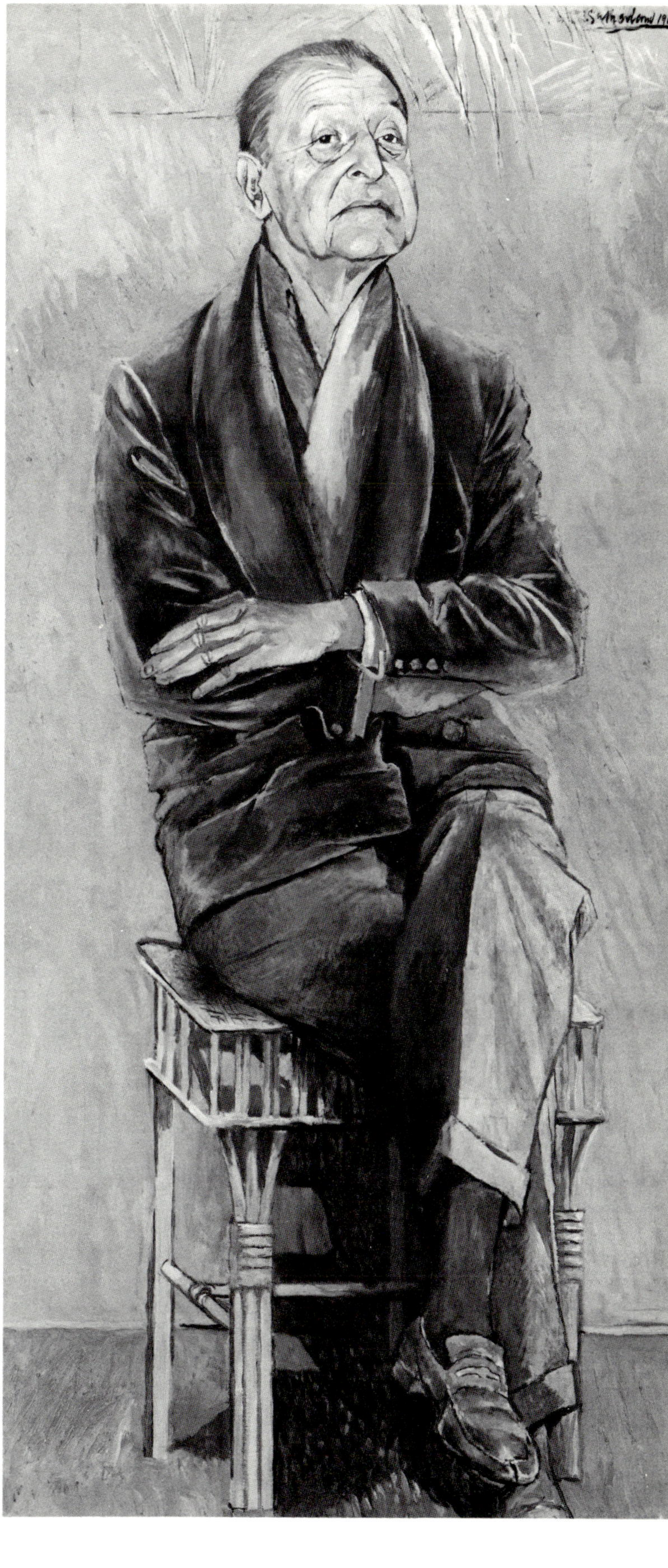

27

28
Sketch of head in profile to left
Black chalk
$8\frac{5}{16} \times 8$ (21.1 × 20.3)
Signed, dated and inscribed upper right: *W.S.M. / G.S. 1952*

A study of Maugham in the act of stammering.

Lent by Mrs Graham Sutherland

29
Study of head facing half right
Black chalk and pencil, with some gouache, on tracing paper
$7\frac{1}{4} \times 6\frac{3}{16}$ (18.4 × 15.7)
Executed in 1953

Study for the lithograph (No. 32) commissioned by Messrs Heinemann for an edition of *Cakes and Ale* to celebrate Maugham's eightieth birthday.

Lent by Mrs Graham Sutherland

30
Study of head facing half right
Black chalk on tracing paper
$6\frac{1}{4} \times 5$ (15.9 × 12.7) irregular
Executed in 1953

LITERATURE: Francesco Arcangeli, *Graham Sutherland*, New York, 1975, p.41, plate 224.

Study for the lithograph (No. 32). A trial lithograph was made, including coat and collar, as depicted here, but this was abandoned.

Lent by Mrs Graham Sutherland

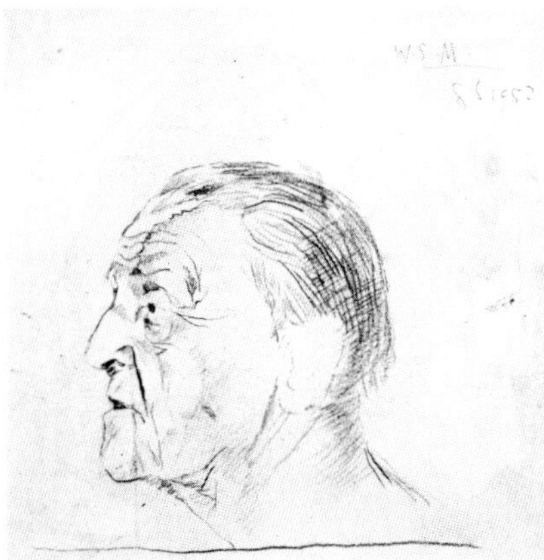

28

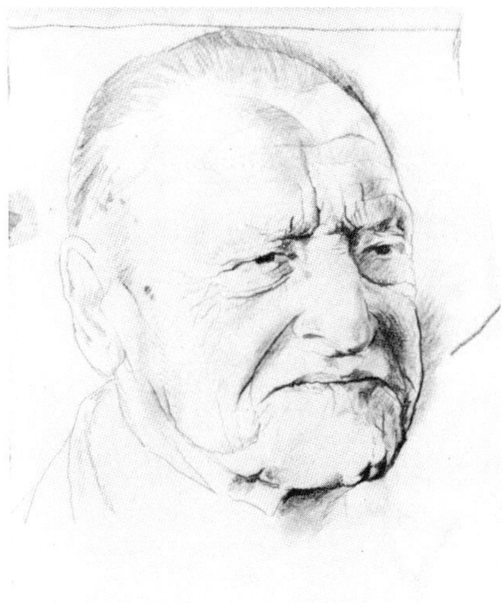

29

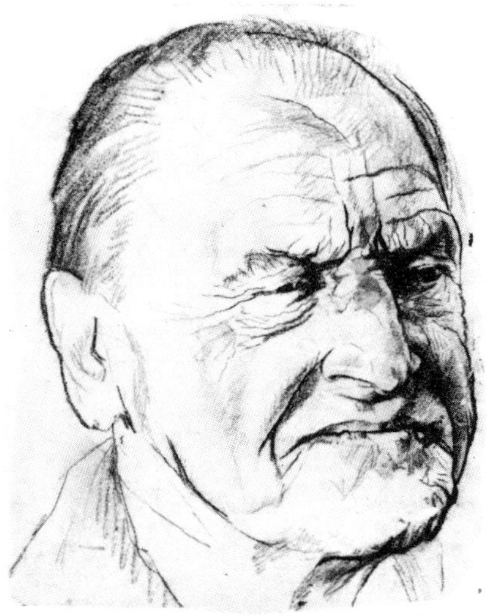

30

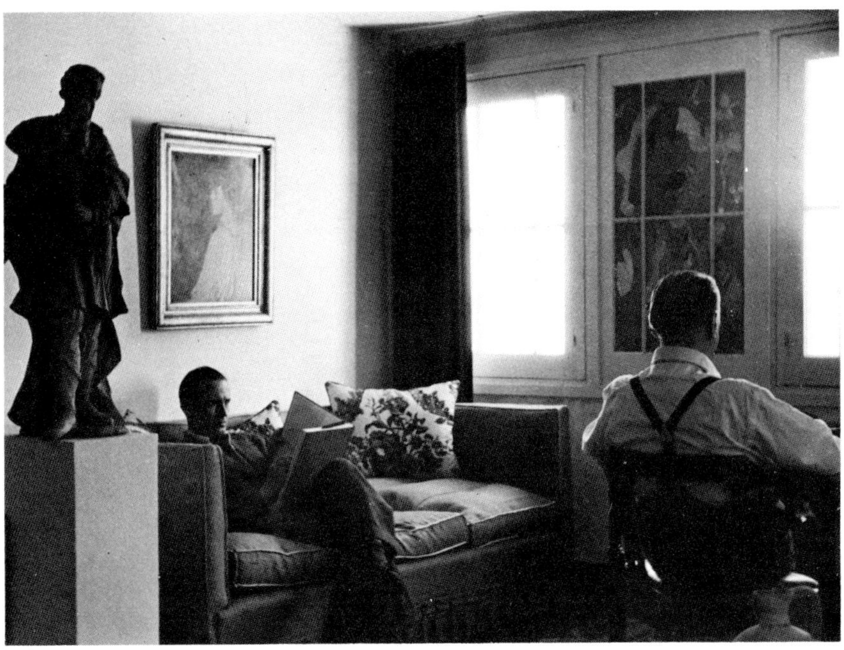

Figure 3
Sutherland sketching Somerset Maugham for the lithograph (No. 32) at the Villa Mauresque, St Jean Cap Ferrat, 1953 (Photograph: Felix H. Man)

31
Study of head facing half right
Black and red chalk
$8\frac{13}{16} \times 5\frac{15}{16}$ (22.4 × 15.1)
Dated upper right: *28. VI. 53*

The definitive working drawing for the lithograph (No. 32).

Lent by Mrs Graham Sutherland

32
Head facing half right
Lithograph
$7\frac{1}{2} \times 6\frac{5}{8}$ (19.1 × 16.8)
Executed in 1953

LITERATURE: Published as the frontispiece to the eightieth birthday edition of *Cakes and Ale,* London, n.d. (=1954); Douglas Cooper, *The Work of Graham Sutherland,* London, 1961, p. 56, Felix H. Man, *Graham Sutherland Das Graphische Werk 1922–70,* Munich, 1970, No. 57.

Artist's proof. The published edition is dated 7 July 1953.

Lent by Mrs Graham Sutherland

33
Head and shoulders facing half right
Oil on canvas
$27\frac{1}{4} \times 21\frac{1}{4}$ (69.2 × 54)
Signed, dated and inscribed upper right: *W.S.M./SUTHERLAND. 1954–5*

PROVENANCE: Purchased by Lord Beaverbrook 1955, and presented by him.
LITERATURE: *Paintings*, Beaverbrook Art Gallery, Fredericton, 1959, p. 65, plate 56.

A portrait which Sutherland subsequently painted for his own satisfaction, based on the drawings from life made for the lithograph (No. 32).

Lent by the Beaverbrook Foundation, Beaverbrook Art Gallery, Fredericton, New Brunswick (59.242)

34
Sketch of head facing half right and of left and right ears
Pencil
12 × $9\frac{1}{4}$ (30.5 × 23.5)
Executed in 1955. Inscribed upper right: *Sketch of W.S.M/laughing*
Verso: the start of a similar sketch

Lent by Mrs Graham Sutherland

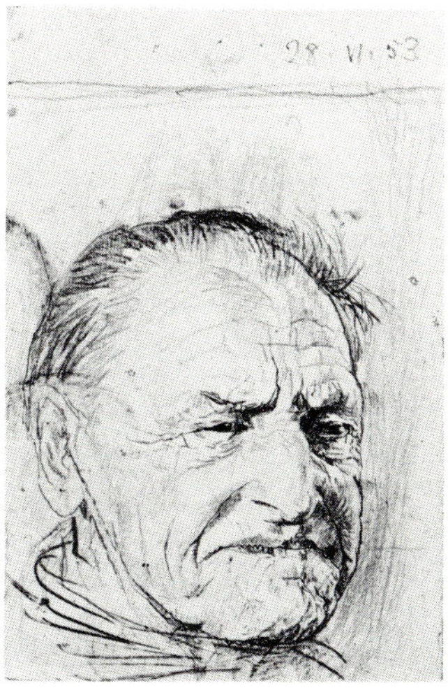

31

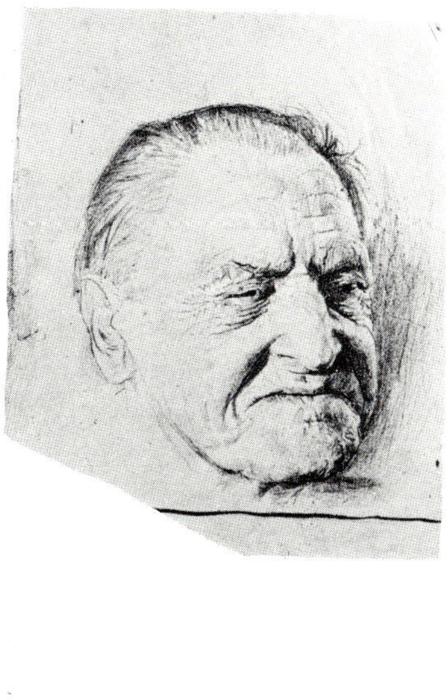
32

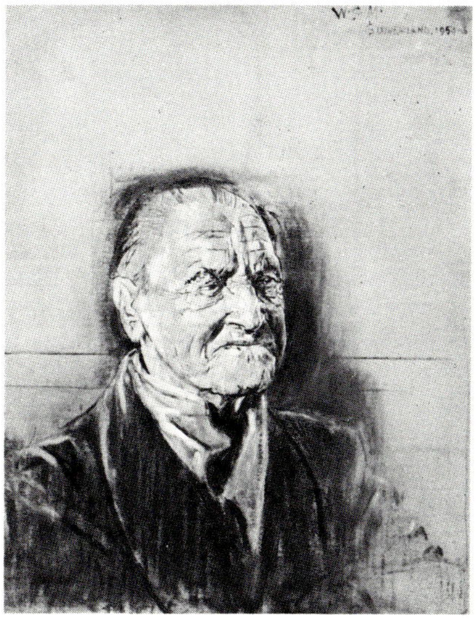
33

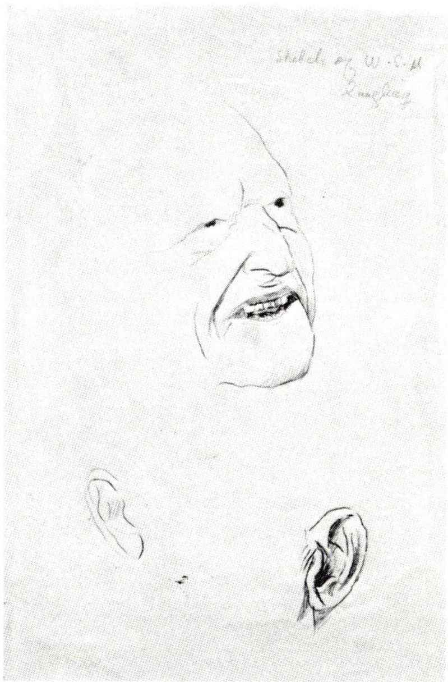
34

Lord Beaverbrook
1879–1964

Canadian; statesman, writer and newspaper proprietor; held ministerial posts in the Churchill wartime government, 1940–5.

Lord Beaverbrook invited Sutherland to paint his portrait after seeing the *Somerset Maugham*. The commission was begun in 1950. The definitive portrait, which is now in the Beaverbrook Art Gallery, was started in May 1951 and finished in November.

35
Study of head facing half left
Oil on canvas
20 × 16 (50.8 × 40.6)
Signed and dated lower right: *Sutherland. 1950*

PROVENANCE: Purchased by Lord Beaverbrook 1955, and presented by him.
EXHIBITED: Institute of Contemporary Arts, Boston, Houston and Palm Beach, 1953–4.
LITERATURE: *Paintings*, Beaverbrook Art Gallery, Fredericton, p. 64; Douglas Cooper, *The Work of Graham Sutherland*, London, 1961, p. 58 Note.

A final study of the head, made before starting work on the final canvas, and squared up for transfer. Sutherland's emphasis on, and linear description of, the folds and furrows in Lord Beaverbrook's face are similar to his approach to the *Maugham*.

Lent by the Beaverbrook Foundation, Beaverbrook Art Gallery, Fredericton, New Brunswick (59.220)

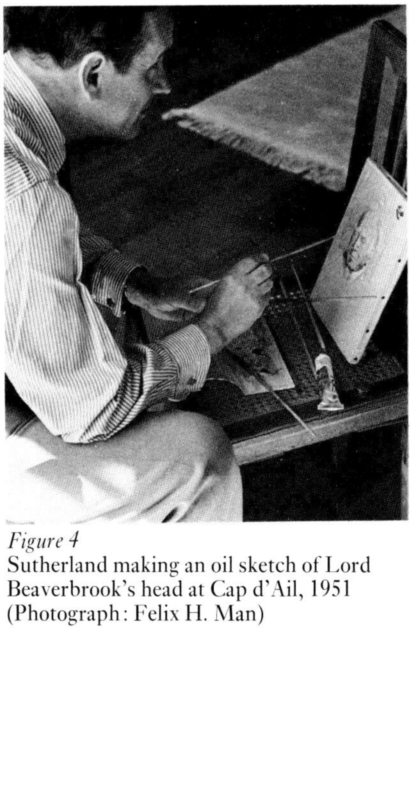

Figure 4
Sutherland making an oil sketch of Lord Beaverbrook's head at Cap d'Ail, 1951 (Photograph: Felix H. Man)

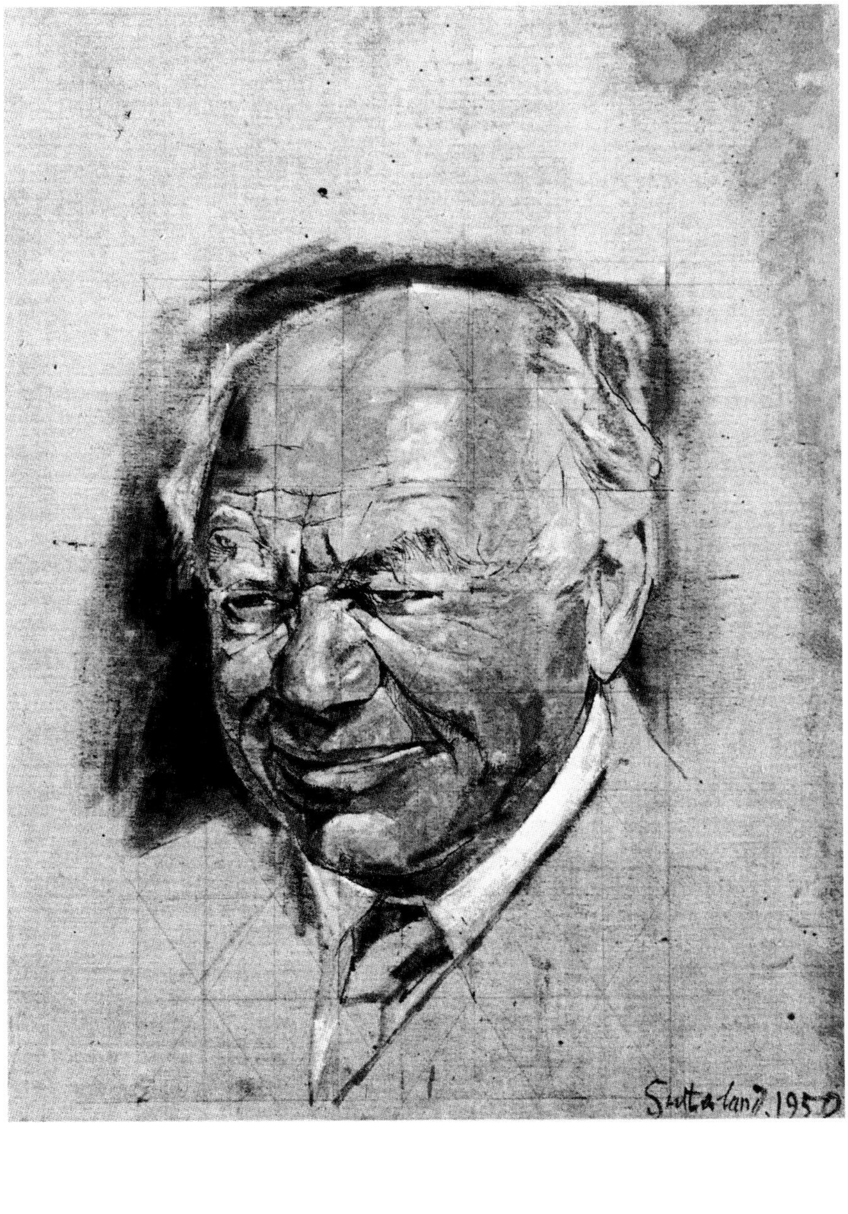

35

Sir Winston Churchill
1874–1965

Statesman, historian and writer; held most of the high offices of state over a period of nearly fifty years; Prime Minister 1940–5 and 1951–5.

The commission was begun in August 1954 and finished in November. The portrait was presented to the sitter as a celebration of his eightieth birthday by past and present members of the House of Lords and House of Commons in Westminister Hall on 30 November 1954. The All-Party Committee had specified that Churchill should be represented as the House of Commons had always known him, and the spotted bow tie, black coat and waistcoat and striped trousers in which Sutherland painted him were indeed the dress familiar to every one of Churchill's parliamentary colleagues. Churchill appeared for sittings on a dais, and on a dais, and as a man who wielded supreme power, Sutherland depicted him, conveying to the full the distinction and tenacity of the elder statesman who had saved the world from tyranny in 1940–5 and whose political life had been spent in combat for causes innumerable. The image was deliberately not conceived with the sharpness, precision and angularity of the Maugham, but the principles governing the portrait, as opposed to the solution of the problems posed by a totally different personality, are similar: nothing detracts from the bulldog pugnacity of the head, the weight of the form is massive, and the figure is set against a background of loosely arranged rectangles.

36
Study at full-length in Garter robes
Oil on canvas
40 × 24 (101.6 × 61)
Signed, dated and inscribed upper left: *GS August 1955/Study for a project of WSC/in Garter Robes* ('1955' a slip for '1954')

PROVENANCE: Purchased by Lord Beaverbrook 1955, and presented by him.
LITERATURE: *Paintings*, Beaverbrook Art Gallery, Fredericton, 1959, p. 65; Douglas Cooper, *The Work of Graham Sutherland*, London, 1961, p. 59 Note.

Churchill would have preferred to have been painted in his robes as Knight of the Garter rather than in his everyday dress as colleagues knew him in the House, and this study was executed right at the start of the commission when Sutherland was experimenting with various possibilities for his interpretation, 'clearing the ground' for what he would ultimately do.

Lent by the Beaverbrook Foundation, Beaverbrook Art Gallery, Fredericton, New Brunswick (59.223)

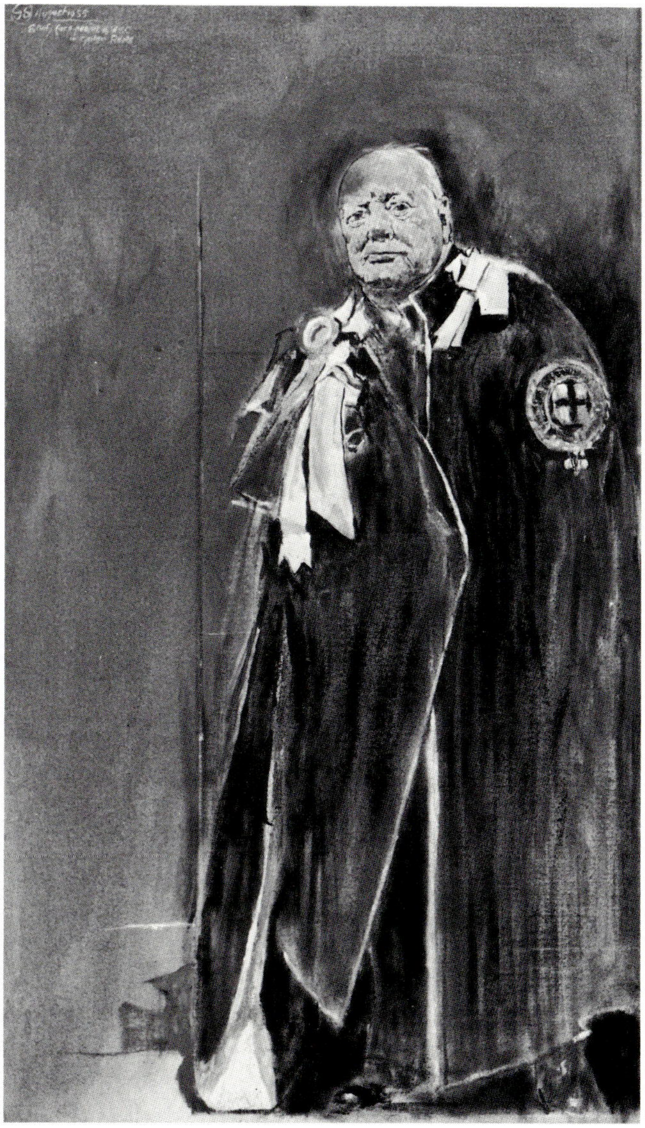

36

37
Study of nose and mouth
Black chalk and pencil
$10 \times 10\frac{3}{4}$ (25.4 × 27.3)
Executed in 1954

PROVENANCE: Purchased by Lord Beaverbrook 1955, and presented by him.
LITERATURE: *Paintings*, Beaverbrook Art Gallery, Fredericton, 1959, plate 54.

A study of the relationship of features for the definitive portrait, squared up for transfer, which has something of the quality of a water-colour by Cézanne done in front of the motif. The essentials of Churchill's bulldog countenance are already clearly stated.

Lent by the Beaverbrook Foundation, Beaverbrook Art Gallery, Fredericton, New Brunswick (59.231)

38
Study of eyes, nose and mouth
Black chalk, pencil and gouache
10 × 13 (25.4 × 33)
Executed in 1954

PROVENANCE: Purchased by Lord Beaverbrook 1955, and presented by him.

A study for the definitive portrait, similar to the previous sketch (No. 37) and also squared for transfer, but including a notation of the eyes as well as of the nose and mouth. Something of the force of the earlier sketch is lacking.

Lent by the Beaverbrook Foundation, Beaverbrook Art Gallery, Fredericton, New Brunswick (59.230)

39
Study of head facing slightly to left
Pen and ink, black chalk, pencil and gouache
$14\frac{3}{4} \times 12$ (37.5 × 30.5)
Executed in 1954

PROVENANCE: Purchased by Lord Beaverbrook 1955, and presented by him.
LITERATURE: *Paintings*, Beaverbrook Art Gallery, Fredericton, 1959, plate 55.

A study for the definitive portrait, developed from the previous sketch (No. 38) and also squared up for transfer.

Lent by the Beaverbrook Foundation, Beaverbrook Art Gallery, Fredericton, New Brunswick (59.229)

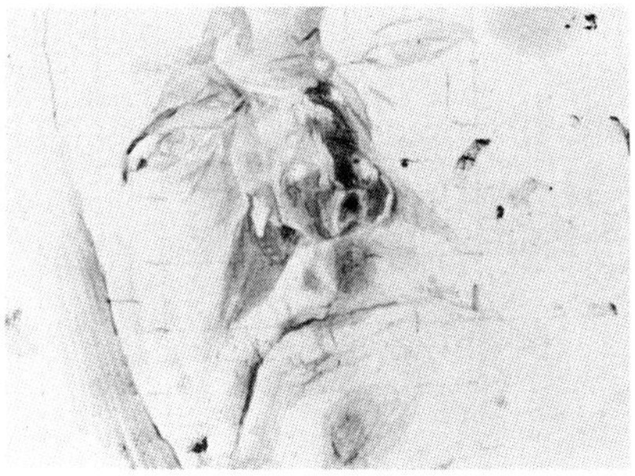
38

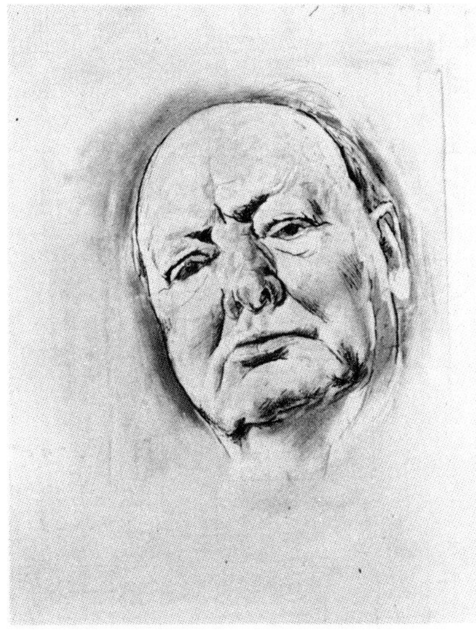
39

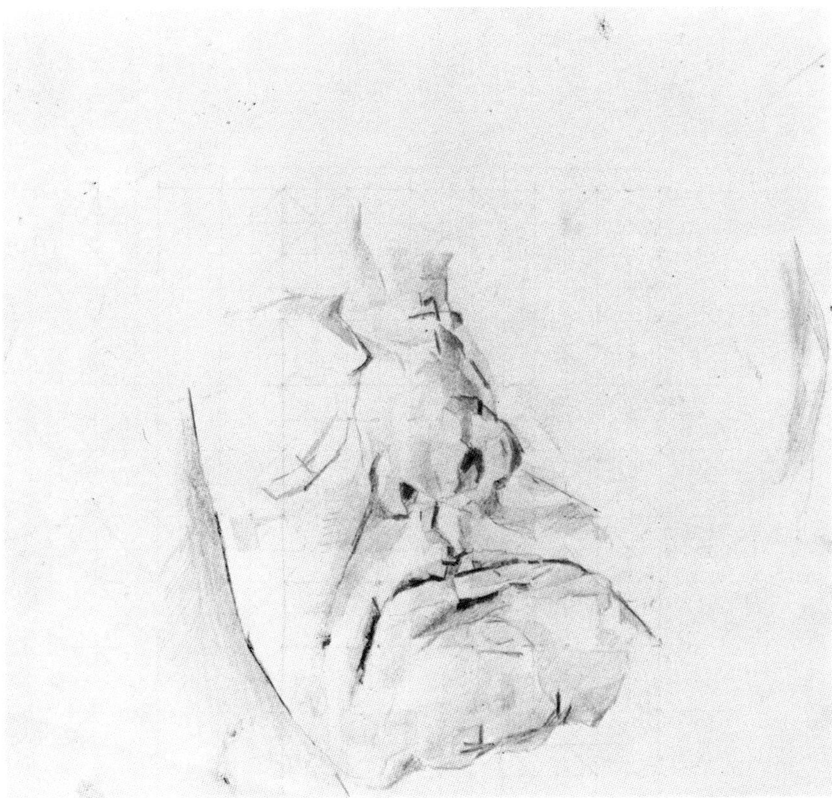
37

40
Study of head facing slightly to left
Oil on canvas
$26\frac{5}{8} \times 17\frac{3}{4}$ (67.6 × 45.1)
Executed in 1954

PROVENANCE: Mr and Mrs Robert Melville.
EXHIBITED: *Paintings and Watercolours by Graham Sutherland*, Lefèvre Gallery, April–May 1975 (12b repr.).
LITERATURE: *Apollo*, May 1975, p.397, fig. 6; *The Burlington Magazine*, June 1975, p.417, fig. 122.

A study for the definitive portrait, derived from the previous sketch (No. 39). A larger head, facing half left, executed on the lower part of the canvas, has been painted out.

Lent from a Private Collection (recto of No. 19)

41
Study of left hand
Pen and ink on tracing paper
$4\frac{7}{8} \times 3\frac{7}{8}$ (12.4 × 9.8)
Executed in 1954

PROVENANCE: Purchased by Lord Beaverbrook 1955, and presented by him.

A study for the definitive portrait. This and the following studies constitute the fullest surviving series of sketches of a sitter's hands for any of Graham Sutherland's portraits.

Lent by the Beaverbrook Canadian Foundation, Beaverbrook Art Gallery, Fredericton, New Brunswick (59.432)

42
Studies of right hand
Pencil and gouache
$14\frac{1}{2} \times 10$ (36.8 × 25.4)
Executed in 1954

PROVENANCE: Presented to Lord Beaverbrook by the artist, 1955.

Four studies of Churchill's right hand, on squared paper, for the definitive portrait.

Lent by the Beaverbrook Foundation, Beaverbrook Art Gallery, Fredericton, New Brunswick (59. 238)

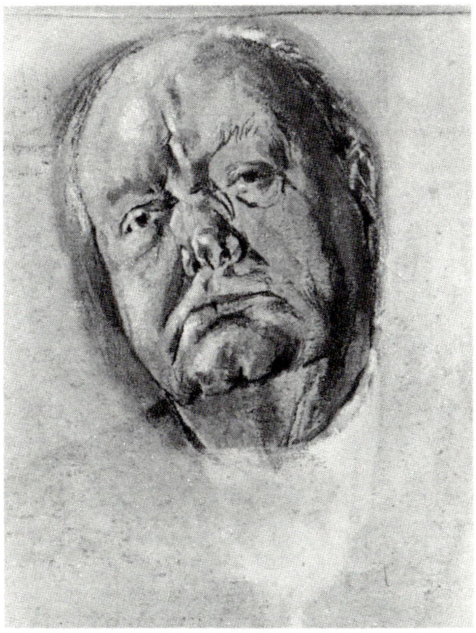

40 *detail*

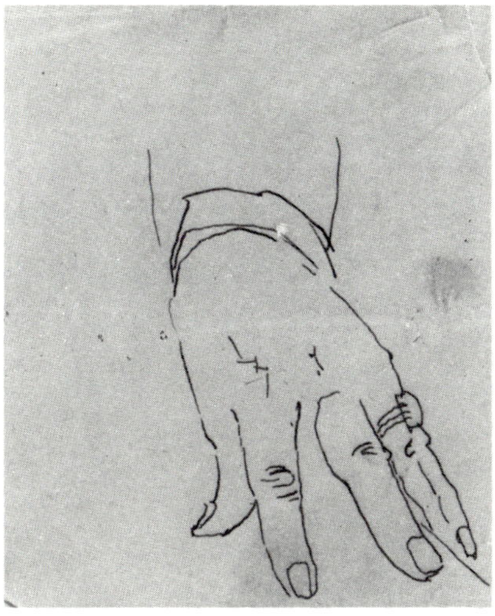

41

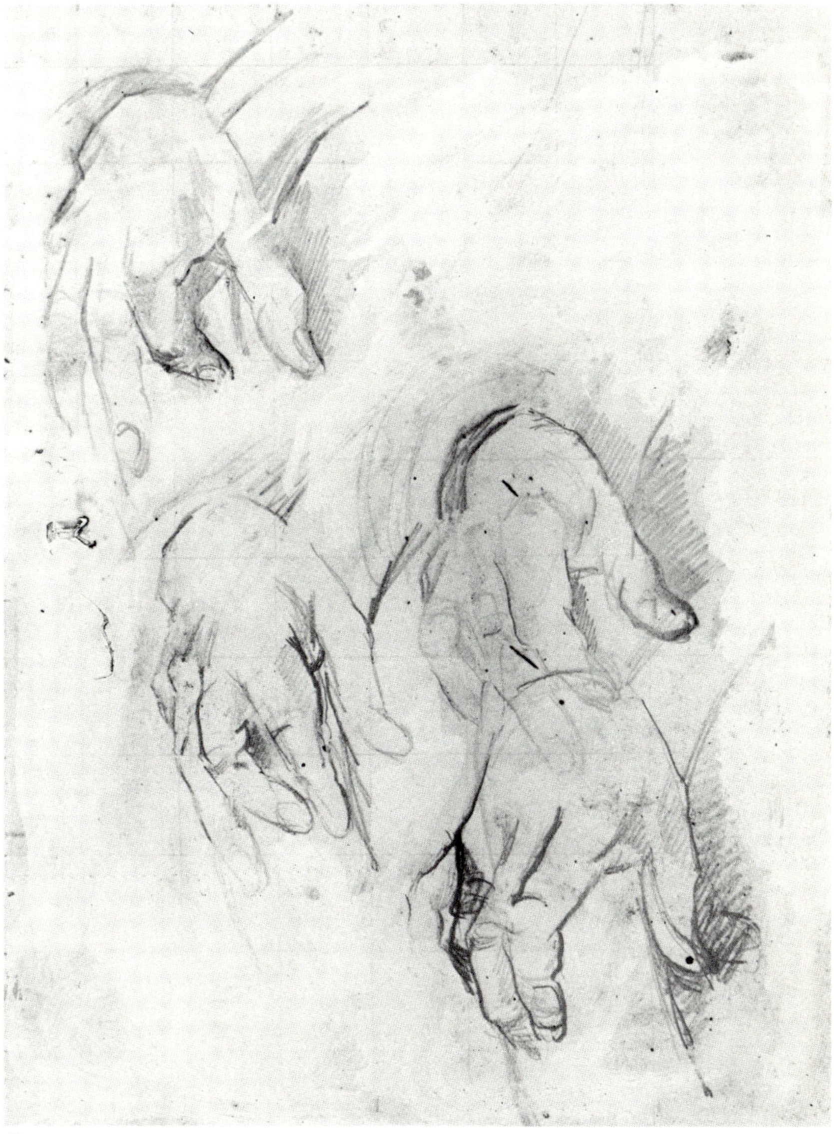

42

43
Studies of right hand
Pen and ink and pencil on tracing paper
$6\frac{1}{4} \times 4\frac{3}{4}$ (15.9×12.1)
Signed and dated lower right: *Dec. 1954/G.S.* (it seems likely that the 'Dec' is a slip, probably for 'Oct', since the finished picture was completed in November. It may be noted here that some of the sketches bought by Lord Beaverbrook in 1955 were inscribed by Sutherland at the time of the purchase).

PROVENANCE: Purchased by Lord Beaverbrook 1955, and presented by him.

Three studies of Churchill's right hand, for the definitive portrait.

Lent by the Beaverbrook Foundation, Beaverbrook Art Gallery, Fredericton, New Brunswick (59.240)

44
Studies of right hand
Black chalk and pencil
$9\frac{1}{2} \times 11\frac{1}{8}$ (24.1×28.3)
Signed and dated upper left: *October 1954, G.S.*

PROVENANCE: Purchased by Lord Beaverbrook 1955, and presented by him.
LITERATURE: Douglas Cooper, *The Work of Graham Sutherland*, London, 1961, p.58 Note and fig. 11.

Two studies of Churchill's right hand, for the definitive portrait.

Lent by the Beaverbrook Foundation, Beaverbrook Art Gallery, Fredericton, New Brunswick (59.236)

45
Studies of right hand
Pen and ink, black chalk and pencil
$9\frac{3}{8} \times 15\frac{3}{8}$ (23.8×39.1)
Signed and dated lower left: *October 1954. G.S.*

PROVENANCE: Purchased by Lord Beaverbrook 1955, and presented by him.

Six studies of Churchill's right hand, for the definitive portrait. The study on the left of the sheet shows the pose substantially as adopted.

Lent by the Beaverbrook Foundation, Beaverbrook Art Gallery, Fredericton, New Brunswick (59.239)

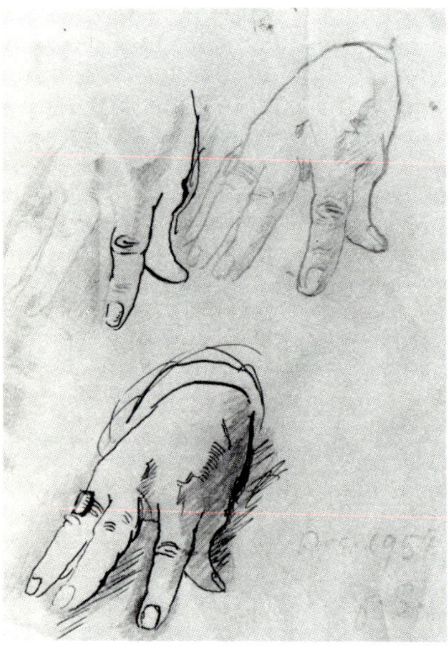

43

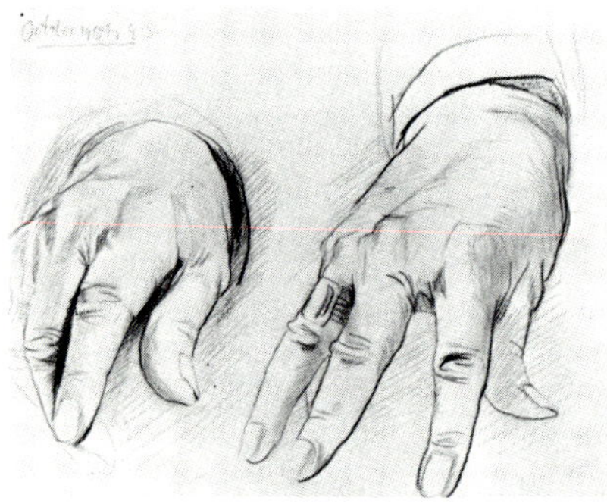

44

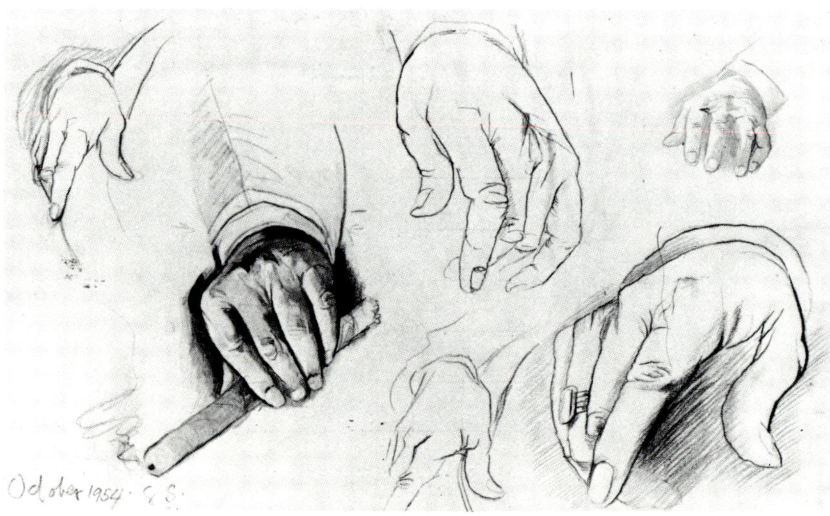

45

46
Studies of right hand
Pen and ink and pencil
$9\frac{3}{8} \times 7\frac{7}{16}$ (23.8 × 18.9)
Executed in 1954

Two studies of Churchill's right hand, for the definitive portrait. The upper of the two drawings is close to the pose as finally adopted.

Lent by Mrs Graham Sutherland

47
Studies of right eye and mouth
Black chalk and pencil
$14\frac{1}{2} \times 10$ (36.8 × 25.4)
Dated and inscribed bottom: *Chequers 14th November 1954.* Inscribed top: *Done while W.S.C was playing cards with Soames.* (this is followed by elaborate colour notes).

PROVENANCE: Purchased by Lord Beaverbrook 1955, and presented by him.

Three studies of Churchill's right eye, and slighter sketches of his mouth, for the definitive portrait. Sutherland has made detailed colour notes which relate to the features and subtle variations of complexion in Churchill's face. The sheet dates from only six days before the completion of the final portrait, and is an example of Sutherland's increasing concern to refresh his memory about details of tints – in other words, scrupulous concern for accuracy – during the course of finishing a commission.

Lent by the Beaverbrook Foundation, Beaverbrook Art Gallery, Fredericton, New Brunswick (59.232)

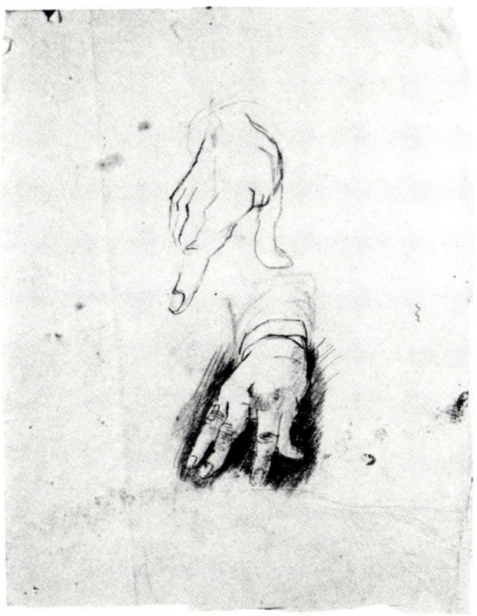

46

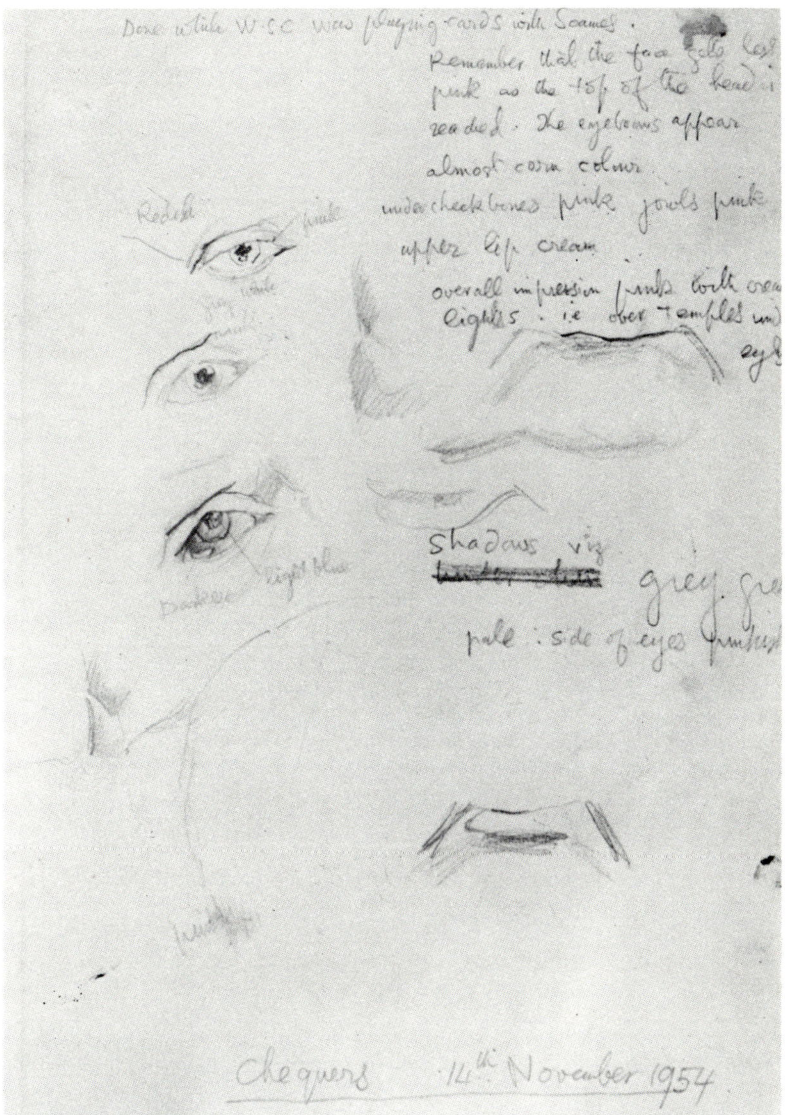

47

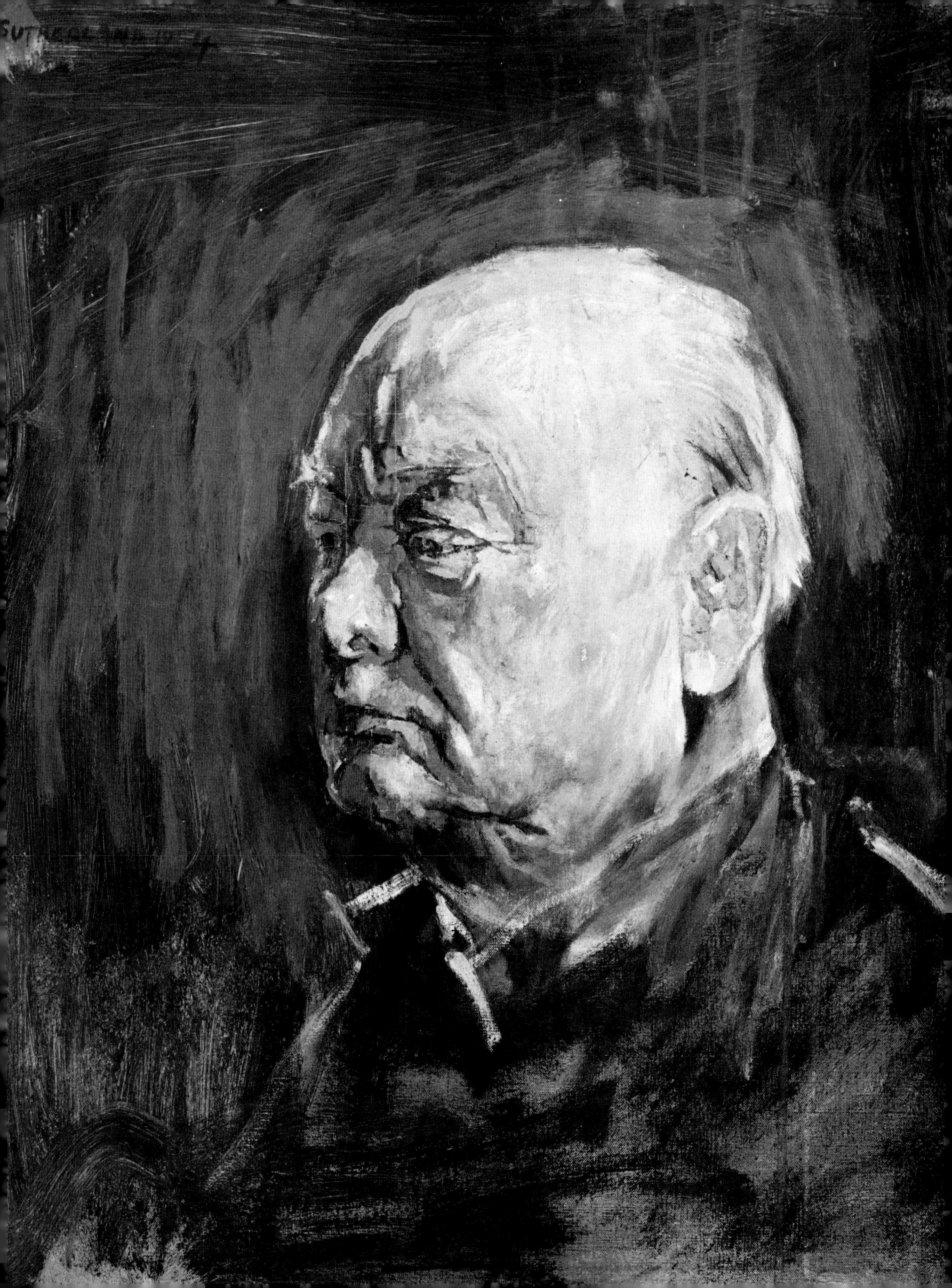

48
Study of head facing half left
Oil on canvas
24 × 20 (61 × 50.8)
Signed and dated upper left:
SUTHERLAND 1954

PROVENANCE: Beaverbrook Art Gallery.
EXHIBITED: *Sutherland*, Galleria Civica d'Arte Moderna, Turin, October – November 1965 (98 repr.); *Graham Sutherland*, Kunsthalle, Basel, February – March 1966 (87 repr.).
LITERATURE: *Paintings*, Beaverbrook Art Gallery, Fredericton, 1959, p. 65, plate 51; Douglas Cooper, *The Work of Graham Sutherland*, London, 1961, p. 83, plate 168; Francesco Arcangeli, *Graham Sutherland*, New York, 1975, p. 41, plate 223.

A brilliant oil sketch from life of the great warrior, showing him in one of his characteristic moods, abstracted and brooding. After lunch one day Churchill had agreed to be photographed by Felix Man, at the same time as he was dictating letters to his secretary; he had gone over to the window and, as the sun was low, his skin seemed transparent, an effect most sensitively conveyed by Sutherland in this oil study (see also, for Sutherland's account of his sittings with Churchill, Giorgio Soavi, *Protagonisti*, Milan, 1969, pp. 165–6).

Lent by Mrs Graham Sutherland

49
Study of head facing frontally
Black chalk with some pencil
$15\frac{3}{8} \times 14\frac{1}{4}$ (39.1 × 36.2)
Executed in 1954
Signed and inscribed lower right:
W.S.C./G.S. Chartwell

An effective study of Churchill's features in repose; he is shown asleep still wearing his spectacles.

Lent by Mrs Graham Sutherland

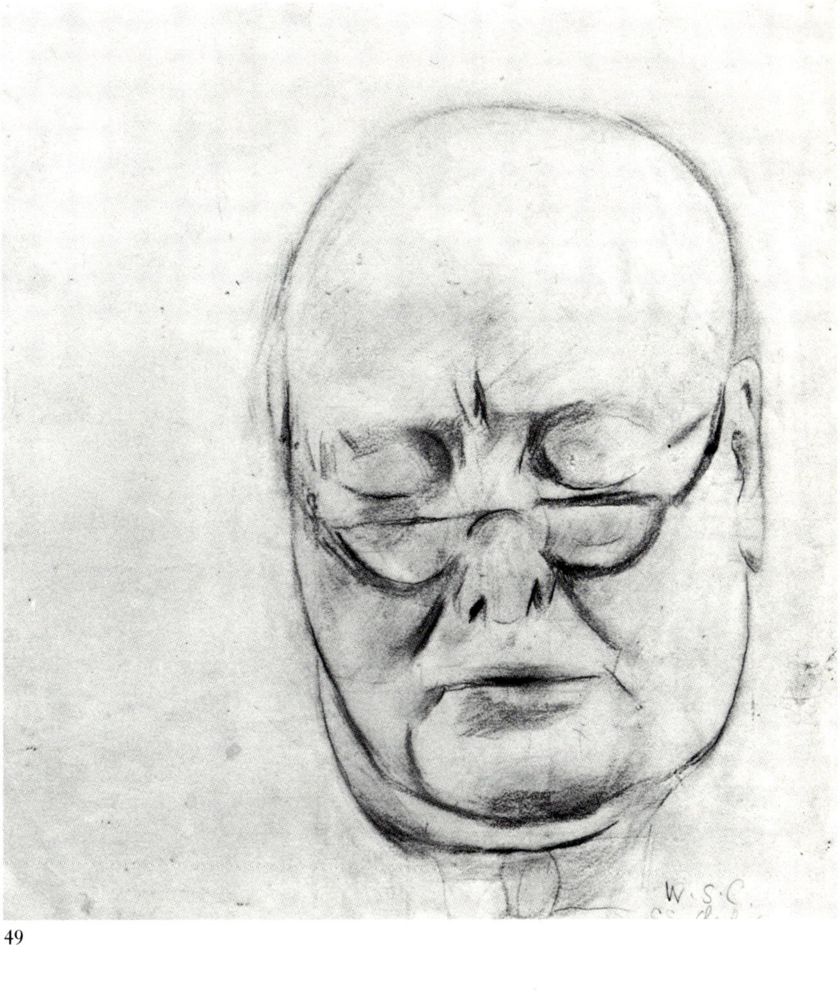

49

48

Edward Sackville-West, later Lord Sackville
1901–65

Writer, musicologist and heir to Knole.

The commission, undertaken for Mrs Ian Phillips, was begun in November 1953 and finished in December 1954. A smaller portrait was executed in 1957.

50
Study of head facing slightly to left
Black chalk and gouache on grey paper
$15\frac{3}{8} \times 10\frac{1}{4}$ (39.1 × 26)
Executed in 1953

PROVENANCE: Purchased by Lord Beaverbrook 1955, and presented by him.

A study for the definitive portrait, in the pose adopted, and squared up for transfer. The tension and relationship of the features is brilliantly rendered.

Lent by the Beaverbrook Foundation, Beaverbrook Art Gallery, Fredericton, New Brunswick (59.246)

51
The definitive portrait
(Colour plate 2, page 23)
Oil on canvas
$66\frac{3}{4} \times 30\frac{3}{8}$ (169.5 × 77.2)
Executed in 1954
Signed and dated on the back: *Portrait of/Hon. E. Sackville-West/1955/G. Sutherland*

EXHIBITED: *British Portraits*, Royal Academy, 1956–7 (794); *Modern British Portraits*, Arts Council (Cambridge, Newcastle, Torquay, Nottingham, Newport and Bolton), 1960–1 (35); *Sutherland*, Galleria Civica d'Arte Moderna, Turin, October – November 1965 (95 repr.); *Graham Sutherland*, Kunsthalle, Basel, February – March 1966 (84); *Graham Sutherland*, Munich, The Hague, Berlin and Cologne, March – November 1967 (47 repr.).

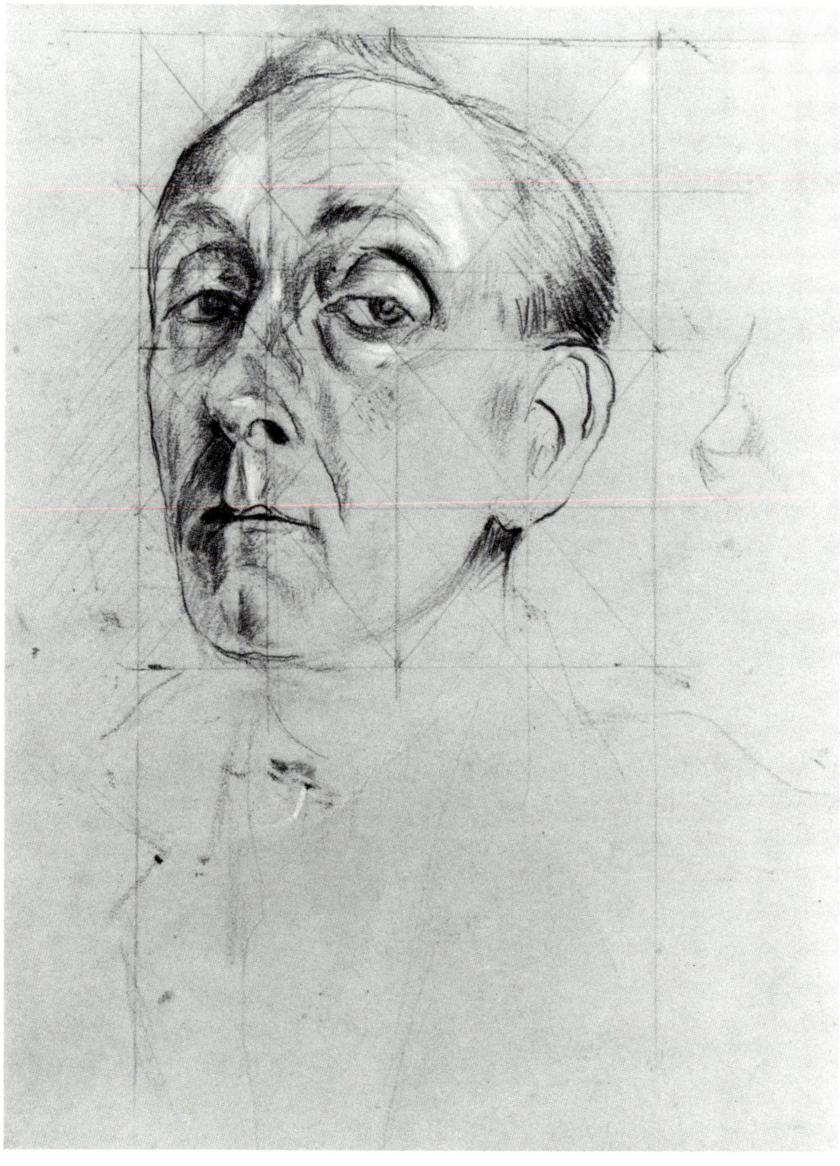

50

LITERATURE: 'Some little-known Portraits at the Royal Academy', *The Burlington Magazine*, January 1957, p. 27, fig. 32; Douglas Cooper, *The Work of Graham Sutherland*, London, 1961, pp. 56–8, 67 and 83, plate 169a; Andrew Révai, *Graham Sutherland* (The Masters Series), 1966, pp. 2 and 6, plate IX; John Rothenstein, *Modern English Painters*, Vol. 3, London, 1974, pp. 67–8.

Sutherland's first three completed portraits, those of Maugham, Beaverbrook and Churchill, were all vigorous and dynamic, as befitted their worldly subjects. Edward Sackville-West was hypersensitive and highly strung, and seemed, as Lord Clark writes, 'to stand permanently on the threshold of death's door'. Sutherland's portrait of him is, appropriately, far subtler than his previous works: not only in characterisation, but in composition, in modelling, in its muted colour scheme based on the dark red priming evident throughout, and in its tonal nuances. The sitter is perched on a high stool, his hands nervously clasped (the habit of kneading his fingers was a characteristic nervous compulsion), and his expression tense, almost anguished; notwithstanding, as Sutherland says, he 'sat like a rock'. The impression of imbalance is corrected by the placing of the background rectangles, the first use of a wholly abstract setting in Sutherland's portraits. In the lower part of the canvas Sutherland tried to create 'an impalpable atmosphere', which accounts for the sketchiness of handling. These formal decisions were the product of Sutherland's profound psychological insight into an individual whom he knew well. The sitter's relative and admirer, Benedict Nicolson, described the portrait as a 'magnificent image of controlled distress' (*The Burlington Magazine*, op. cit.). The only analogy is with the portraits of Goya.

Lent from a Private Collection

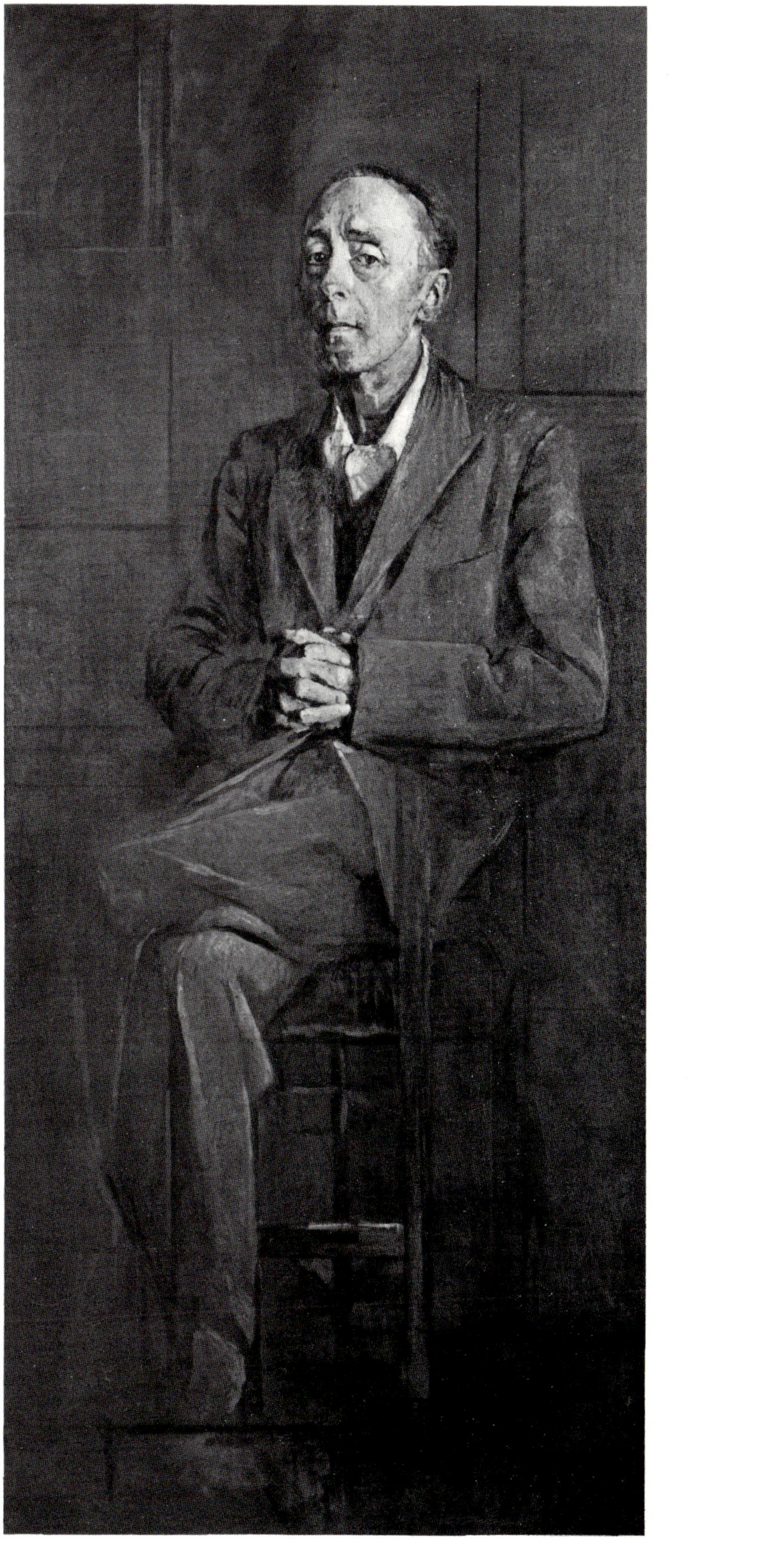

51

52

Study of head facing half left

Pencil with some gouache

$8\frac{9}{16} \times 6\frac{3}{16}$ (21.8 × 15.7)

Signed and inscribed lower right: *E.S.W/G.S.*

Drawn in 1957

A study, recalling Sutherland's admiration of Holbein in its economy of line, for a projected portrait of Sackville-West in bed.

Lent by Mrs Graham Sutherland

53

Head and shoulders facing half left

Oil on canvas

24 × 24 (61 × 61)

Signed and dated lower right: *G.S.1957*

PROVENANCE: Purchased from the artist, 1958.

EXHIBITED: *Primitives to Picasso*, Royal Academy, 1962 (262); *Graham Sutherland*, Munich, The Hague, Berlin and Cologne, March–November 1967 (48 repr.); *British Portraits*, British Council, National Museum of Western Art, Tokyo, October–December 1975 (70 repr.).

LITERATURE: *Emporium*, March 1959, p. 135; Douglas Cooper, *The Work of Graham Sutherland*, London, 1961, pp. 56 and 83, plate 169b; *Catalogue of Paintings*, City Museum and Art Gallery, Birmingham, n.d. (=1961), p. 142, plate 48; John Rothenstein, *Modern English Painters*, Vol. 3, London, 1974, pp. 67–8; Francesco Arcangeli, *Graham Sutherland*, New York, 1975, p. 41, plate 225.

A rather less tense portrait than the full-length of 1954, but displaying nonetheless Sackville-West's nervous, ever-questioning disposition. Eyes, nostrils and mouth are all intensely alert.

Lent by the City Museum and Art Gallery, Birmingham (P.10' 58)

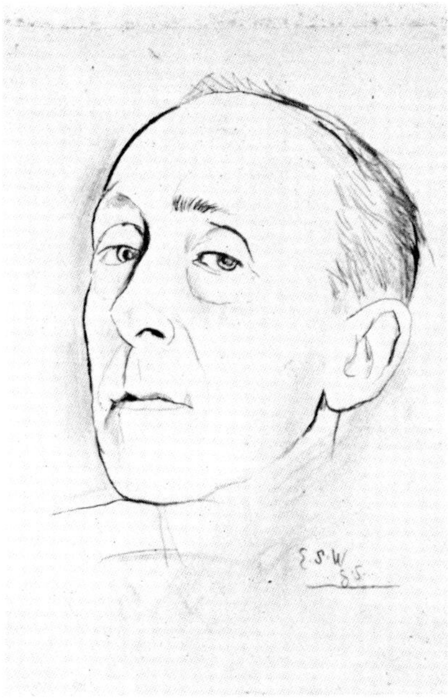

52

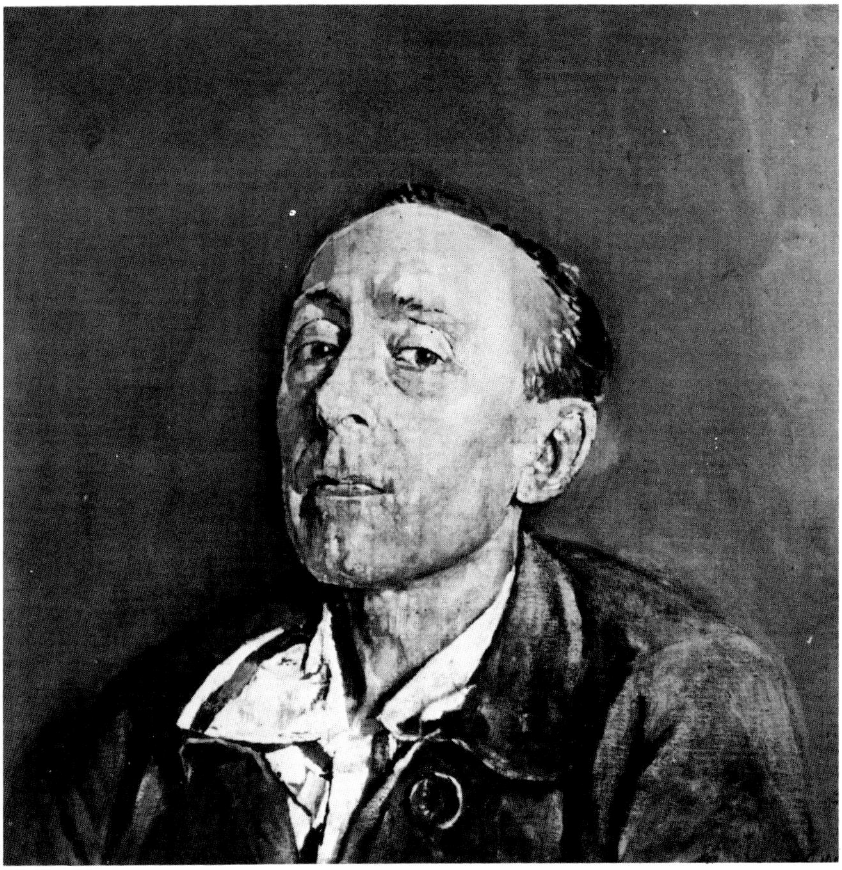

53

Arthur Jeffress
1904 – 61

American; collector and art dealer.

The commission was begun in July 1954 and finished in May 1955.

54
Study of head and shoulders facing half right
Oil on canvas
$15\frac{3}{4} \times 11\frac{3}{4}$ (40 × 29.9)
Dated and inscribed upper right:
Outdoor Study of AJ/Venice July/1954

EXHIBITED: *Paintings and Watercolours by Graham Sutherland*, Lefevre Gallery, April–May 1975 (14 repr.).
LITERATURE: Douglas Cooper, *The Work of Graham Sutherland*, London, 1961, p. 59 Note; 'Southampton Art Gallery: The Arthur Jeffress Bequest', *The Burlington Magazine*, January 1965, p. 53; *The Burlington Magazine*, June 1975, p. 417.

A brilliant study from life revealing the more introverted characteristics of Jeffress's complex personality, qualities which were responsible for his tragic suicide in Paris in November 1961.

Lent from a Private Collection

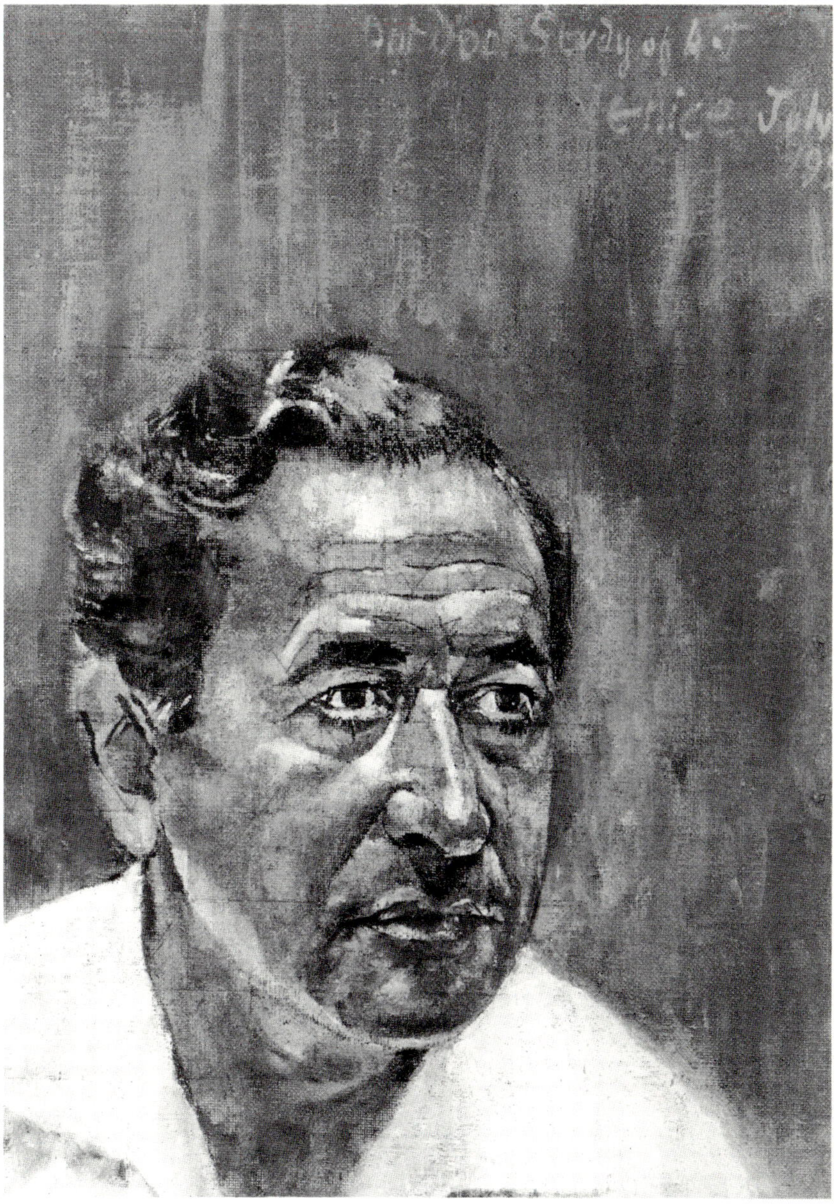

54

55
Study of head facing slightly to right
Oil on canvas
16 × 12 (40.6 × 30.5)
Signed, dated and inscribed upper left: *Sketch for A. J. indoors/Venice July 1954/G.S*

PROVENANCE: Bequeathed by the sitter, 1961.
EXHIBITED: *Graham Sutherland*, Arthur Jeffress Gallery, May–June 1955 (2); *Modern British Portraits*, Arts Council (Cambridge, Newcastle, Torquay, Nottingham, Newport and Bolton), 1960–1 (34); *The Arthur Jeffress Collection*, Worthing Art Gallery, July–August 1974 (24).
LITERATURE: Douglas Cooper, *The Work of Graham Sutherland*, London, 1961, p. 59 Note; *The Arthur Jeffress Bequest*, Southampton Art Gallery, n.d. (=1964), pp. 4–5 and 10; 'Southampton Art Gallery: The Arthur Jeffress Bequest', *The Burlington Magazine*, January 1965, p. 53.

An equally brilliant study from life recording the opposite polarity to the characteristics portrayed in the previous sketch (No. 54): Jeffress's liveliness, sense of mischief and appetite for life – note the glint in the eyes, as well as the vital, almost mercurial, set of nose and mouth. This pose and expression was substantially that adopted by Sutherland for the definitive portrait.

Lent by Southampton Art Gallery

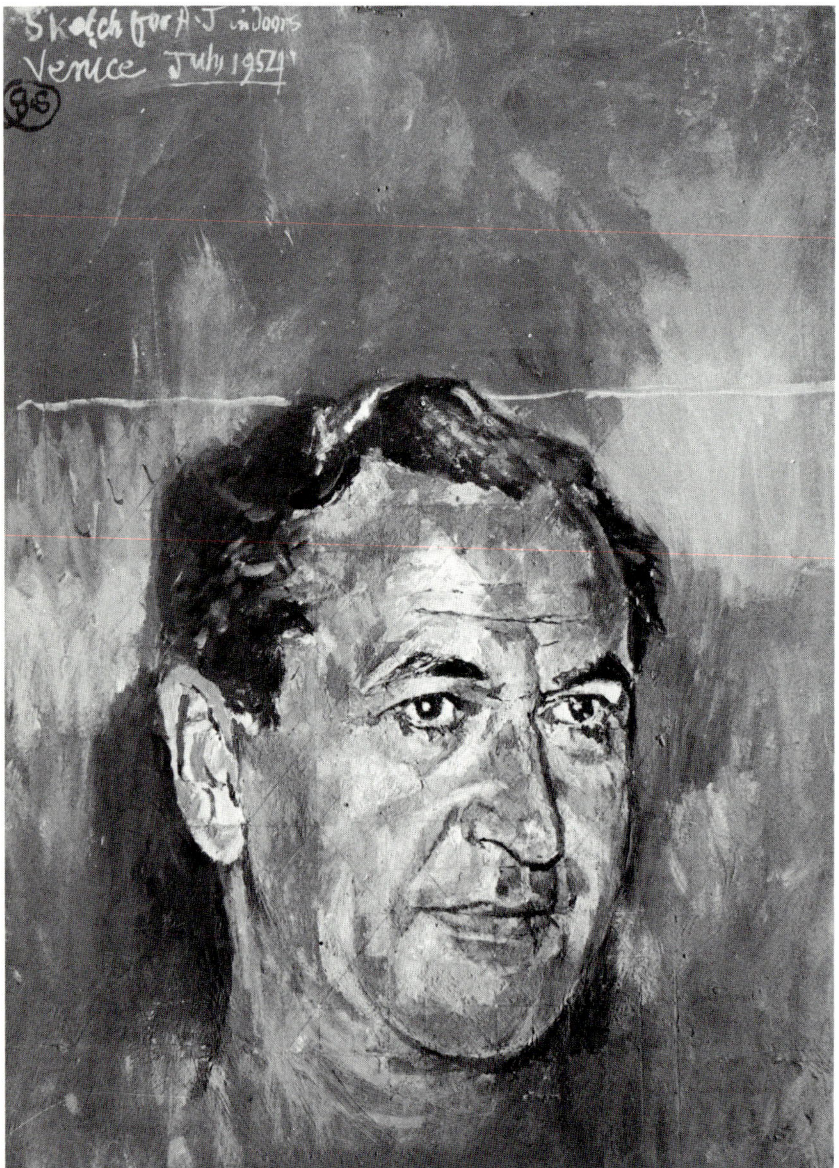

55

56
The definitive portrait
Oil on canvas
$56\frac{1}{2} \times 47\frac{1}{2}$ (143.5 × 120.7)
Signed and dated lower right:
Sutherland. Venice 1955.

PROVENANCE: Bequeathed by the sitter, 1961.
EXHIBITED: *Graham Sutherland,* Arthur Jeffress Gallery, May–June 1955 (1); *Masters of British Painting 1800–1950,* British Council (Museum of Modern Art, New York, St Louis and San Francisco), 1956–7 (108), repr. p. 139; *Inaugural Exhibition,* Rhodes National Gallery, Salisbury, Rhodesia; *Three Masters of British Painting,* Arts Council (Plymouth, Sheffield, Leeds, Manchester and Cheltenham), June–October 1961 (61 plate VI); *Menschenbilder,* Kunsthalle, Darmstadt, September–November 1968, repr. p. 55; *The Arthur Jeffress Collection,* Worthing Art Gallery, July–August 1974 (26).
LITERATURE: Douglas Cooper, *The Work of Graham Sutherland,* London, 1961, pp. 59 and 83, plate 170; *The Arthur Jeffress Bequest,* Southampton Art Gallery, n.d. (= 1964), pp. 3, 4–5, 11 and repr. cover; 'Southampton Art Gallery: The Arthur Jeffress Bequest', *The Burlington Magazine,* January 1965, p. 53.

Sutherland described Jeffress as 'Romantic, even exotic, the physical character of his countenance – with its black humorous eyes and (especially after the long summer sun) its warm brown colouring – reminded one strongly of the faces of certain figures in the paintings of Eugene Delacroix, whose works he admired so much'. Though the composition is dominated by the elaborate, decorative foliated fabric behind the sitter and by the reversed iron garden chair upon which Jeffress is nonchalantly seated, the emphasis is still, as in all Sutherland's previous portraits, on the head, now more broadly painted and even more lively. These changes reflect the differences between the nuances marked down in a sketch from life and the demands of a large-scale composition. The legs are scarcely more than indicated (indeed, visually, the chair legs take their place), and the spectator's eye is drawn inexorably to the upper half of the canvas. The rich material against which Jeffress is painted is suggestive of the backcloth to a Bellini Madonna, or to the throne in Giorgione's celebrated altarpiece at Castelfranco, close to Jeffress's beloved Venice; but, though these may have been ideas latent in Sutherland's subconscious, the fabric (and colour scheme) is in fact an allusion to Jeffress's exoticism, suggestive in particular of the red damask which decorated the walls and covered the bed in his lavish 'Empire' bedroom.

Lent by Southampton Art Gallery

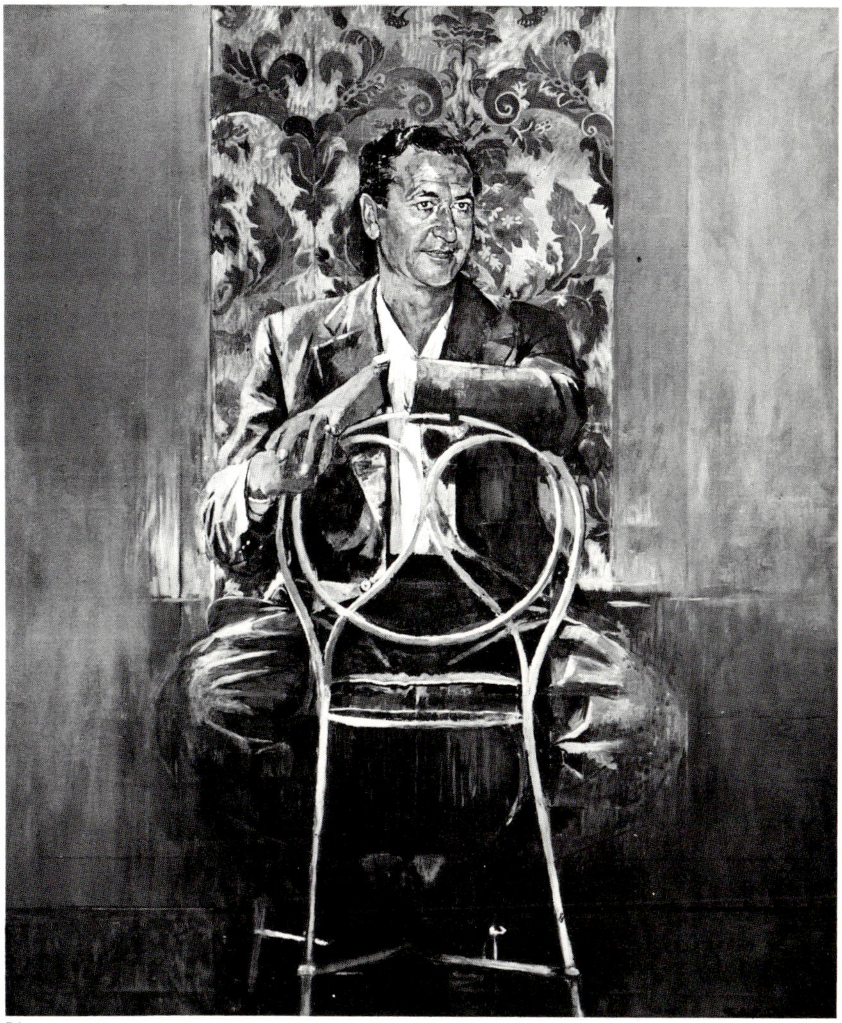

56

Dr Paul Sacher

Swiss; conductor; founder and conductor of the Basle Chamber Orchestra and Choir.

The commission was begun in November 1955 and finished in October 1956.

57
Study of head in profile to right
Oil on canvas
$10\frac{3}{4} \times 8\frac{11}{16}$ (27.3 × 22.1)
Signed, dated and inscribed lower right: *GS. Schönenberg./Nov. 1955*

An exploratory study of the head made in front of the sitter at the start of the commission, 'clearing the ground', as it were, before any compositional ideas began to form in Sutherland's mind. The concentration and pent-up energy revealed in this penetrating sketch is reminiscent of such Renaissance profiles as Pisanello's portrait of Filippo Maria Visconti, Duke of Milan.

Lent by Mrs Graham Sutherland

58
One of the two definitive portraits
Oil on canvas
$50\frac{1}{8} \times 40\frac{1}{8}$ (127.3 × 101.9)
Signed and dated lower right: *Sutherland 1956.*

EXHIBITED: *Graham Sutherland*, Kunsthalle, Basel, February – March 1966 (92 repr.); *Graham Sutherland*, Munich, The Hague, Berlin and Cologne, March – November 1967 (51 repr.).
LITERATURE: Douglas Cooper, *The Work of Graham Sutherland*, London, 1961, pp. 60 and Note and 83, plate 174.

Sutherland studied Sacher on the rostrum, and this portrait most successfully suggests – in every aspect of the pose, but notably in the hands – not only the tension and sensitivity of the sitter, but the latent power and control which Sacher exerted over, and precision of musical interpretation which he expected from, his players. The white shirt is painted with unusually thick impasto; the trousers, on the other hand, are scarcely more than outlined. The orange tints round the head mediate between the subdued, greyish flesh tones and the bright, emerald green background. Sutherland worked on a second portrait of Sacher simultaneously, in which the conductor is also depicted on the rostrum, but is seen in profile facing left.

Lent from a Private Collection, Basel

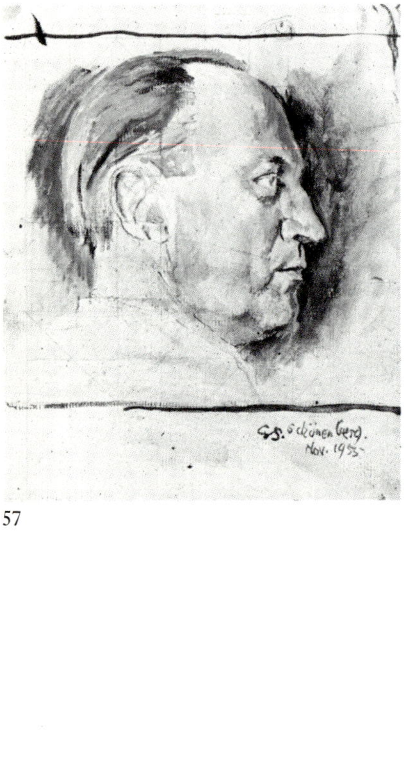

57

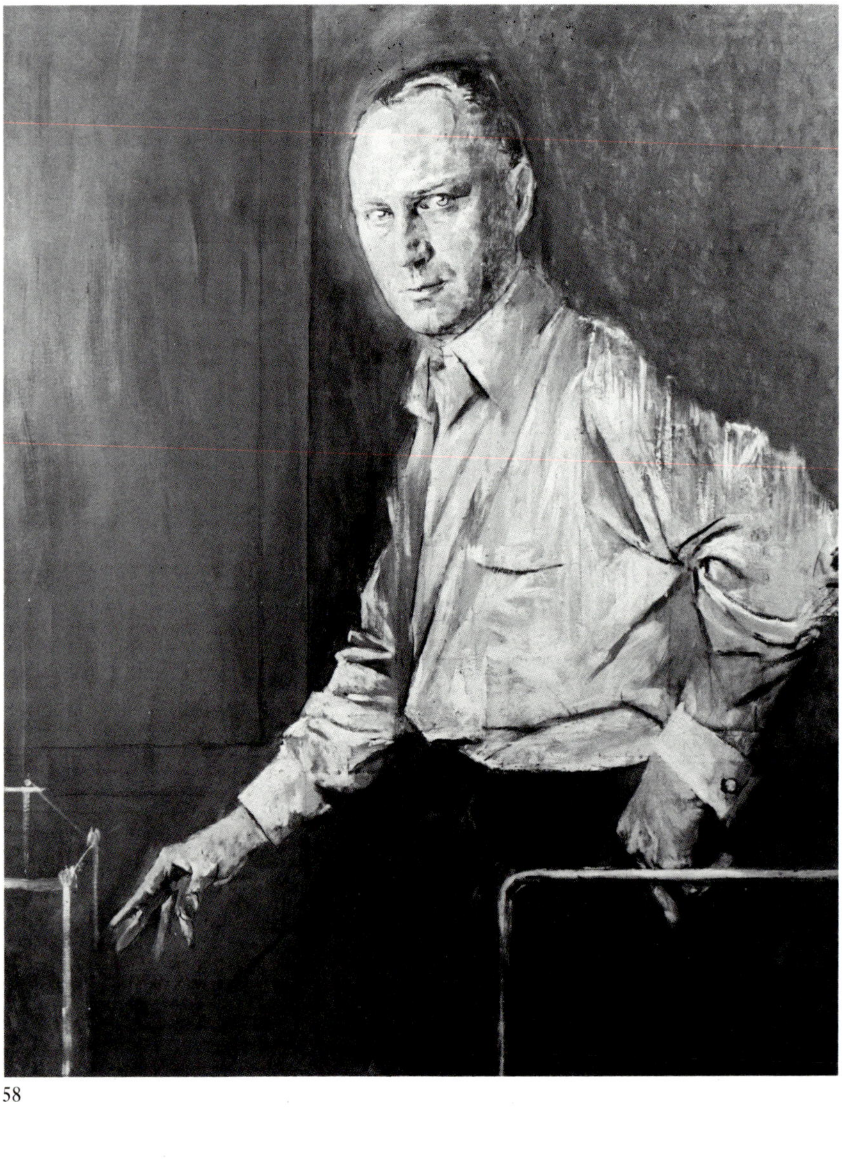

58

Helena Rubinstein (Princess Gourielli)
1871–1965

Australian; research chemist, beauty specialist, cosmetics manufacturer and business woman; collector and patron of the arts.

The commission was begun in April 1956 and completed in April 1957.

59
Study of head facing half left, with hat
Black chalk on tracing paper
$9\frac{1}{4} \times 9\frac{3}{16}$ (23.5 × 23.3)
Executed in 1956

One of a number of studies of Helena Rubinstein wearing the hat which she wore on her way to her Paris salon at the time of the sittings.

Lent by Mrs Graham Sutherland

60
Studies of head facing half left
Pen and ink and black chalk, with some red chalk
$10\frac{7}{16} \times 11\frac{1}{2}$ (26.5 × 29.2)
Executed in 1956
Verso: similar head, unfinished

Three studies on the same sheet; the sketch top right is the clearest statement of the sitter's strong and dominant personality, but the more subdued and more finished study lower right is most closely related to the portraits as executed.

Lent by Mrs Graham Sutherland

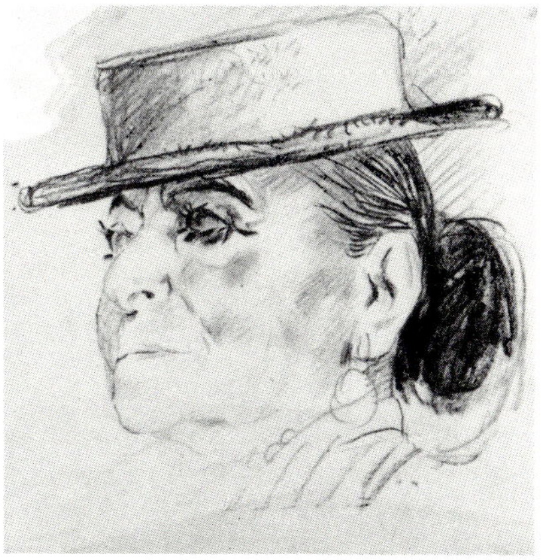
59

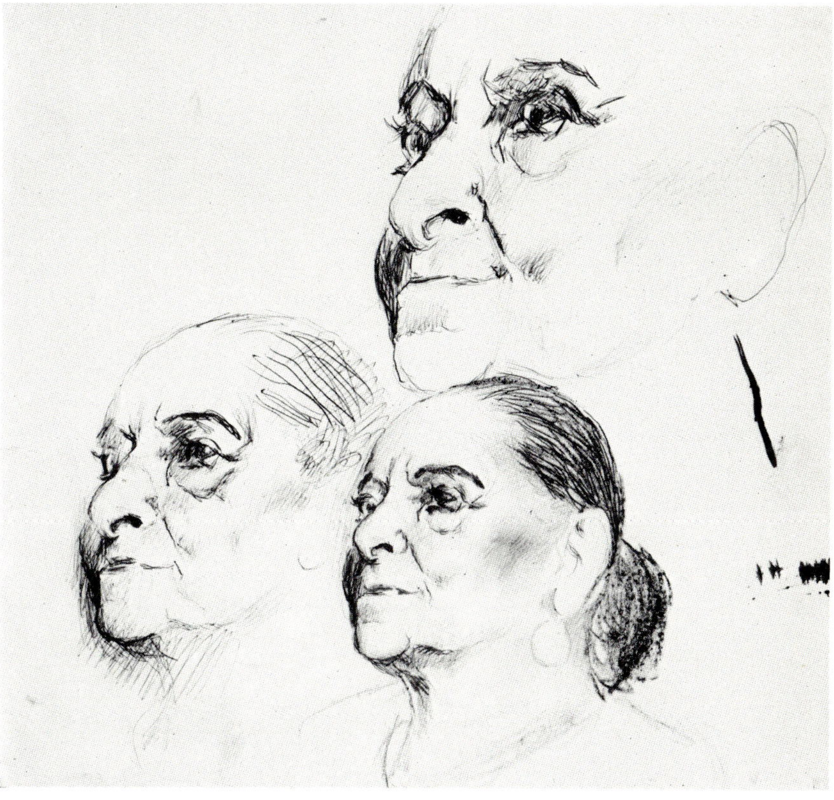
60

61
Study of left eye
Pencil
$3\frac{3}{8} \times 3\frac{13}{16}$ (8.6 × 9.7)
Executed in 1956

A detailed study of the eye and eyelashes.

Lent by Mrs Graham Sutherland

62
Composition study
Pen and ink, black chalk, pencil and gouache
$11\frac{3}{8} \times 6\frac{1}{4}$ (28.9 × 15.9)
Dated and inscribed lower right: *Paris May 1956* (the '6' superimposed upon a '7' written in error). Inscribed upper left: *Remember the/whiteness of the/pearls against the red/dress*

LITERATURE: *Paintings*, Beaverbrook Art Gallery, Fredericton, 1959, p. 63.

A composition study in which the sitter is wearing the same dress and strings of pearls as in both the finished portraits. The pose of the head and the way in which the arms are linked, are, however, comparatively relaxed and informal compared with the portraits as finally executed; only gradually did the sitter shed the appearance of a business woman occupied with her day-to-day worries and become an empress-type figure. This study, and those for Dr Adolf Jann (Nos. 88, 89 and 91), are amongst the few surviving sketches for the layout of one of Sutherland's portrait compositions.

Lent by the Beaverbrook Foundation, Beaverbrook Art Gallery, Fredericton, New Brunswick (59.433)

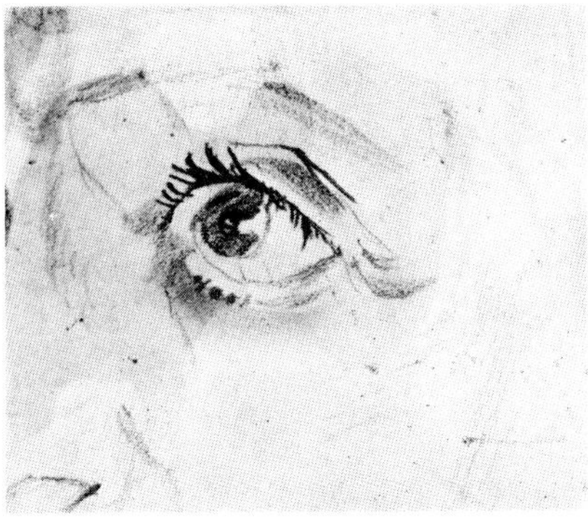
61

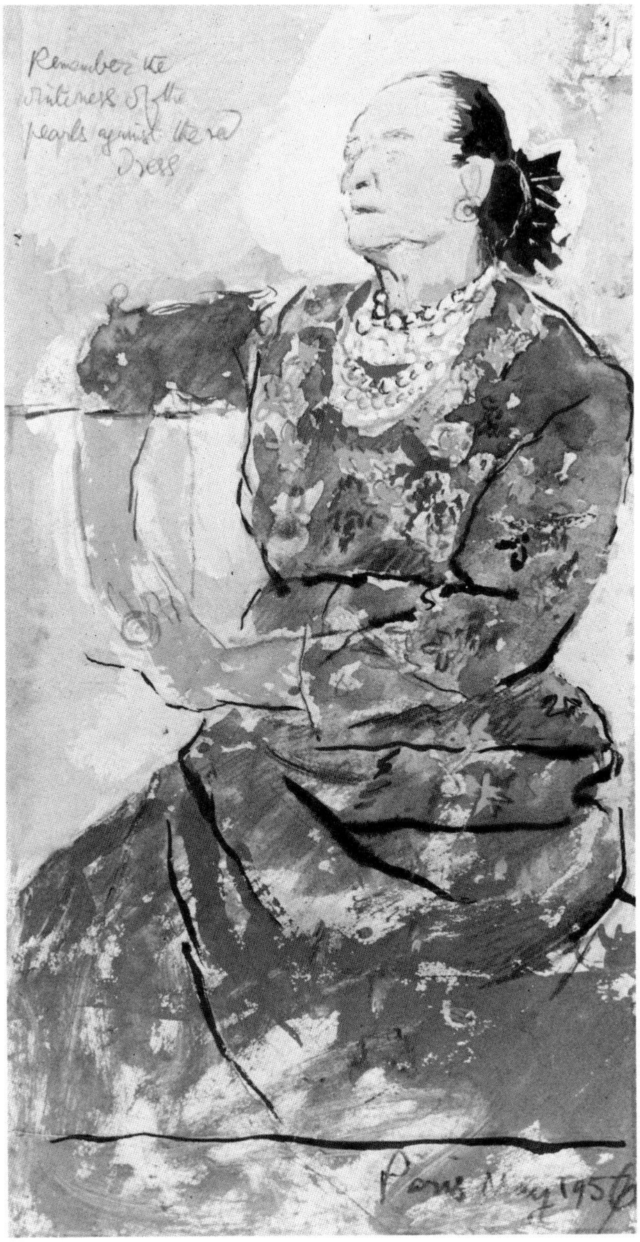

62

63
One of the two definitive portraits
Oil on canvas
$61\frac{3}{4} \times 36\frac{1}{2}$ (156.8 × 92.7)
Signed and dated lower right:
Sutherland 1957

EXHIBITED: *Graham Sutherland*, Munich, The Hague, Berlin and Cologne, March–November 1967 (57 repr.); *Portraits of Helena Rubinstein*, Metropolitan Museum of Art, New York, Palm Springs and Los Angeles, January – June 1976 (repr.); *Portraits of Helena Rubinstein*, National Portrait Gallery, May–June 1977 (17 repr.).
LITERATURE: *Paintings*, Beaverbrook Art Gallery, Fredericton, 1959, p. 63, plate 50; Douglas Cooper, *The Work of Graham Sutherland*, London, 1961, p. 60; Francesco Arcangeli, *Graham Sutherland*, New York, 1975, p. 41, plate 227.

Helena Rubinstein is painted seated, wearing a bright red Balenciaga brocade gown, overlaid with sequins and semiprecious stones; though the arms are depicted in repose, the forms nonetheless build up inexorably towards the imperious head, silhouetted against a plain background. In this it is the exact opposite of Ingres's Madame Moitessier, where the forms flow downwards. The standing portrait of the same size, and in the same dress, in the Beaverbrook Art Gallery, upon which Sutherland worked concurrently, is more obviously powerful, from the sheer weight of the form and the commanding gesture of the left arm held to the hip; but it conveys an image of the sitter which borders on the vulgar and the truculent and is, to this extent, less successful in communicating an impression of regality.

Lent by the Helena Rubinstein Foundation

64
Head facing half right
Lithograph
$10\frac{1}{2} \times 9\frac{3}{8}$ (26.7 × 23.8)
Dated (in reverse): *4.XII.60*

LITERATURE: Felix H. Man, *Graham Sutherland Das Graphische Werk 1922–70*, Munich, 1970, No. 64 (repr.).

Artist's proof. Only trial proofs were made; the lithograph was never published because the grey half-tones did not come out sufficiently well in printing.

Lent by Mrs Graham Sutherland

65
Head facing half left
Lithographic chalk and ink wash
$8\frac{1}{2} \times 8\frac{5}{8}$ (21.6 × 21.9)
Executed in 1960

No impressions were made from this study. The pose is identical with that adopted for the definitive portraits of 1957. Two other lithographs of Helena Rubinstein facing left, but in different poses or costume, were also executed in 1960: only trial proofs of these were made.

Lent by Mrs Graham Sutherland

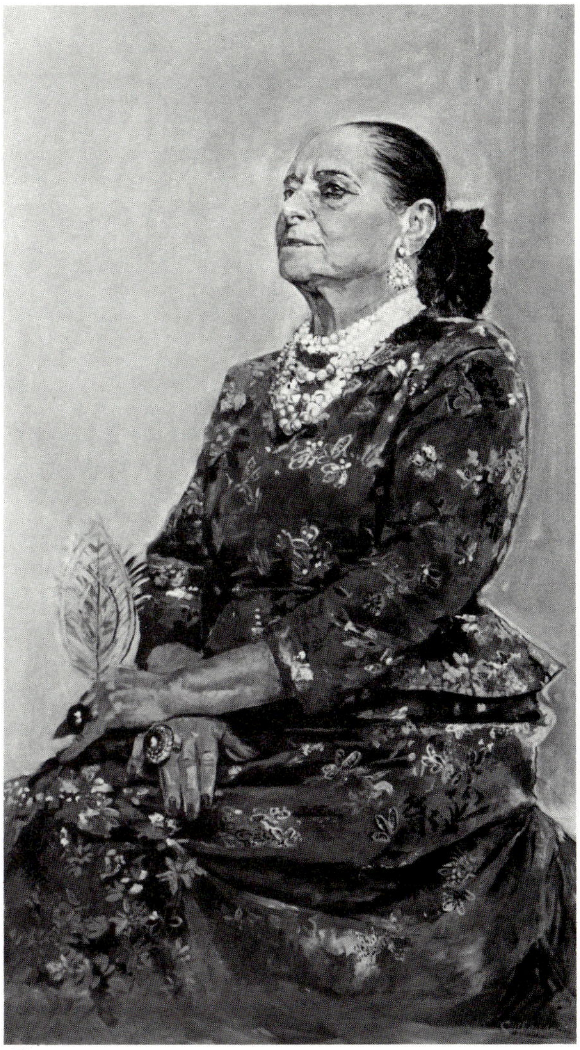
63

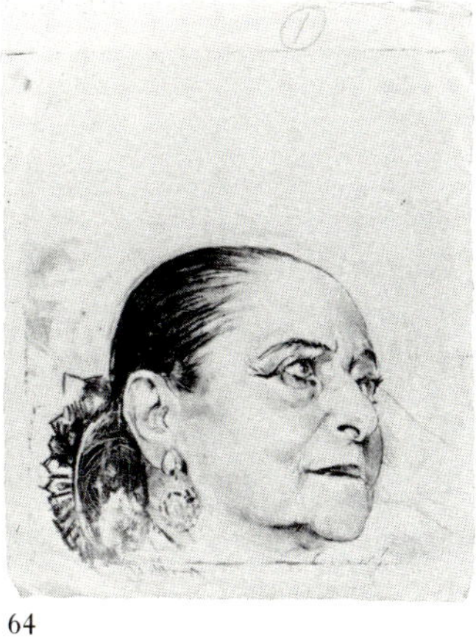
64

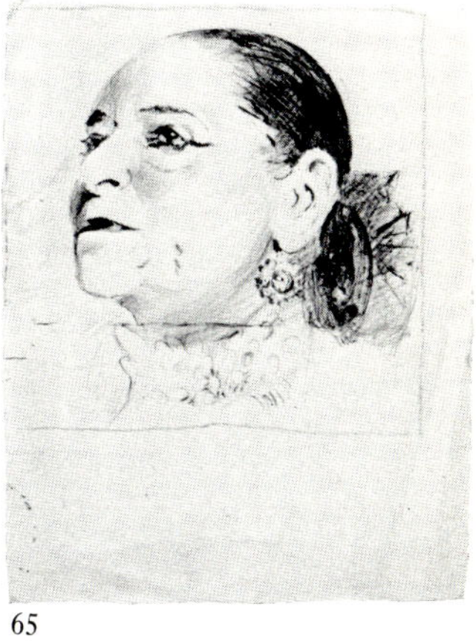
65

Max Egon, Prince von Fürstenberg

German; Bavarian aristocrat and landowner; patron of modern music, and founder of the Donaueschingen Festival.

The commission was begun in July 1958 and completed in March 1959.

66
Study of coat facing half left
Pencil
$12\frac{3}{4} \times 9\frac{3}{8}$ (32.4 × 23.8)
Executed in 1958

A study for the definitive portrait. This sketch demonstrates Sutherland's initial breadth of conception for the coat – which is substantially as finally painted, an instructive contrast to his 'picturesque' preoccupation with the elaboration of folds and creases in the clothes of the *Somerset Maugham* and *Lord Beaverbrook*.

Lent by Mrs Graham Sutherland

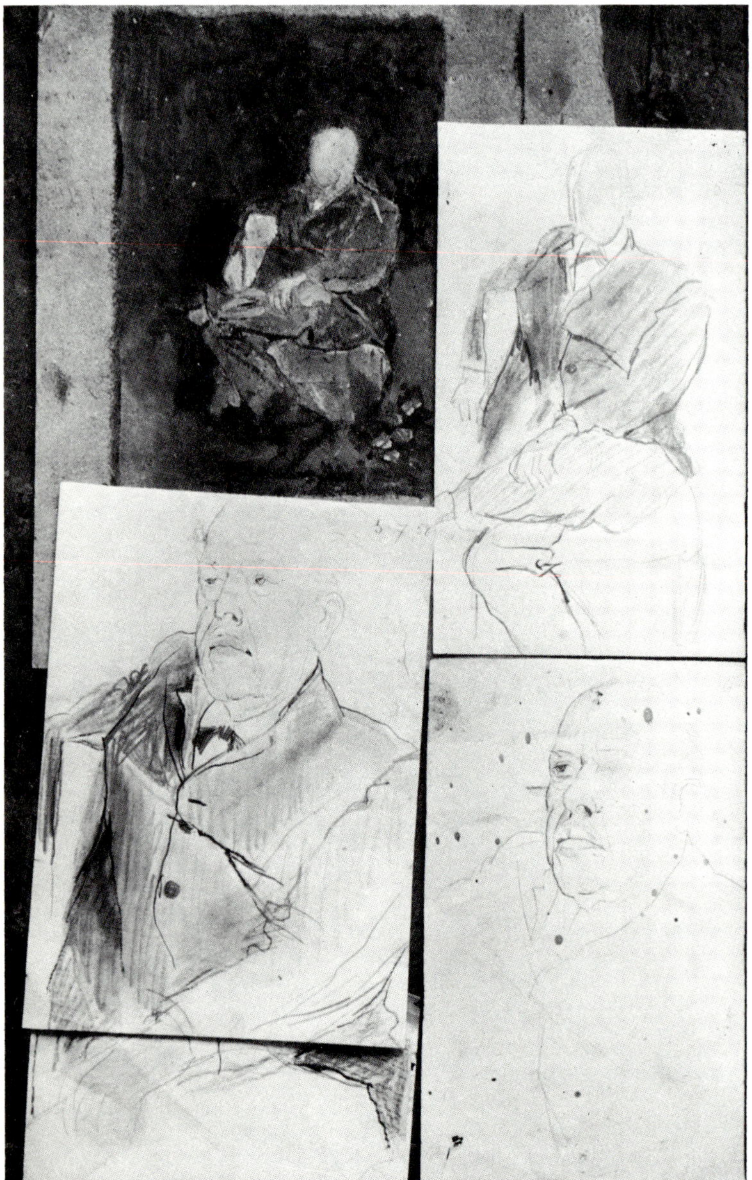

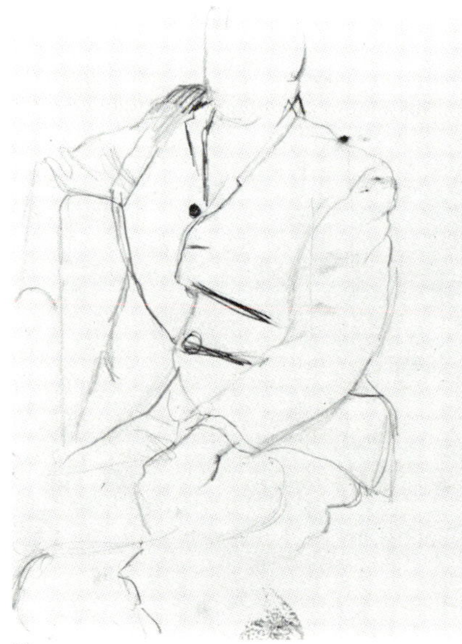

66

Figure 5
Group of sketches of Prince von Fürstenberg, 1958
(Photograph: Felix H. Man)

67

Study of head facing half left, with studies of nose and left eye

Pencil

$12\frac{7}{8} \times 9\frac{3}{8}$ (32.7 × 23.8)

Executed in 1958

Verso: two sketches of the left arm

Studies for the definitive portrait. Meticulous drawings inscribed with colour notes relating to the features and complexion, and the reflection from the collar.

Lent by Mrs Graham Sutherland

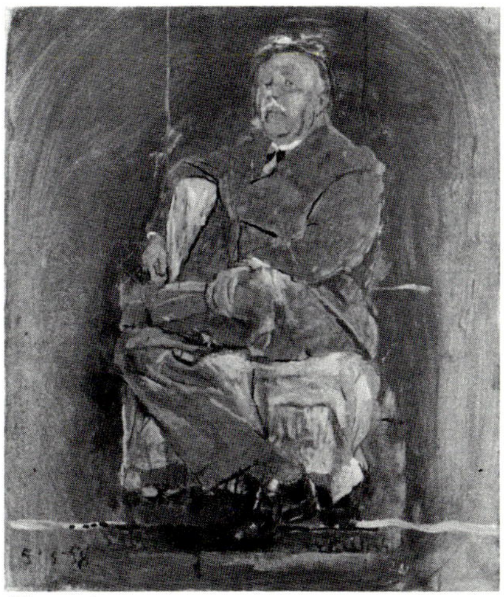

Figure 6

Oil study for the pose in the portrait of Prince von Fürstenberg, dated 5 August 1958 (Photograph: Felix H. Man)

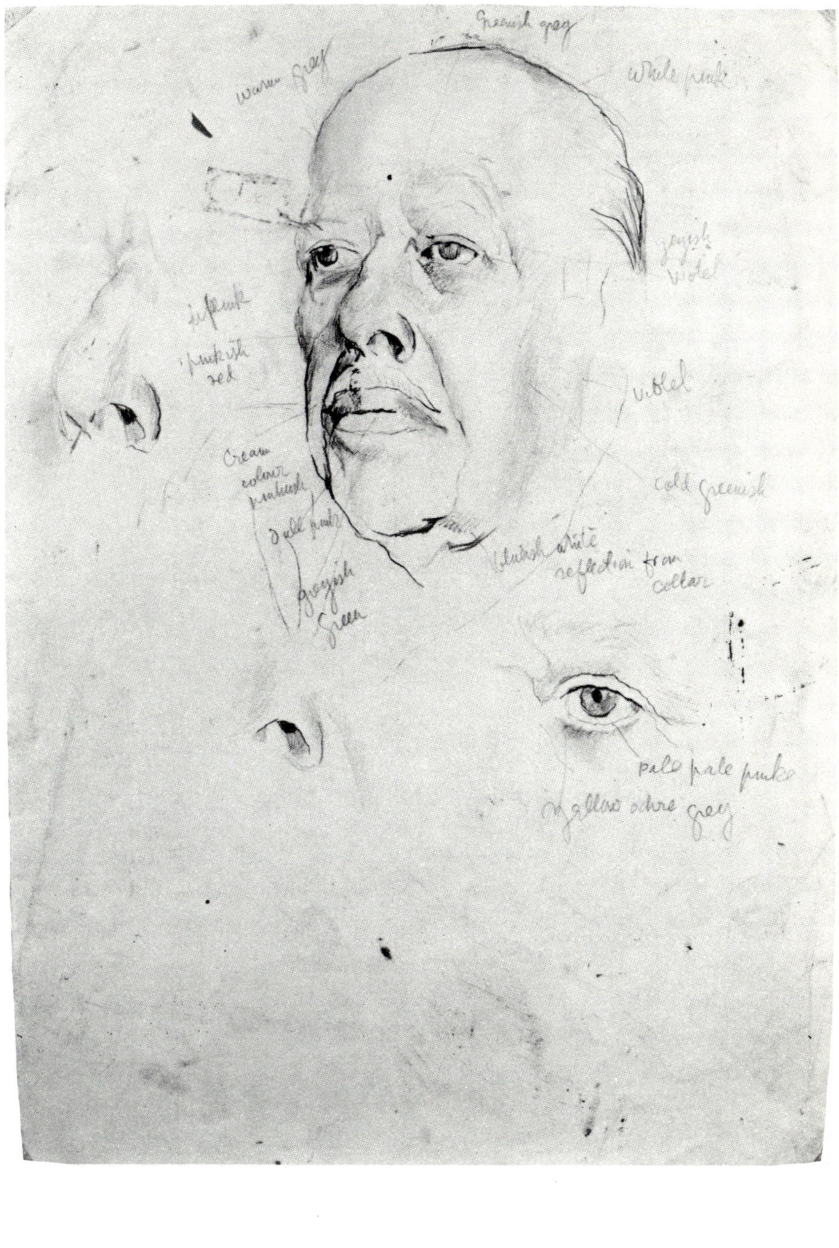

67

68
Study of head and shoulders facing half left
Oil on canvas
20 × 17 (50.8 × 43.2)
Signed and dated lower right:
Sutherland – /7.viii. / 58
Verso: sketch of the left hand in the position as adopted

An unfinished oil sketch for the definitive portrait, done in front of the sitter, in which the set of the head is almost as finally determined. Neither this nor the previous drawing (No. 67), however, shows the eyes with the upward gaze of the finished portrait.

Lent by Mrs Graham Sutherland

69
Study of head and shoulders facing half left
Oil on canvas
$23\frac{5}{8} \times 19\frac{5}{8}$ (60 × 49.8)
Signed and dated lower right:
Sutherland/1958–

In this final oil sketch for the definitive portrait, also painted from life, which Sutherland used for comparison when he was working on the canvas in his studio (see Figure 8), the head has been turned very slightly to the left and the sitter is shown looking upwards. The result of these slight alterations is startling: the expression of authority and determination has been transfigured. In the finished picture (No. 70), the elaborate modelling of the head is simplified to great effect.

Lent from a Private Collection, Germany

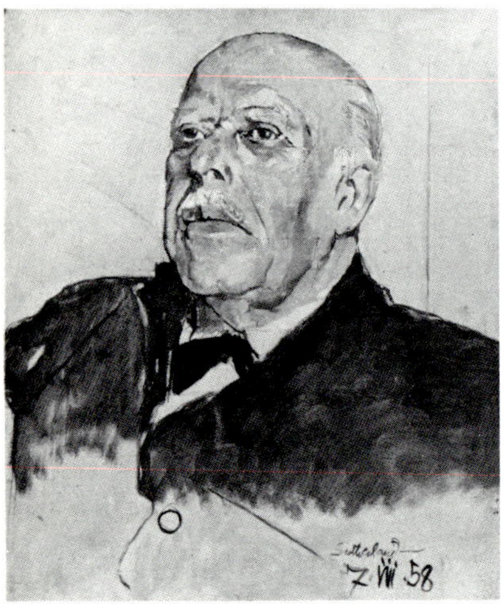

68

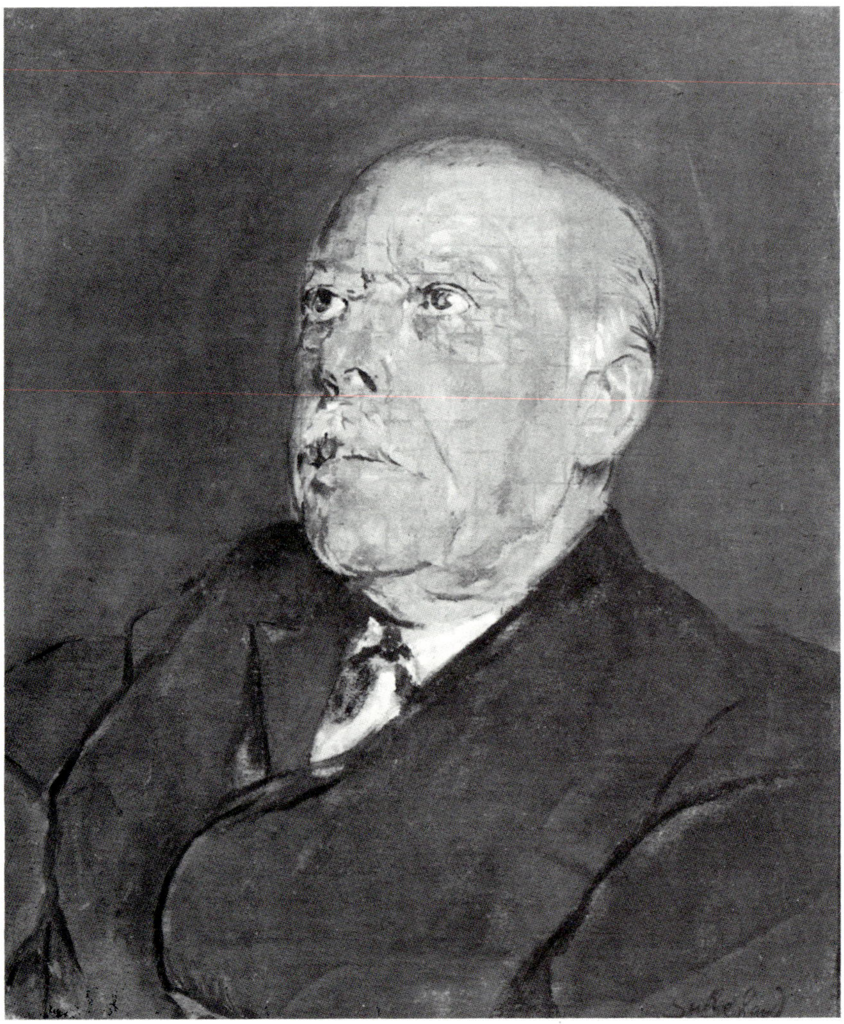

69

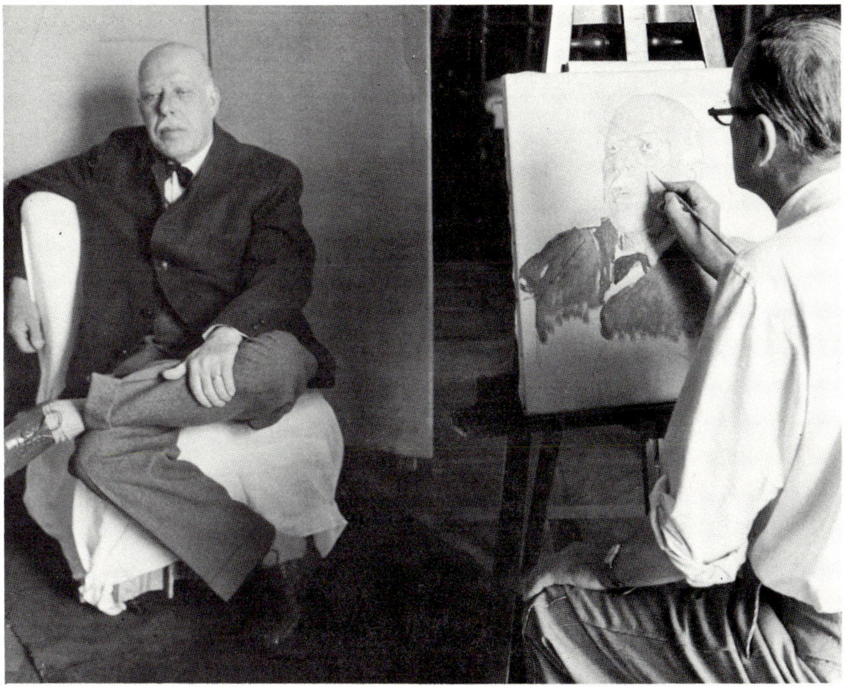

Figure 7
Sutherland making an oil sketch of Prince von Fürstenberg (No. 68) at Donaueschingen, 1958
(Photograph: Felix H. Man)

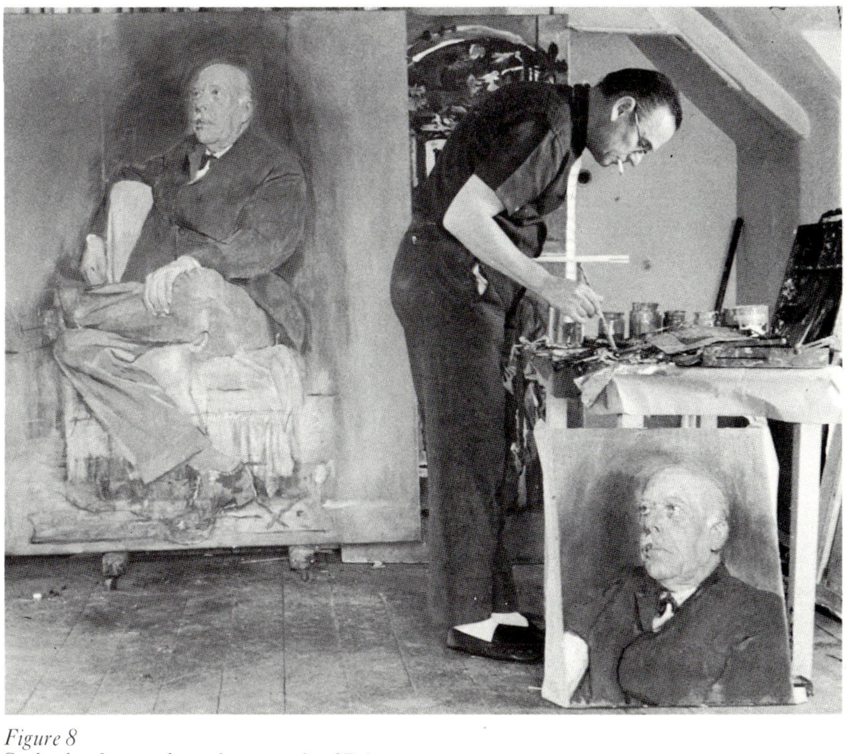

Figure 8
Sutherland at work on the portrait of Prince von Fürstenberg (No. 70) in his studio at Trottiscliffe, 1959. Notice the tape-measure round his neck. The oil sketch done in front of the sitter (No. 69) is by his side for reference (Photograph: Felix H. Man)

70
The definitive portrait
(Colour plate: cover)
Oil on canvas
65 × 55 (165.1 × 139.7)
Signed and dated lower left:
Sutherland/20.3.59

EXHIBITED: *Sutherland*, Galleria Civica d'Arte Moderna, Turin, October–November 1965 (114 repr.); *Graham Sutherland*, Kunsthalle, Basel, February–March 1966 (103 repr.); *Graham Sutherland*, Munich, The Hague, Berlin and Cologne, March–November 1967 (62 repr.).
LITERATURE: Douglas Cooper, *The Work of Graham Sutherland*, London, 1961, pp. 60 and 84, plate XV; John Woodward, *British Painting*, London, 1962, p. 157 (repr.); Francesco Arcangeli, *Graham Sutherland*, New York, 1975, p. 41, plate 228.

The Prince spontaneously adopted the pose which Sutherland has used and, with characteristic German thoroughness and discipline, maintained it every day without the slightest effort. Position, head, arms, hands, feet, all suited Sutherland's interpretation perfectly; uniquely so. Pencil sketches, of which one is dated 5 July 1958, show Sutherland experimenting with the turn of the head (Figure 5). The pose itself is recorded in a composition sketch executed in the studio just a month later, and dated 5 August 1958 (Figure 6): the only alteration made subsequently was in fact in the set of the head (see Nos. 68–69) – in the composition sketch the sitter is shown in a slightly more frontal position, with his eyes turned towards the artist. What is of particular interest from the point of view of Sutherland's technique is that compositional emphases such as the background verticals are clearly stated in this oil sketch made almost at the outset of the artist's work on the portrait, and in precisely the same relationship to the figure as finally painted. The guttering candle on the right was not included in the preparatory studies, and was added at a later stage as a 'picturesque' accent (it is still not seen in the photograph of Sutherland at work on the finished portrait taken by Felix Man (Figure 8). An oil study of the head and shoulders, painted in front of the sitter, was used by Sutherland for comparison whilst he was working on the portrait in his studio at Trottiscliffe (No. 69). The pose, though original, daring and relaxed, tends – and just for these reasons – to emphasise the magisterial quality of the head of this modern Maecenas. Such a design could never have been envisaged by Titian, but the powerful rendering of the head, comparable to the *Pietro Aretino* in the Frick Collection, calls no other portraitist to mind but the greatest of all the Venetians. The handling is economical, and the light brown priming is used throughout as the basis of the modelling.

Lent by Joachim, Fürst zu Fürstenberg

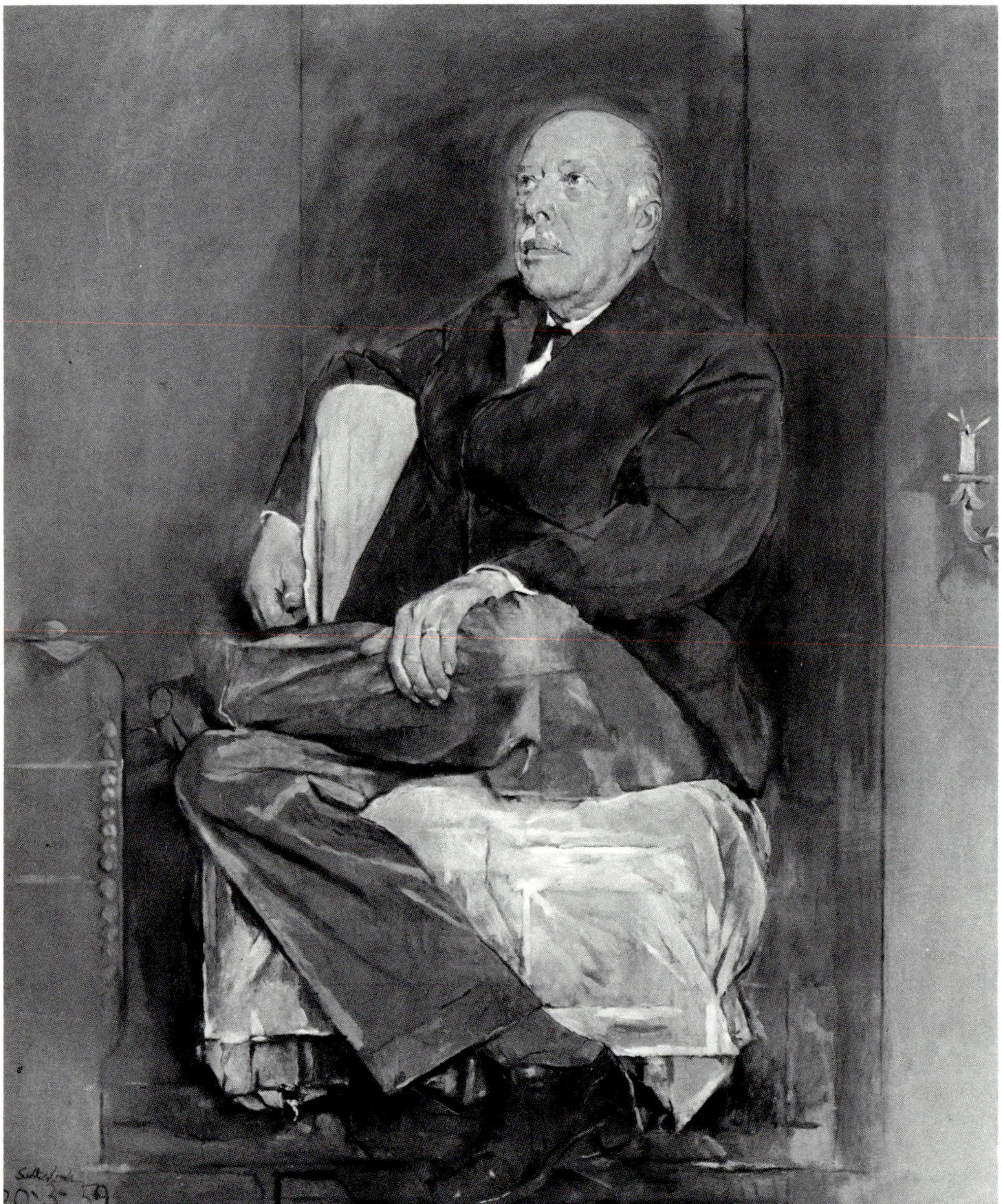

70

Maja Sacher

Swiss; patroness of modern art and music.

The commission was begun in England, a month after that for Prince von Fürstenberg, in August 1958, shortly after her husband had conducted Stravinsky's *The Rake's Progress* at Glyndebourne; it was completed in February 1959.

71
Study of head facing half left
Oil on cardboard
$12\frac{5}{8} \times 11\frac{7}{16}$ (32.1 × 29.1)
Executed in 1958

A preliminary study from life.

Lent by Mrs Graham Sutherland

72
Study of head and shoulders facing half left
Oil on cardboard
$12\frac{1}{16} \times 12\frac{11}{16}$ (30.6 × 32.2)
Inscribed on the back: *Study for/portrait of/Frau Maja Sacher*
Executed in 1958

A final study, also from life, in the pose, and with the expression, adopted for the definitive portrait.

Lent by Mrs Graham Sutherland

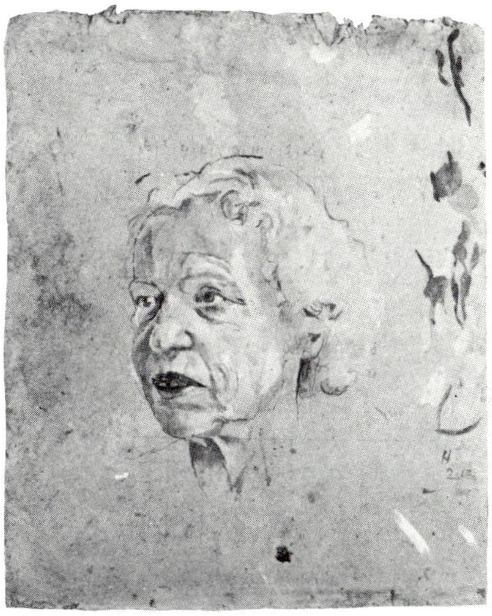

71

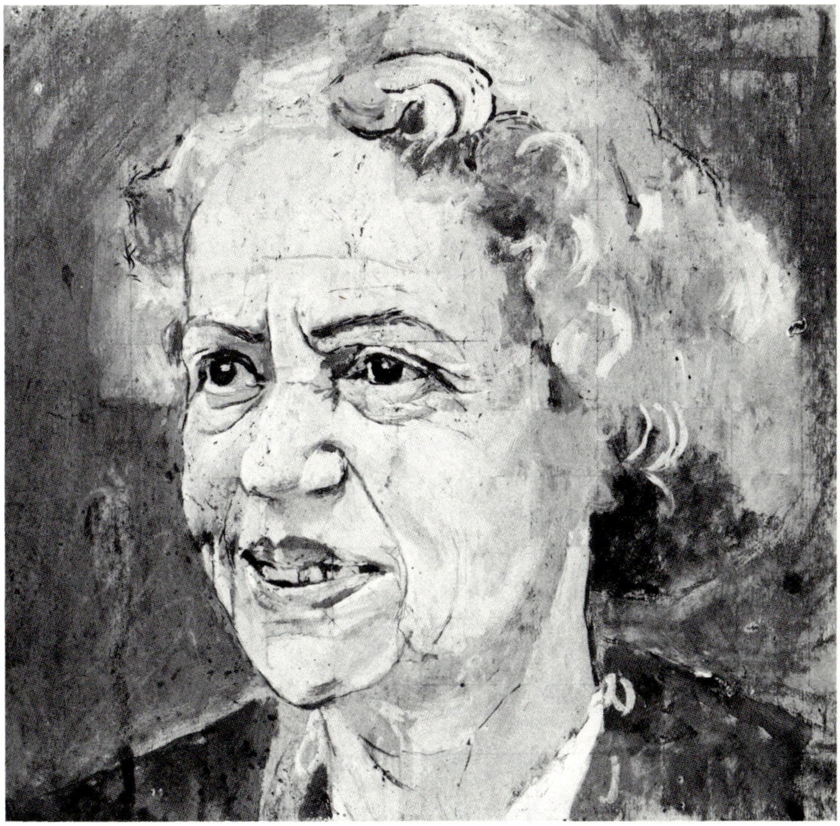

72

Dr Arpad Plesch
1890–1974

Hungarian; financier and merchant; collector of rare botanical books for his foundation, the Stiftung für Botanik.

The commission was begun in December 1961 and completed in March 1962.

73
Study for the definitive portrait
(Colour plate 3, page 26)
Oil on canvas
$26\frac{1}{2} \times 25\frac{5}{8}$ (67.3 × 65.1)
Signed and dated lower right:
Sutherland./13. xii. 61/20. iii. 62
Inscribed on the back of the canvas:
STUDY/FOR/A PORTRAIT/OF ARPAD PLESCH/GS

LITERATURE: Francesco Arcangeli, *Graham Sutherland,* New York, 1975, p. 41, plate 229.

The sitter is shown with his arm on the rail of a pair of library steps. His powerful personality – impressed upon the spectator by the domed forehead, the taut, decisive expression and gimlet eyes – is further heightened by the rectilinear design, the firm horizontal of the left arm and, perhaps above all, by the strong fingers of each of the sitter's hands upon which Sutherland has laid so particular an emphasis. The slim red volume which the sitter holds is symbolic of his passion for collecting rare books; such a device is a traditional one in European portraiture (compare in particular Moroni's portrait of Giovanni Antonio Pantera in the Uffizi). The pose itself is reminiscent of a number of literary, theatrical and musical portraits by Reynolds and Gainsborough. The apparently abstract background, fiery in colour as well as in connotation, and perfect foil to the clarity of the portrait design, is in fact a loose rendering of a curtain, painted in this sketchy manner to add vibrancy to the composition. The definitive portrait is similar in pose, but vertical in format.

Lent by Madame Arpad Plesch

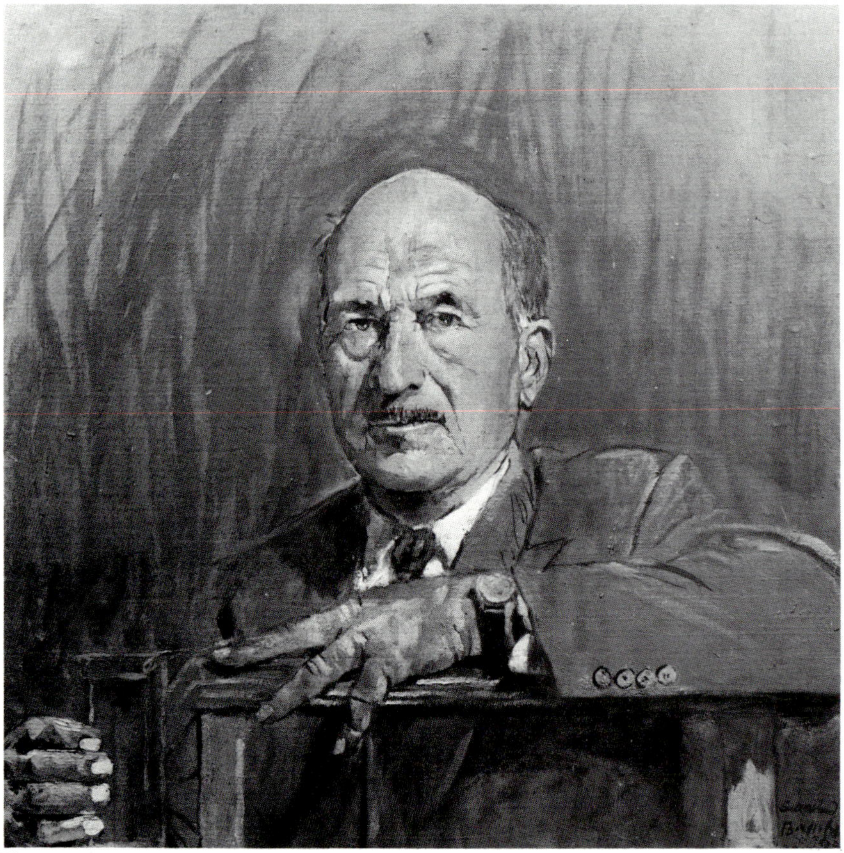

73

Lord Clark of Saltwood,
O.M., C.H.

Art historian, writer, collector, and successively Director of the National Gallery, Chairman of the Arts Council and Chairman of the Independent Television Authority. Intimate friend of the artist for over forty years.

Work on the portraits was begun in February 1962 and completed in December 1964. The studies were made in the garden at Trottiscliffe.

74
Study of head facing almost right
Oil on canvas
$5\frac{11}{16} \times 4\frac{1}{16}$ (14.5 × 10.3)
Signed lower left: *G.S*

An exquisitely finished study of the head for the large threequarter-length study with right hand upraised ($51 \times 38\frac{1}{4}$ inches) in the collection of the Hon Alan Clark. The position and turn of the head, and the expression, are substantially as painted.

Lent by the Hon Alan Clark

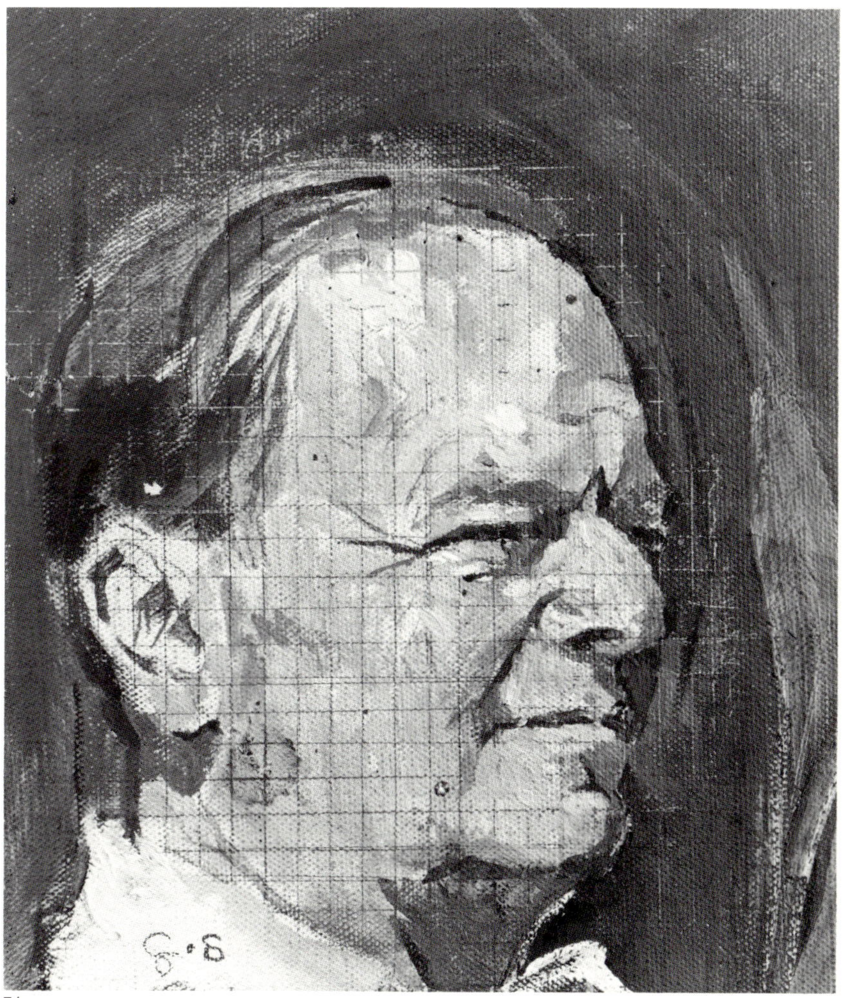

74

75
Study of head in profile to right
Pencil
$8\frac{13}{16} \times 5\frac{15}{16}$ (22.4 × 15.1)
Inscribed upper right: *Trottiscliffe*

Study of the head for the definitive portrait. The pose is as finally adopted.

Lent by the Hon Alan Clark

76
The definitive portrait
Oil on canvas
$21\frac{1}{2} \times 18$ (54.6 × 45.7)
Signed and dated lower right: *G.S. 1963–4*

PROVENANCE: Lord Clark; the Hon Colin Clark.
EXHIBITED: *Paintings and Watercolours by Graham Sutherland*, Lefèvre Gallery, April–May 1975 (18 repr.).
LITERATURE: *The Burlington Magazine*, June 1975, p. 417, fig. 120.

The choice of a profile pose, and the limitation of the figure to a head and shoulders, almost inevitably brings to mind the celebrated diptych of Federigo da Montefeltro, Duke of Urbino, and his wife Battista Sforza, painted by Piero della Francesca, the subject of one of Lord Clark's books. Certainly the design consciously echoes the fifteenth-century Italian tradition of the profile portrait. The slight upward tilt of the head emphasises the sitter's inclination to detachment, and the shrewd expression his relish for the comedy of life.

Lent from a Private Collection

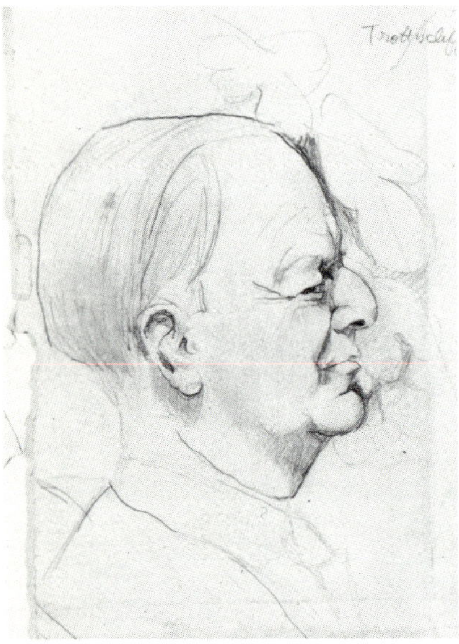

75

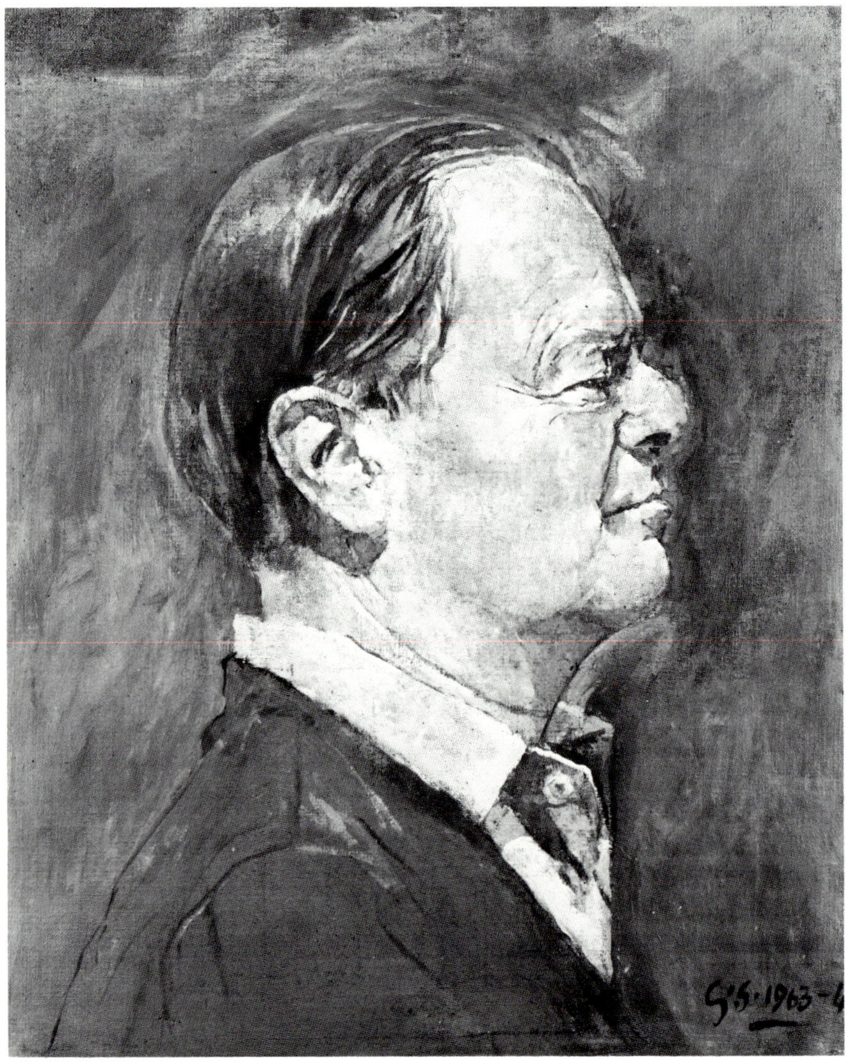

76

Dr Konrad Adenauer
1876 –1967

German; statesman; Chancellor of the Federal German Republic, 1949–63.

The commission was begun in September 1963. The finished portrait was started in May 1964 and completed in February 1965. Sutherland had nine or ten sittings, each lasting about an hour, at the Villa Collina, Adenauer's home in Cadenabbia on Lake Como. A drypoint was executed later.

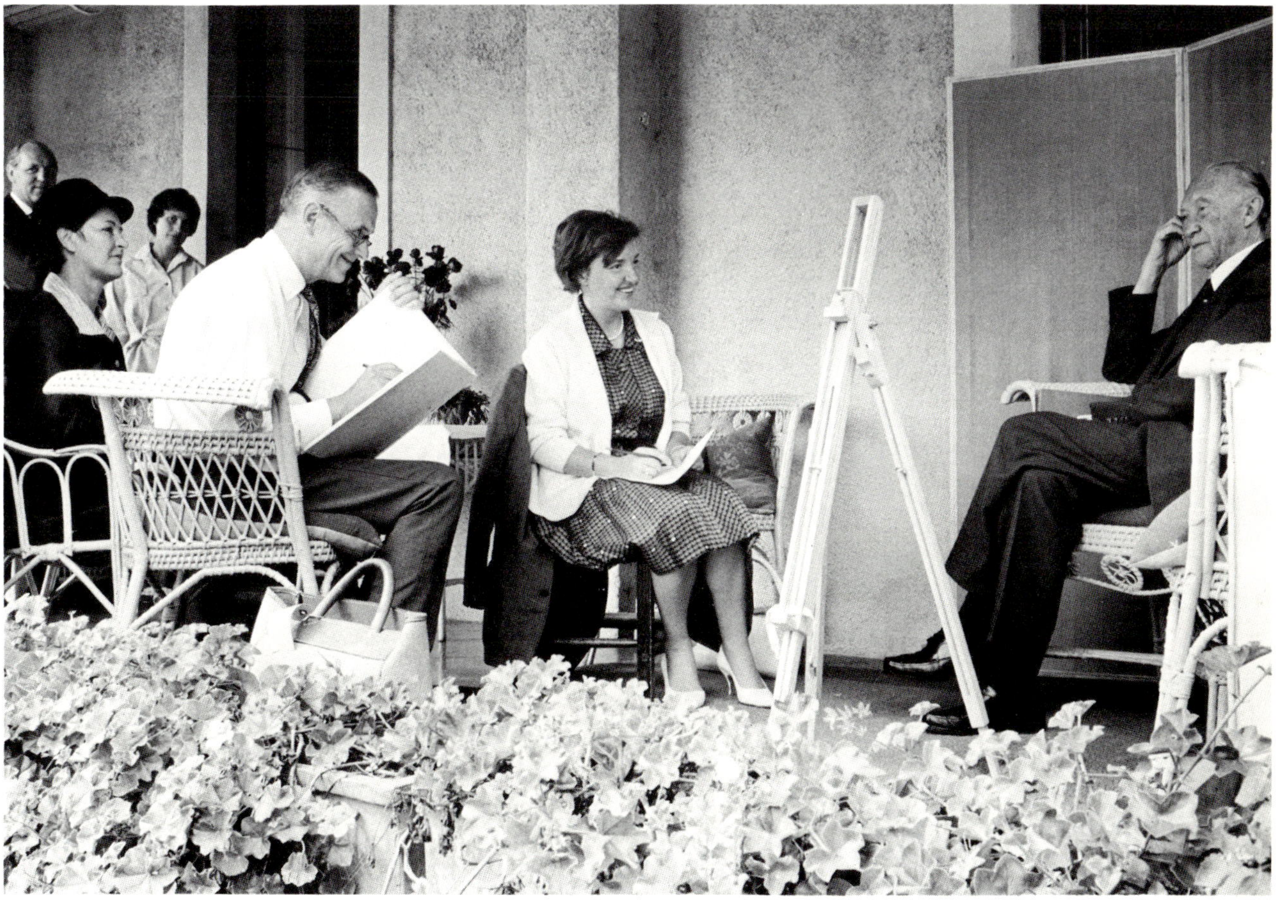

Figure 9
Sutherland sketching Dr Adenauer at the Villa Collina, Cadenabbia, 1963. Notice the easel, and frame above, which allowed the artist to concentrate on the sitter's head. Mrs Sutherland is sitting immediately behind her husband
(Photograph: Felix H. Man)

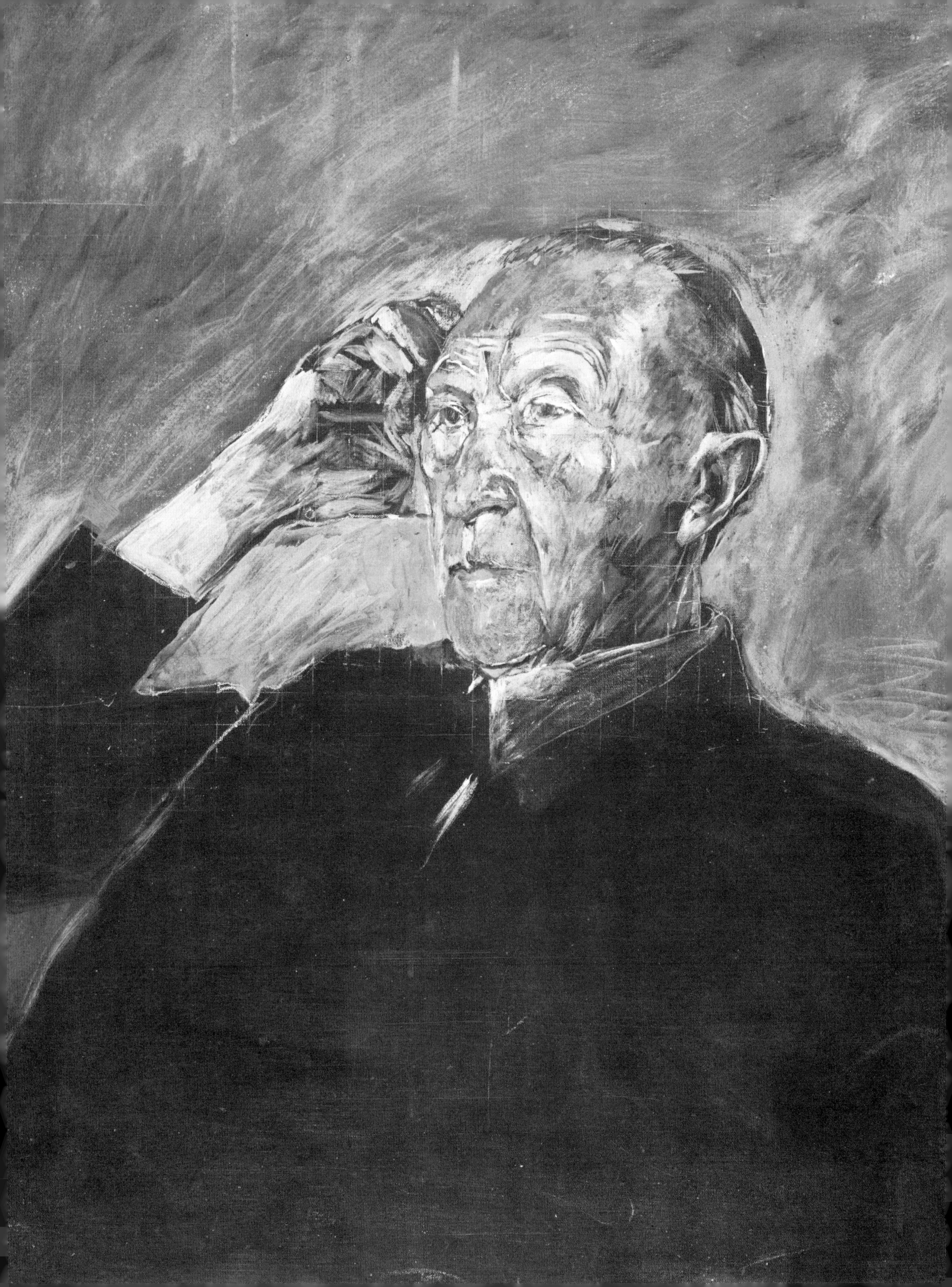

77

Half-length study facing half left

Oil on canvas

$28\frac{3}{4} \times 23\frac{5}{8}$ (73 × 60)

Executed in 1963

EXHIBITED: *Graham Sutherland,* Kunsthalle, Basel, February – March 1966 (131); *Graham Sutherland,* Munich, The Hague, Berlin and Cologne, March – November 1967 (88 repr.); *Menschenbilder,* Kunsthalle, Darmstadt, September – November 1968, repr. p. 54.

LITERATURE: Francesco Arcangeli, *Graham Sutherland,* New York, 1975, p. 41, plate 226.

A brilliant study painted in front of the sitter – perhaps the most brilliant and effective of all Sutherland's studies from the life – which captures the very essence of Adenauer's personality: the detachment, the austerity, the contemplative and visionary and the hard-headed grasp of affairs. The handling, which is in no way 'overclogged' and indeed almost impressionistic, notably in the painting of the hand and wrist, effectively combines mobility of expression and firmness of structure. Sutherland made a more finished oil study based on this sketch, in the studio, using a more rectangular format so that he could try out the effect of painting the sitter lower in the canvas.

Lent by the Kultusministeriums Baden-Württemburg (on permanent loan to the Staatsgalerie, Stuttgart)

78

Study of head and shoulders facing frontally

Black chalk, with some red chalk

$16\frac{1}{8} \times 11\frac{1}{4}$ (41 × 28.6)

Executed in 1963

Study for the definitive portrait. The frontal pose emphasises the searching eyes and the visionary side of Adenauer's personality, as well as his austerity. The lines of the shoulder and the collar play an important part in heightening the tautness of the image.

Lent by Mrs Graham Sutherland

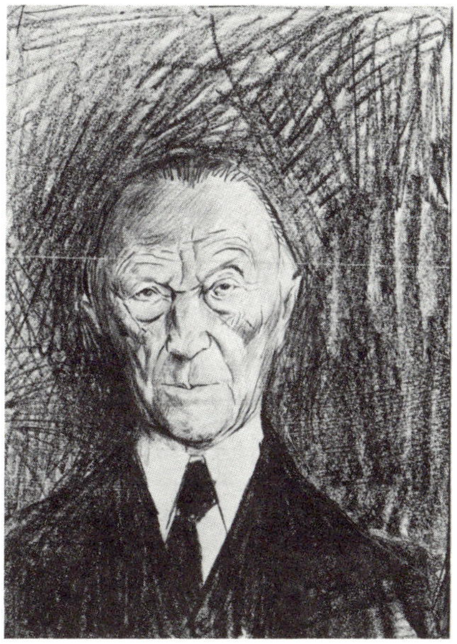

78

77

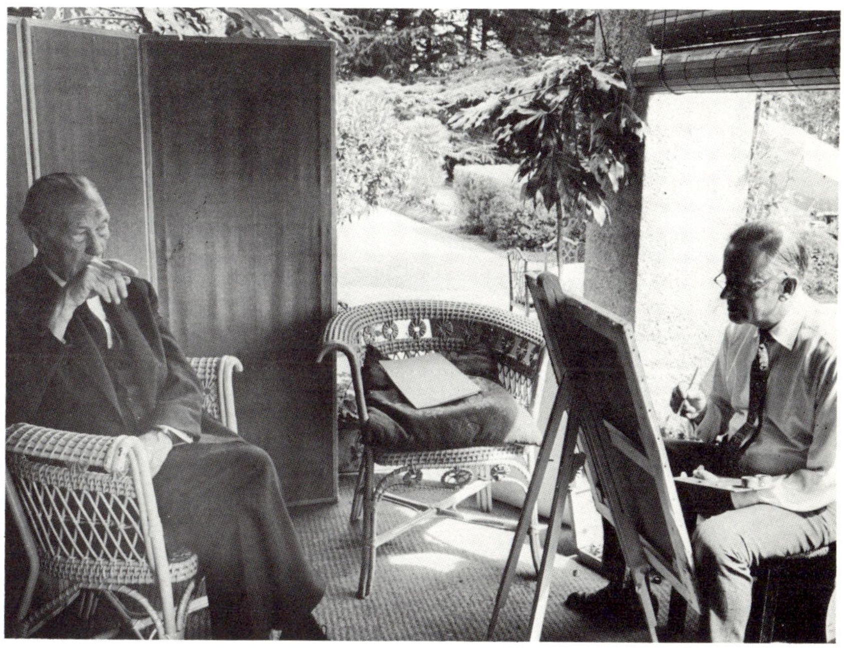

Figure 10

Sutherland making an oil sketch of Dr Adenauer at the Villa Collina, Cadenabbia, 1963 (Photograph: Felix H. Man)

79
The definitive portrait
Oil on canvas
$56\frac{5}{8} \times 48\frac{1}{2}$ (143.9 × 123.2)
Signed and dated upper right:
Sutherland./*1965*

EXHIBITED: *Graham Sutherland*, Kunsthalle, Basel, February – March 1966 (132 repr.); *Graham Sutherland*, Munich, The Hague, Berlin and Cologne, March – November 1967 (89 repr.).

In the finished work the head is tilted very slightly to one side, and the right arm is more relaxed than in the Stuttgart sketch (No. 77), echoing the limpness of the left arm resting on the knee. The effect of these subtle and carefully calculated changes is to reduce the impression of intensity apparent in both the studies and the lithograph; the figure is erect and noble, but less severe. The placing of the sitter in the canvas is masterly, and both this and the background of leaves – similar to those in Sutherland's paintings of fountains of 1964-5 – contribute to the deeper humanity of the final conception. Adenauer delighted in gardens, and constantly talked about his own, and the setting was devised by Sutherland because it was a reflection of the sitter's personal taste. The former Chancellor liked the finished portrait, with its motif of the hand held to the forehead (a traditional gesture in European portraits of writers and philosophers), and is reported to have said that he was glad that 'Sutherland had painted him as a thinking man'.

Lent by Mrs Reiners-Adenauer

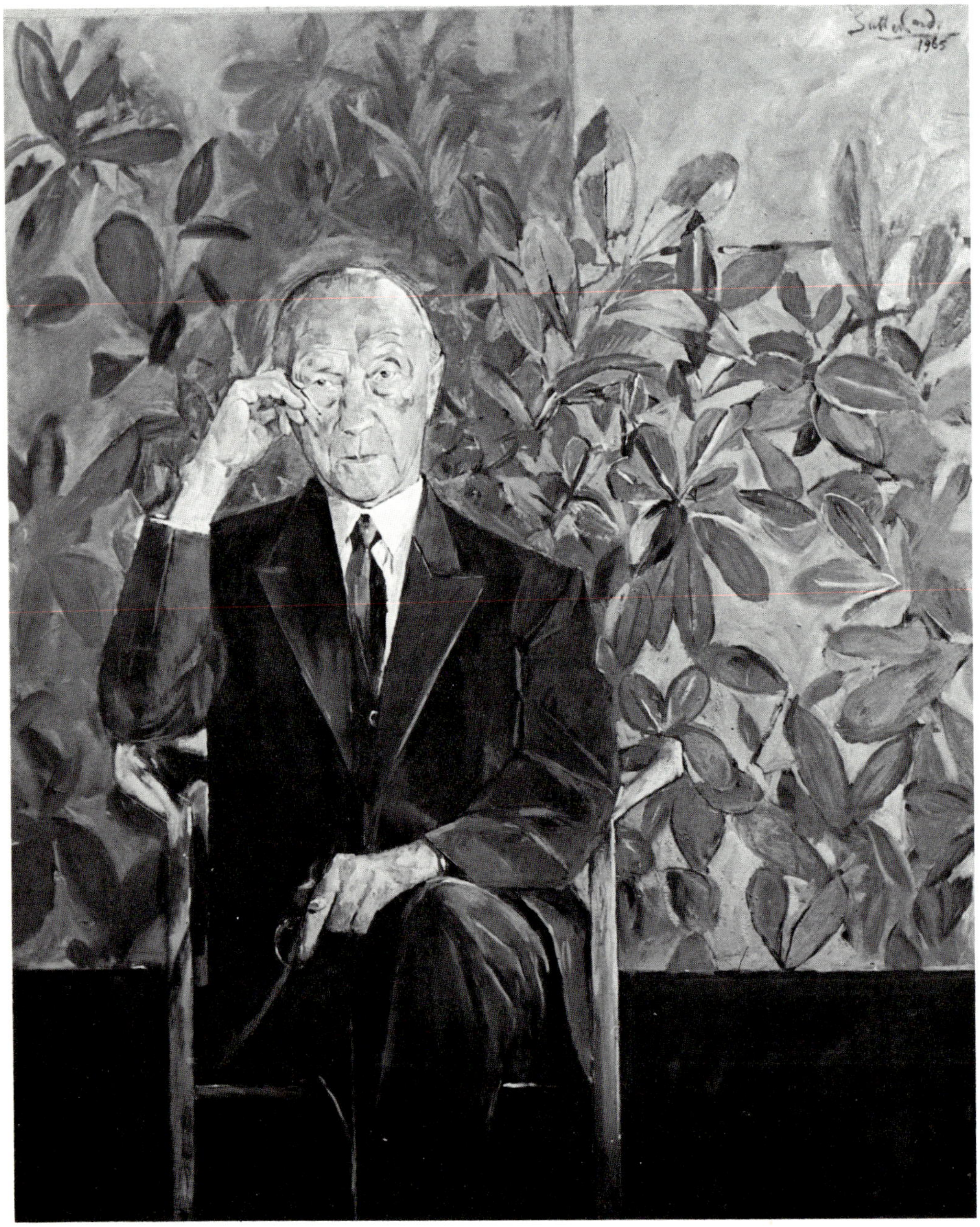

79

80
Half-length facing half left
Lithograph
$21\frac{7}{8} \times 15\frac{5}{8}$ (55.6 × 39.7)
Dated lower right: *29.iii.65.*
Signed and inscribed bottom left: *G.S. 1st state/1st proof*
Unpublished. Only three trial proofs were made.

LITERATURE: Felix H. Man, *Graham Sutherland Das Graphische Werk 1922–70*, Munich, 1970, No. 67 (repr.).

The pose is derived from the sketches culminating in the Stuttgart oil study (No. 77), but the arm and hand held to the forehead are omitted. Adenauer's head was an ideal subject for graphic art – for interpretation in line – and, in this medium, the inclusion of the upraised arm, so compelling a gesture in the painted portraits, would have detracted from the effect. The robustness of the figure is indicated by a simple outline, and additional vitality is imparted to the image by the rough mesh of lines opening up the 'space' of the white paper in the background behind the head.

Lent by Mrs Graham Sutherland

81
Study of head and shoulders facing frontally
Black and red chalk and pencil
$17\frac{3}{16} \times 13\frac{1}{2}$ (43.7 × 34.3)
Executed in 1967

Study for the drypoint, based on the earlier chalk drawing (No. 78).

Lent by Mrs Graham Sutherland

82
Head and shoulders facing frontally
Drypoint
$11\frac{5}{16} \times 9\frac{9}{16}$ (28.7 × 24.3)
Executed in 1967
Inscribed lower right beneath the platemark: *1st state. 3rd print. GS.*

In the drypoint the features have been emphasised by a greater use of chiaroscuro, and the concentration on the head is demonstrated by its larger scale in relation to the sheet and by the elision of the shoulders. The image has thus become more immediate and intense. It is perhaps not wholly fanciful to equate this powerful print with the lion's head Sutherland drew for his *Bestiary* in the same year, 1967 (see No. 7). The exceptional force and broad outlines of the image are remarkably similar.

Lent by Mrs Graham Sutherland

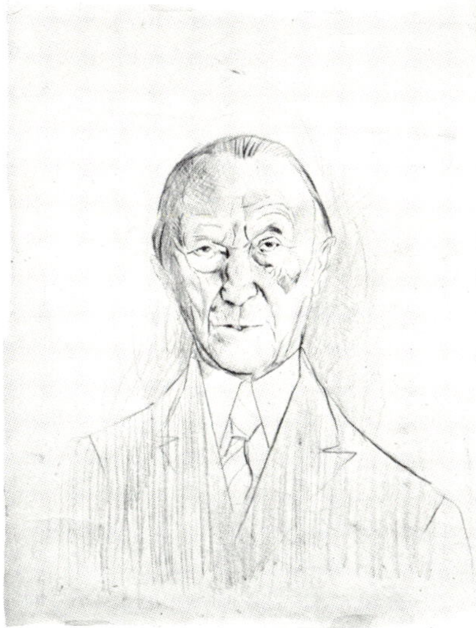

81

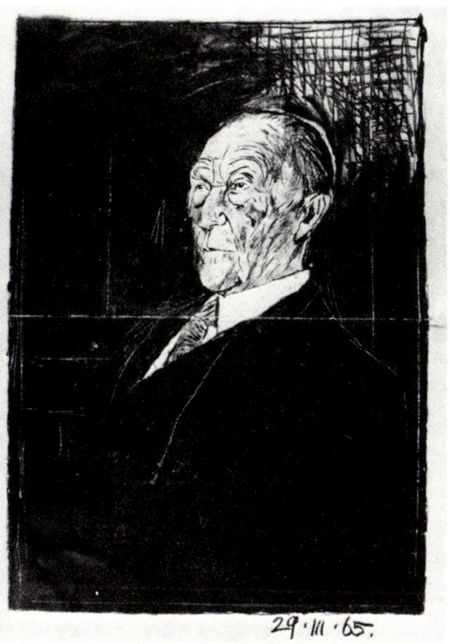

80

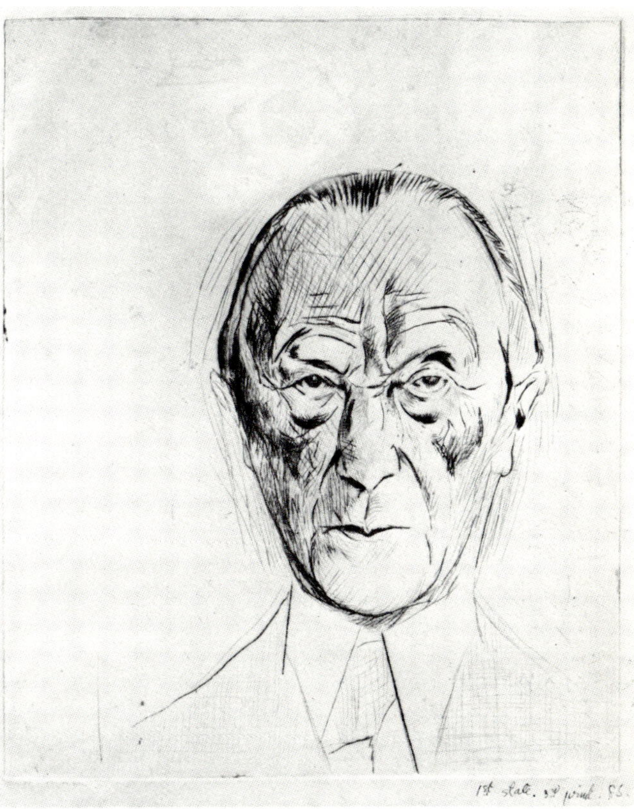

82

Emery Reves

Literary agent, entrepreneur, collector and connoisseur; intimate friend of Sir Winston Churchill, and for many years his host in the South of France.

The commission was begun in 1965. The finished portrait was started in March 1966 and completed in June.

83
Study of head and shoulders facing frontally
Gouache on hardboard
$15 \times 11\frac{3}{4}$ (38×30)
Signed and dated lower right: *G.S 1965–6*

A rough, oil sketch done in front of the sitter in which Sutherland concentrated wholly upon the expression. As far as the costume goes, there is just a suggestion of the bow tie which Reves was wearing (see No. 84).

Lent by Mr and Mrs Emery Reves

84
The definitive portrait
Oil on canvas
$25\frac{5}{8} \times 21\frac{1}{4}$ (65×54)
Signed and dated upper right: *Sutherland/1966*. Signed, dated and inscribed on the back: *GS. 1966. E.R*

Though Reves sat to Sutherland in a white coat and the yellow spotted bow tie which he often wore, the final portrait shows him in a dark coat and an open-necked shirt. The dark tonality, characteristic of the background as well as the coat, exceptional in Sutherland's work – and which gives this portrait a particular distinction – was adopted in relationship to the sitter's complexion. The placing of the hand, with the forefinger raised to the temple, is in the tradition of such literary portraits as Reynolds's *Laurence Sterne*.

Lent by Mr and Mrs Emery Reves

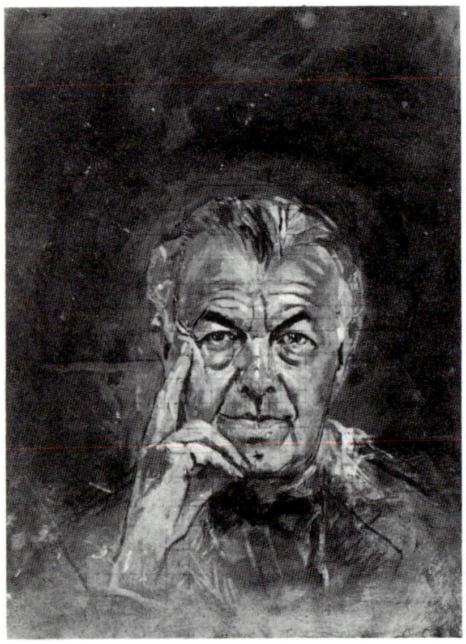

83

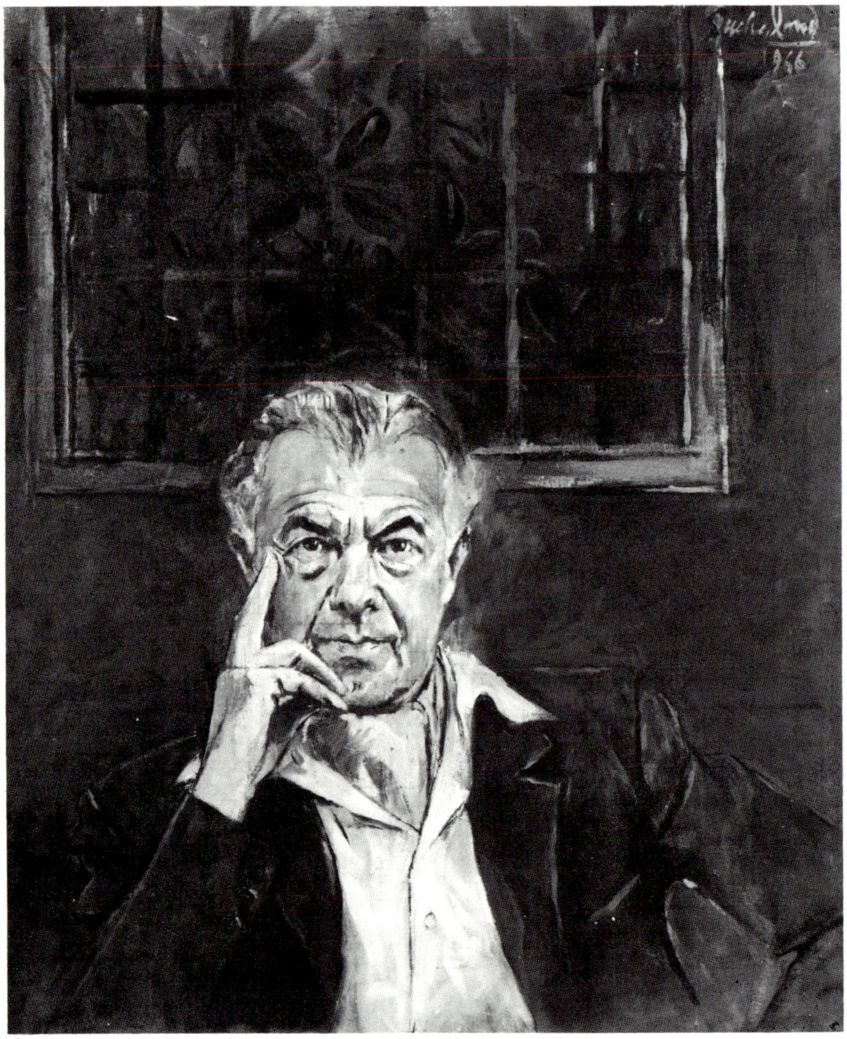

84

Lord Rayne of Prince's Meadows

Financier; Chairman of London Merchant Securities; Chairman of the National Theatre Board and of the Festival Ballet; patron and benefactor of education, medicine and the arts.

The commission was begun in October 1966 and completed in July 1970.

85
One of the two definitive portraits
(Colour plate 4, page 27)
Oil on canvas
$71\frac{3}{4} \times 43\frac{1}{4}$ (182.2 × 109.9)
Signed, dated and inscribed on the back: *Portrait of/M.R./G.S. 1968–9*

The composition is as hieratic as the *Somerset Maugham* (No. 27) but – in contrast to the world-weary image of the successful novelist, the story-teller who became the darling of the lending libraries – it is both dynamic and rhythmic. The sitter is not placed to one side as in the *Adenauer* (No. 79), and confronts the spectator head on, vigorous and alert, leaning slightly forward, and with his right knee and leg projecting firmly outwards beyond the confines of the picture. The proportions of the head, enlarged as though by the distortion of a photographic lens, are determined by this powerful concept of the man of affairs; and the vertical of the left leg and shoe presses inexorably on the base of the canvas in such a way as to seem the very spring which sets the whole design in motion. The arms, linked by the strong, firmly clasped hands, establish a lively counter-rhythm in the centre of the picture echoed by the abstract arc on the left of the right arm and by the similar rhythms of the tie and the left lapel. Withal, the image is elegant, even dapper, as well as virile. The background is painted in a greyish-brown tonality to accord with the brickwork of the College Hall in which the painting hangs. Sutherland executed a similar, but more intimate, version of this splendid 'state' portrait for Lord Rayne himself, which is signed and dated 1967–70.

Lent by the Master and Fellows of Darwin College, Cambridge

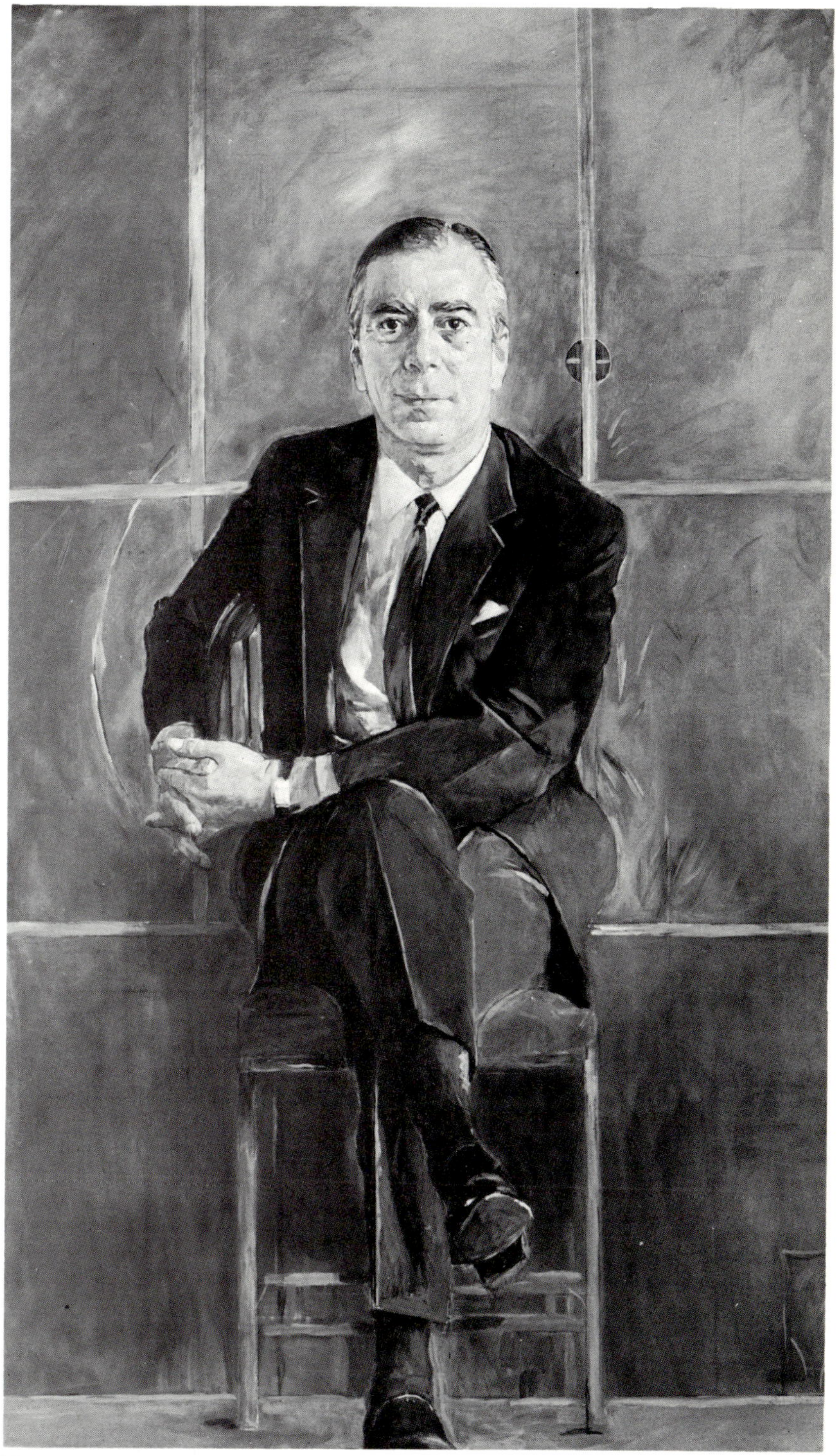

85

Baron Elie de Rothschild

French; merchant banker, vineyard owner, connoisseur, collector and sportsman.

The commission was begun in 1968 and completed in March 1969.

86
One of the two definitive portraits
Oil on canvas
$57\frac{1}{2} \times 47\frac{5}{8}$ (146.1 × 121)
Signed and dated lower right:
Sutherland/68
Signed, dated and inscribed on the back: *MONSIEUR/LE BARON ELIE DE ROTHSCHILD/G:S OCT 1968*

As in the portrait of Lord Rayne (No. 85), the pose is both central and frontal, the blue eyes are similarly piercing, and the right knee and leg project outwards towards the spectator. But there the similarities end. Where Lord Rayne is portrayed as the man of decisive action, ready at any moment to spring up from the narrow, functional chair of the business world upon which he is seated, Baron Elie de Rothschild has left his financial cares behind him and is shown in a moment of relaxation, comfortably seated, the whole weight of the body taken by the chair, wearing a blue, sleeveless open-necked shirt, with his arms crossed over his knees, a cigarette in his right hand, his gaze open and friendly. The two portraits demonstrate the range of Sutherland's sympathies, and the skill with which his compositions match his interpretations: contrast not only the pose but the broad, horizontal divisions of the background in the Rothschild portrait with the taut compartments in the *Rayne*. The flickering red highlights in the trousers and the chair covering give added vibrancy to the picture.

Lent by the Baron Elie de Rothschild

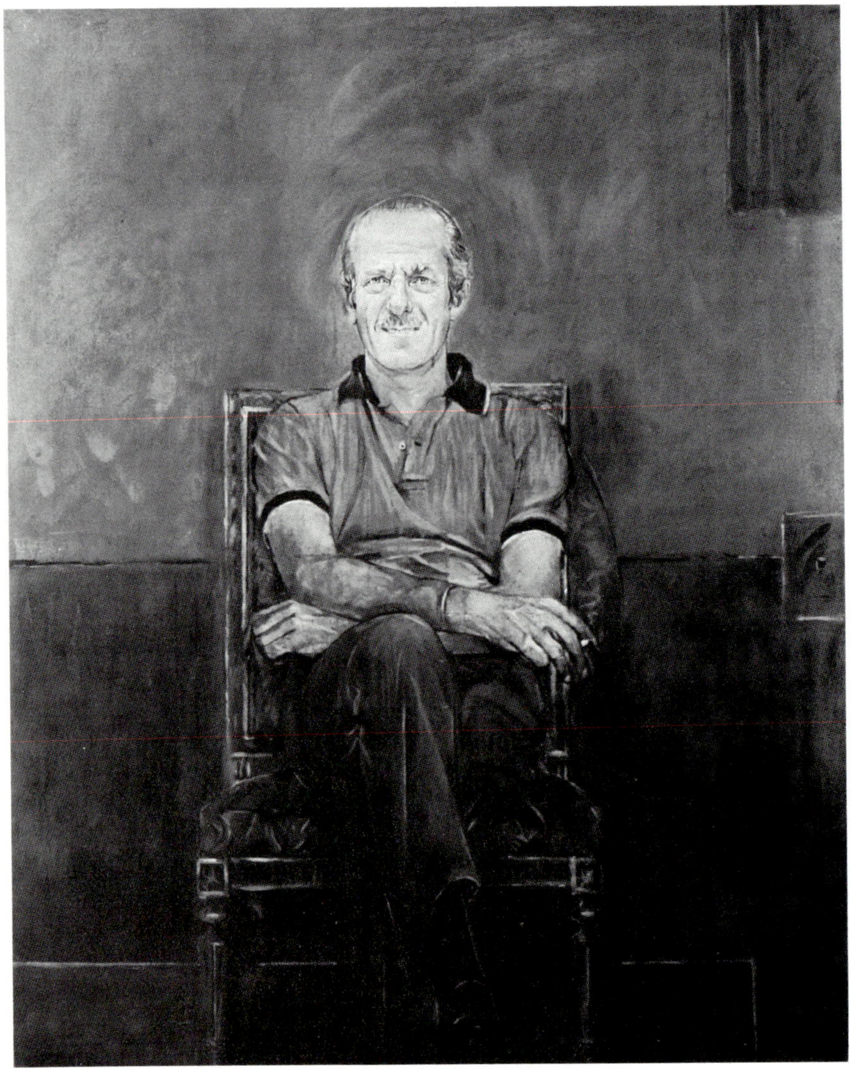

86

87
One of the two definitive portraits
Oil on canvas
$39\frac{3}{8} \times 31\frac{1}{2}$ (100 × 80)
Signed and dated lower right: *GS 69*
Signed, dated and inscribed on the back: *Baron/Elie de Rothschild/GS. 1968* with, on the right: *Nov–Dec* and below: *FEV.MARS 1969*

A more informal and intimate portrait than the larger canvas (No. 86). The tone is lighter, the handling thinner and sketchier (the priming being used as the basis of the colour scheme), the Louis Seize chair has been excluded, and the face is seen at threequarters, thus allowing a more lively rendering of the expression and characteristic smile. The pose, however, is precisely the same, though the sitter is seen from a different angle. (In this connection it is of interest to note that the artist had originally started on a larger canvas, in which the figure would not have appeared so prominent, and had included the feet in the same position; the composition was completed as it is now because the sitter preferred it.)

Lent by the Baron Elie de Rothschild

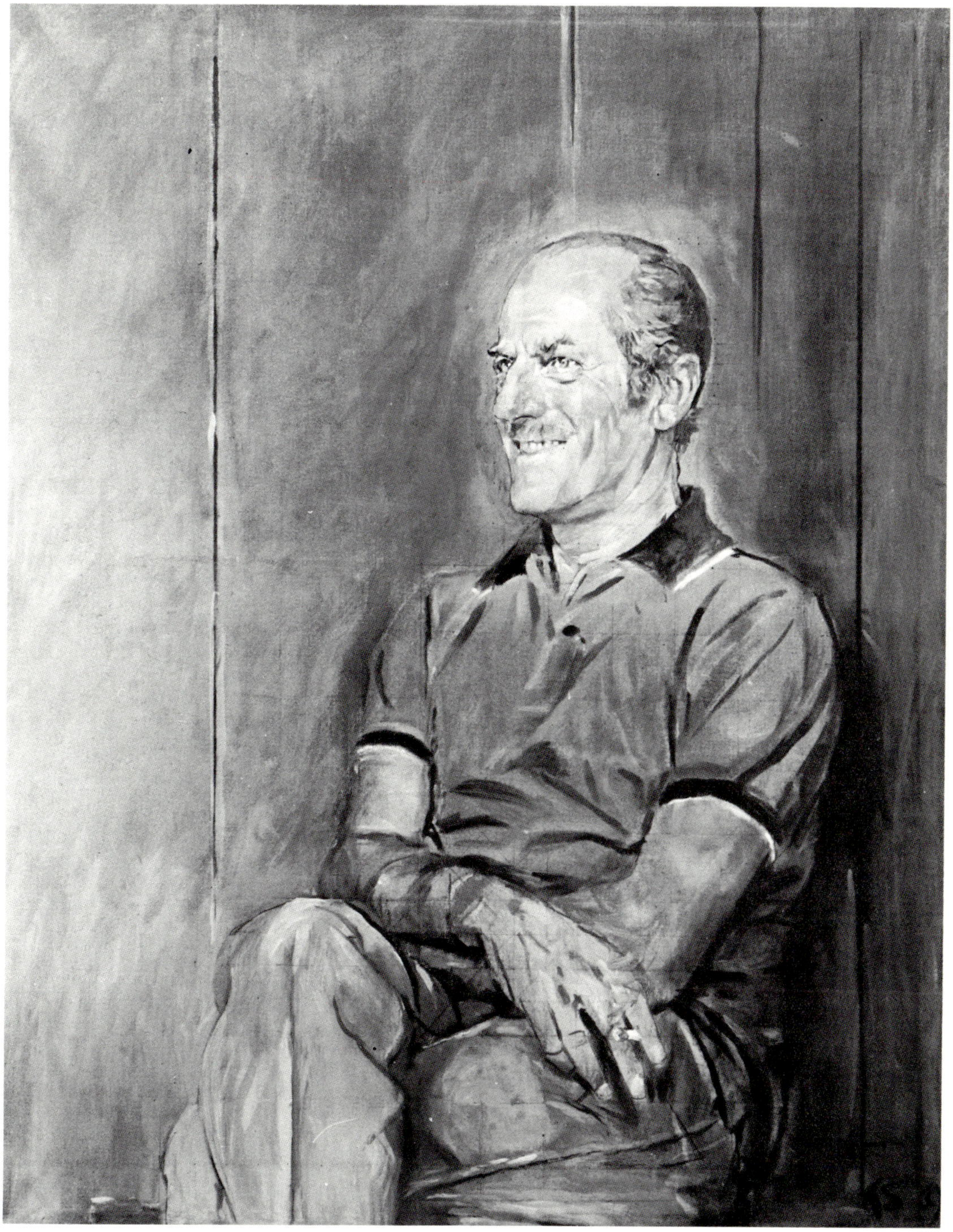

87

Dr Adolf Jann

Swiss; lawyer, banker and President of Hoffman-La Roche.

The commission was begun in January 1968 and completed in 1970.

88
Composition study
Gouache on card
$10\frac{3}{4} \times 8\frac{1}{2}$ (27.3 × 21.6)
Executed in 1968

This study for the definitive portraits shows the composition of both pictures broadly as finally completed but is directly related to the larger version (size $70\frac{1}{2} \times 55$ inches), which was painted first (this work is not included in the exhibition, but is reproduced as Figure 11). Compare No. 89.

Lent by Mrs Graham Sutherland

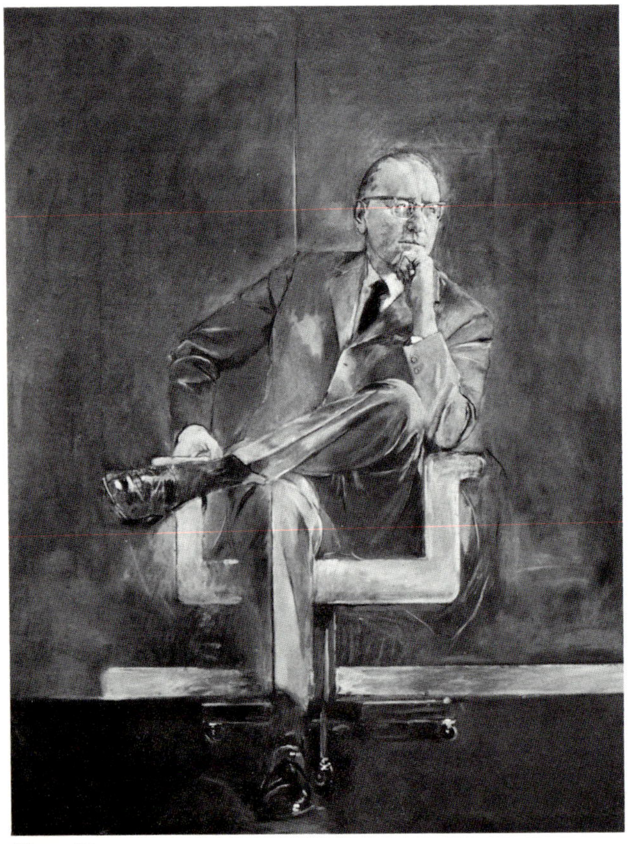

Figure 11
The definitive portrait of Dr Adolf Jann, 1969–70 (not included in the exhibition). See Nos. 88–92

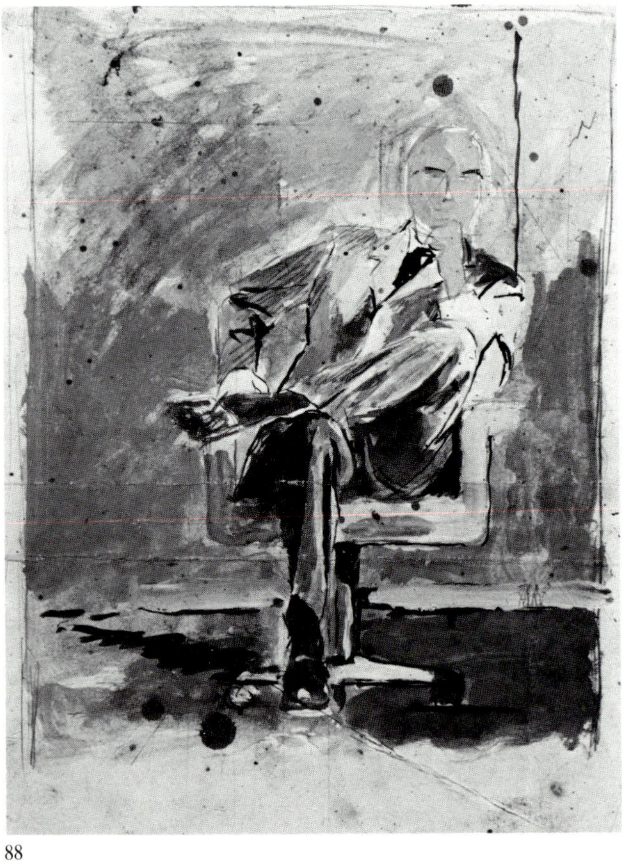

88

89
Composition study
Oil on hardboard
$24\frac{1}{16} \times 17\frac{7}{16}$ (61.1 × 44.3)
Size of the image $18 \times 14\frac{7}{8}$ (45.7 × 37.8)
Inscribed lower right:
G Suth . . . /Wrotham/27/9/6 . . .
Executed in 1968

This study for the first of the definitive portraits includes minor but significant alterations from the previous sketch (No. 88), and shows the composition as finally painted. The head is not seen frontally but turned slightly to the right, the right trouser is altered so that the crease forms an emphatic vertical linking the horizontals of the chair and the background bar below, and the swivel legs of the chair have been brought closer to this bar, thus further emphasising the foot. In the finished portrait (Figure 11) the background vertical line seen behind the sitter's left shoulder in the earlier study (No. 88) has been moved to an almost central position. The emphatic vertical of the right leg is comparable to the similar motif in the portrait of Lord Rayne (No. 85), and has precisely the same effect; in this case, however, the head and torso convey an impression of repose, and form a deliberate contrast to the powerful compositional lines which dominate the lower part of the canvas.

Lent by Mrs Graham Sutherland

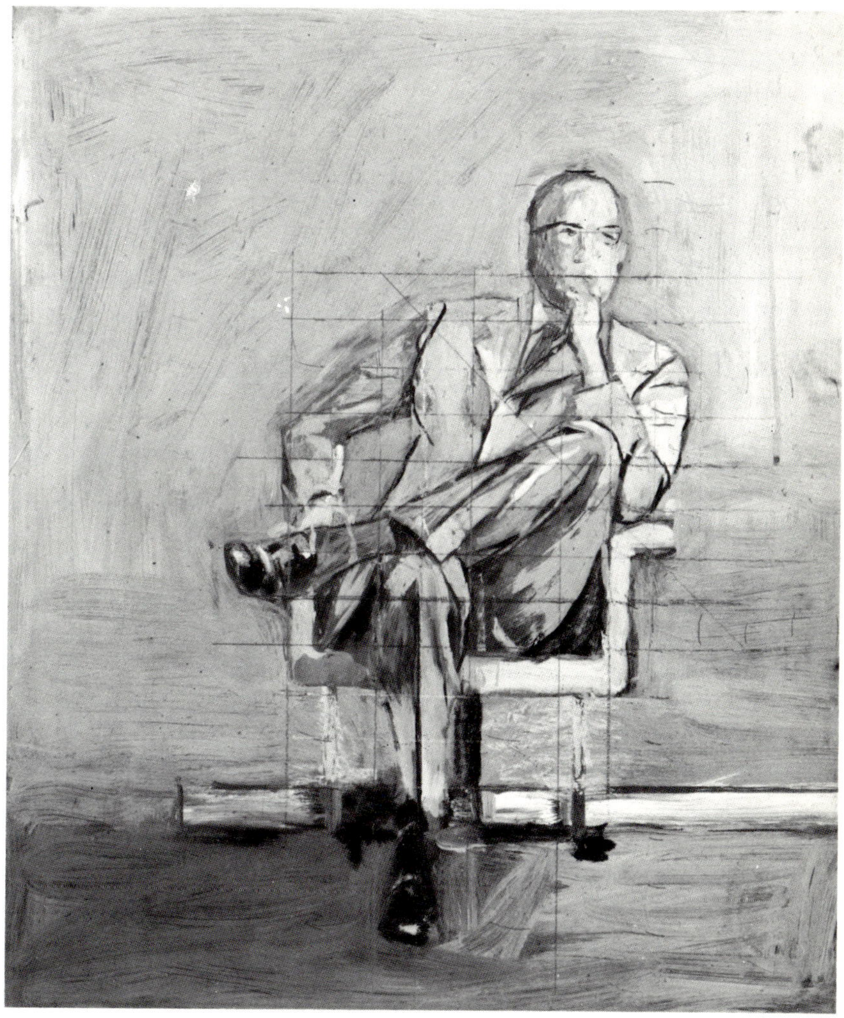

89 *detail*

90
Study of head facing slightly to right
Pencil, water-colour and gouache
$6\frac{15}{16} \times 6\frac{1}{2}$ (17.6 × 16.5)
Executed in 1968

A sensitive study of the head, drawn at a fairly advanced stage of work on the portrait, in which Sutherland is seeking to pin down the essence of the sitter's complexion as it altered under light and shadow and, in particular, the dramatic effect caused by the glint of the slightly tinted spectacles on the flesh tones round the eyes.

Lent by Mrs Graham Sutherland

91
Composition study
Gouache on cardboard
$23\frac{15}{16} \times 18\frac{3}{8}$ (60.8 × 46.7)
Size of the image 15 × 13 (38.1 × 33)
Executed in 1969

In this study for the second of the definitive portraits the sitter is leaning more to the right and his right leg has been shifted further to the left, thus masking one of the verticals of the chair, slight alterations in design which introduce a diagonal rhythm productive of a wholly different effect. Repose has become relaxation.

Lent by Mrs Graham Sutherland

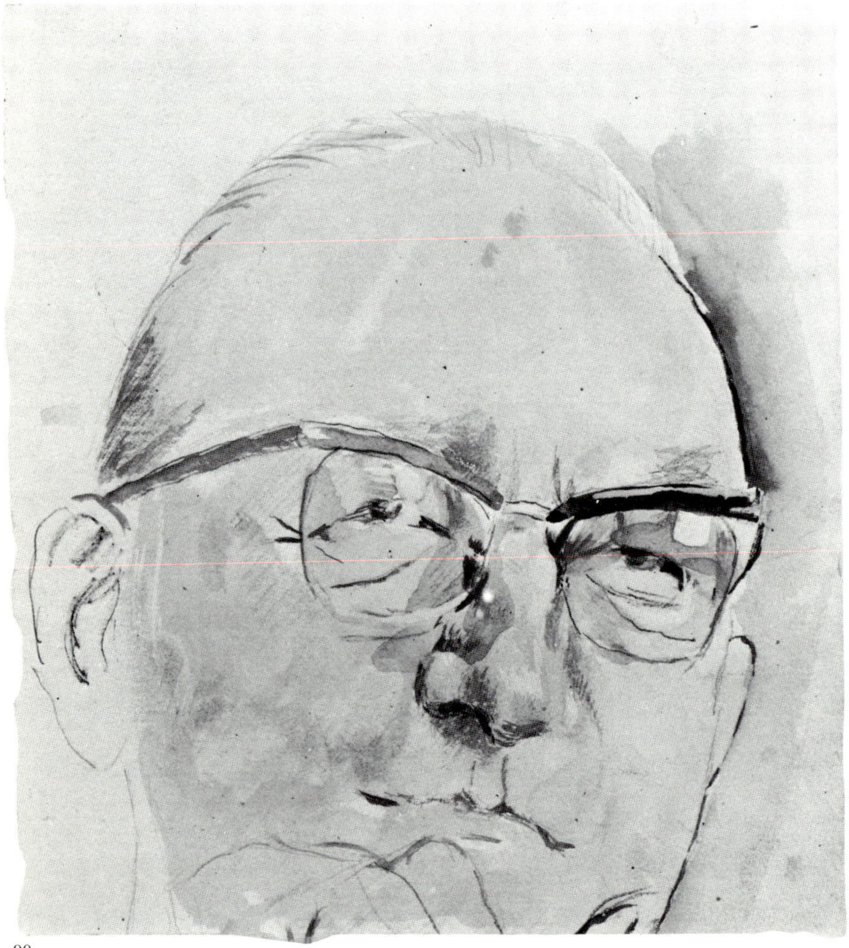

90

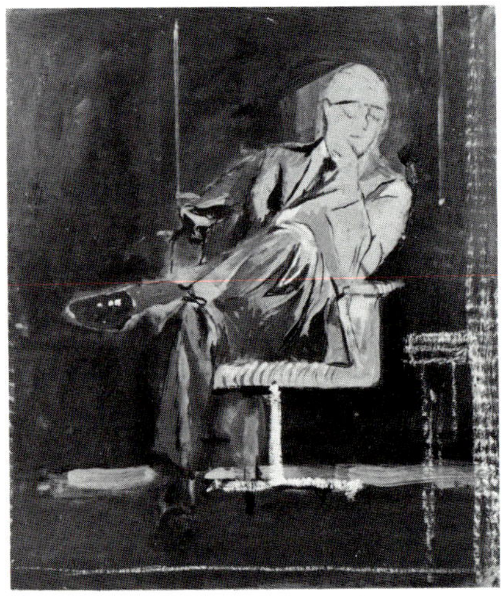

91 *detail*

92
One of the two definitive portraits
Oil on canvas
$49\frac{1}{2} \times 43\frac{5}{8}$ (125.7 × 110.8)
Signed and dated lower right:
Sutherland 1970
Dated and inscribed on the back:
ADOLPH|WALTER|JANN|1970–1971

In this portrait painted for the sitter's private collection Sutherland has concentrated, perhaps because of the smaller canvas, on the informal aspects of the original design, taking up the ideas developed in his fresh study (No. 91) and carrying them still further by 'moving in' upon the sitter. In the first place, the powerful compositional point and counterpoint of the lower part of the canvas has been abandoned and, in order not to reduce the scale of the figure, the right leg and left shoe have been truncated, thus bringing the sitter into closer contact with the spectator. Secondly, the rhythmical diagonal of the new sketch has been emphasised by abstract semicircular lines, only embryonic in the larger canvas, which contain the body within an oval and introduce an extraordinary sense of motion into the portrait, a motion no doubt suggested by the swivel chair; any sense of imbalance is held in check by the vertical line introduced on the extreme right. Sutherland's concern for mobility, expressiveness and structure is admirably held in balance in this superbly controlled image.

Lent by Dr Adolf Jann

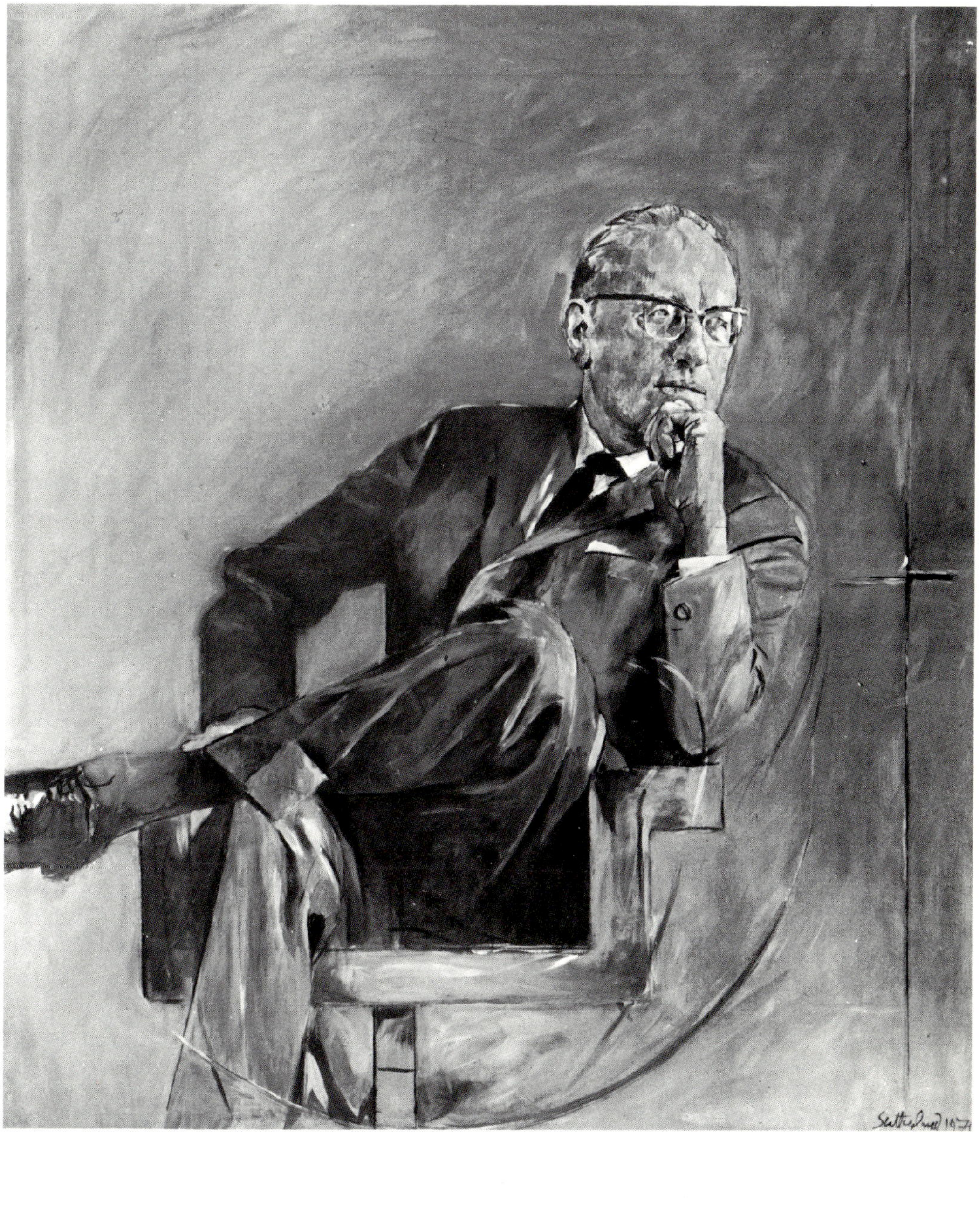

92

Giorgio Soavi

Italian; poet, novelist, designer and photographer.

The commission was begun in July 1968 and completed in August.

93
The definitive portrait
Oil on canvas
$47\frac{1}{4} \times 23\frac{5}{8}$ (120 × 60)
Signed and dated upper left:
G. Sutherland 1968
Signed, dated and inscribed on the back: *Depinta/con amore/G.S. 1968*

LITERATURE: Giorgio Soavi, *Protagonisti: Giacometti Sutherland de Chirico*, Milan, 1969, repr. p.162 (with photograph of the sitter posing).

A taut pose, emphasised by the set of the features and the placing of the lower parts of the legs, only the tips of the shoes touching the ground. The sitter had instinctively put his arms behind the chair, and this action, taken in conjunction with the milieu in which the sittings took place – a building, formerly the laundry of the Cipriani Hotel on the Giudecca, which, visually, resembled a prison – at once reminded Sutherland of Goya's drawings of prisoners. Hence the idea of tying the wrists (incidentally helpful to the sitter in maintaining the pose), which can be seen in the finished portrait. The idea for the background, which gives an impression of prison bars, thus taking the concept further, was suggested by the squares of the shining white tiles in the laundry building upon which the tonality is based.

Lent by Signor Giorgio Soavi

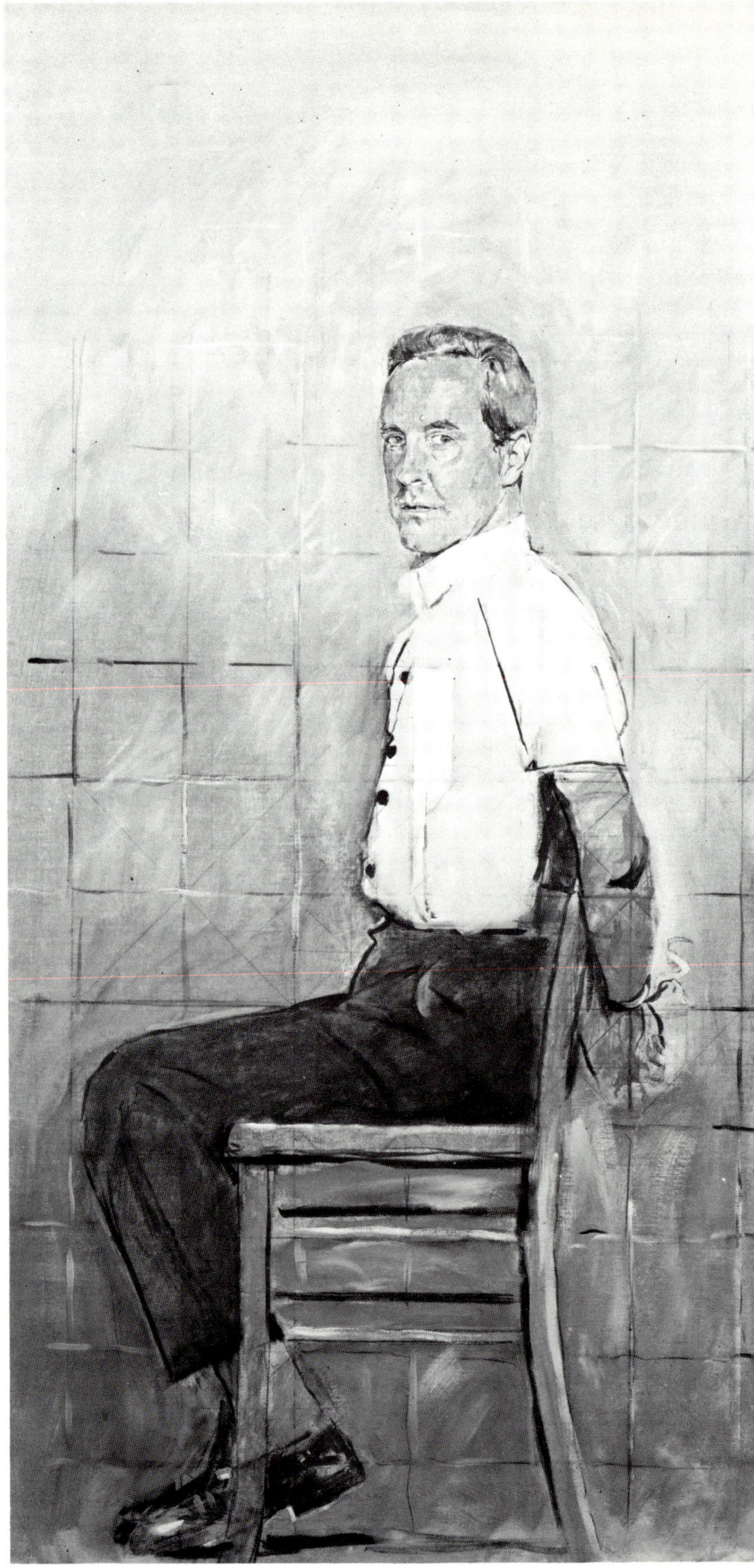

93

Mark Longman
1916–72

Publisher; Chairman of the National Book League.

The commission was begun in November 1968 and completed in 1970.

94
The definitive portrait
Oil on canvas
$56\frac{1}{2} \times 41\frac{1}{4}$ (143.5 × 104.8)
Signed and dated lower right: *G.S. 1970*

An elegant sitter who found it difficult to settle into an elegant pose, and who did not appear for sittings elegantly dressed: the white shirt, for instance, was too long. The design is extraordinarily rhythmical. Although the portrait is contained within a basic framework of verticals and horizontals – the verticals especially pronounced – the dominant rhythm is the serpentine movement of the arms (a variation on the similar motif in the portrait of Arthur Jeffress (No. 56)), and the sitter is shown as just about to speak. A strong impression of nervous vitality is suggested by the broken handling of the shirt and by the highlights flicked in round the outlines of the figure. Mobility, expression and structure are once again brilliantly held in balance.

Lent by the Longman Group

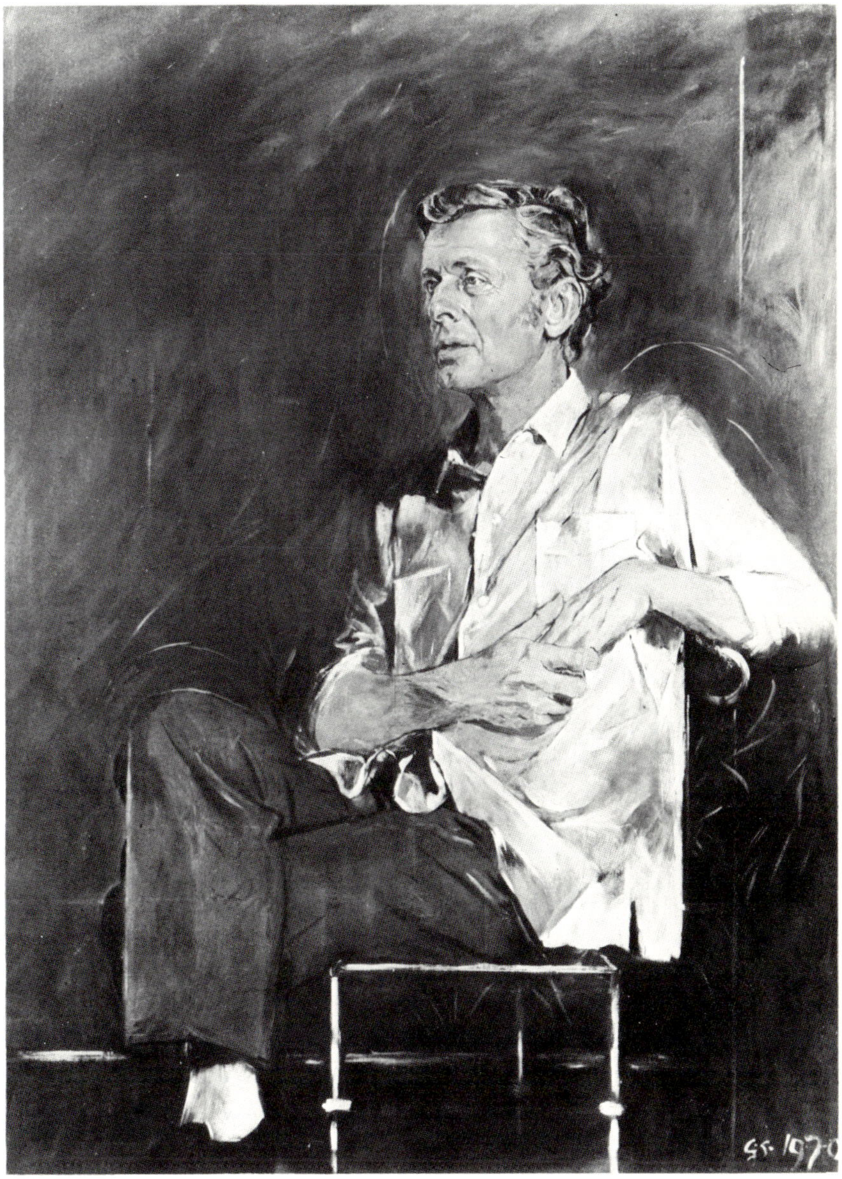

94

Lord Goodman, C.H.

Solicitor, administrator and diplomat; successively Chairman of the Arts Council and Master of University College, Oxford.

The commission was begun in April 1973 and completed in 1974.

95
Study of head facing half left
Pencil and water-colour
$13\frac{9}{16} \times 9\frac{5}{8}$ (34.5 × 24.5)
Executed in 1973

Study for the definitive portraits, in the pose as adopted.

Lent by Mrs Graham Sutherland

96
Study of head facing half left
Pencil and water-colour with some gouache
$13\frac{9}{16} \times 9\frac{5}{8}$ (34.5 × 24.5)
Executed in 1973

Study for the definitive portraits, in the pose as adopted. The ear is less fully modelled, but the nostrils are more accurately drawn, and the hair is shown as finally painted.

Lent by Mrs Graham Sutherland

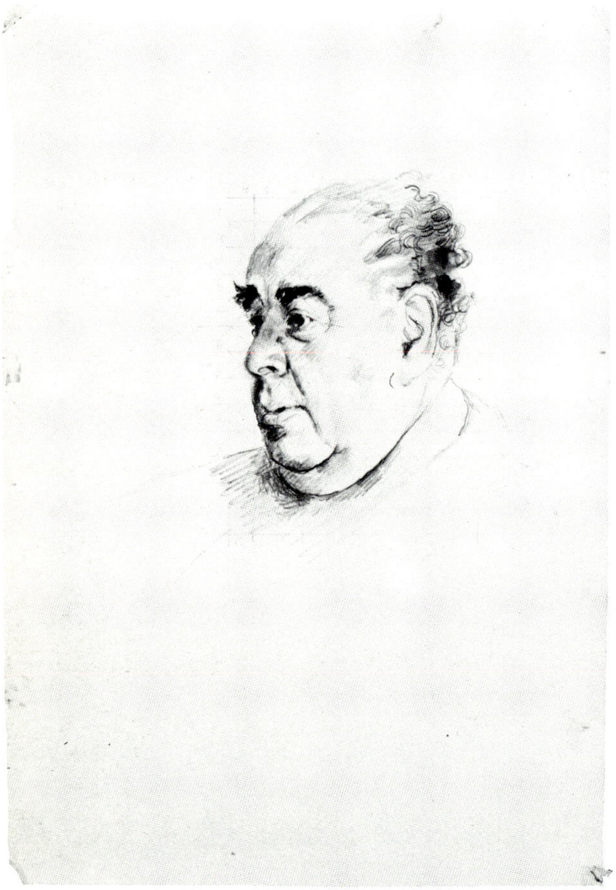

95

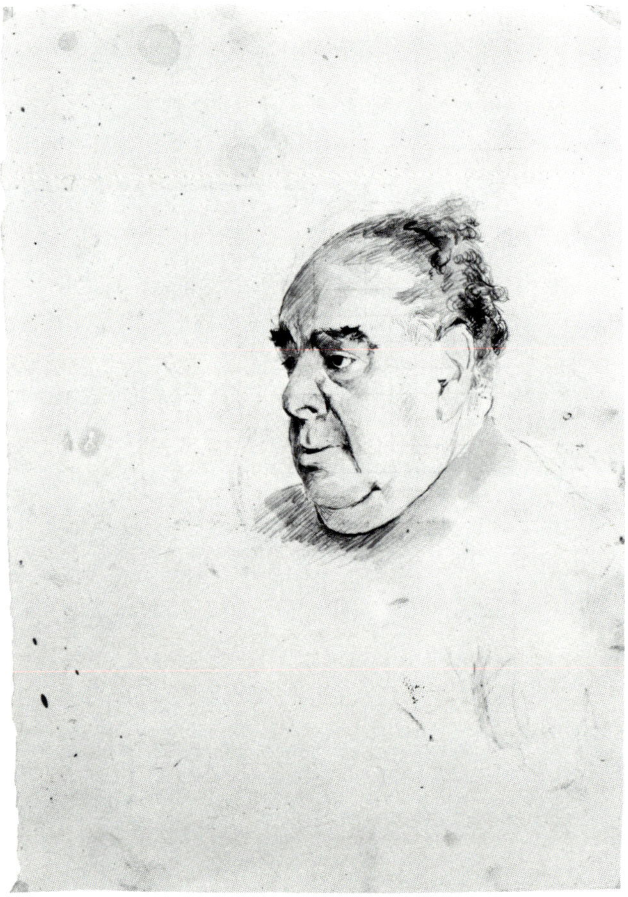

96

97

One of the two definitive portraits
Oil on canvas
$37\frac{3}{4} \times 37\frac{3}{4}$ (95.9 × 95.9)
Executed in 1973

LITERATURE: *Annual Report*, The Friends of the Tate Gallery, 1974–5, p. 23, repr. p. 22; Francesco Arcangeli, *Graham Sutherland*, New York, 1975, p. 41, plate 230; John Sunderland, *Painting in Britain 1525 to 1975*, London, 1976, p. 245, plate 218.

The bulk of Lord Goodman's gigantic frame is suggested not only by the pose, the threequarter view and the weight of the head sunk into the body, but by the choice of a square format for the composition and through placing the sitter low in the canvas. Notice the way in which the wide sleeve of the upper left arm, an essential element in the conception, tails off below the elbow. It is instructive to compare this composition with Ingres's solution for the portrait of Louis-François Bertin, now in the Louvre. Muted red suggested itself as the most appropriate background tone to serve as a foil to the sitter's complexion.

Lent by the Trustees of the Tate Gallery (T1880)

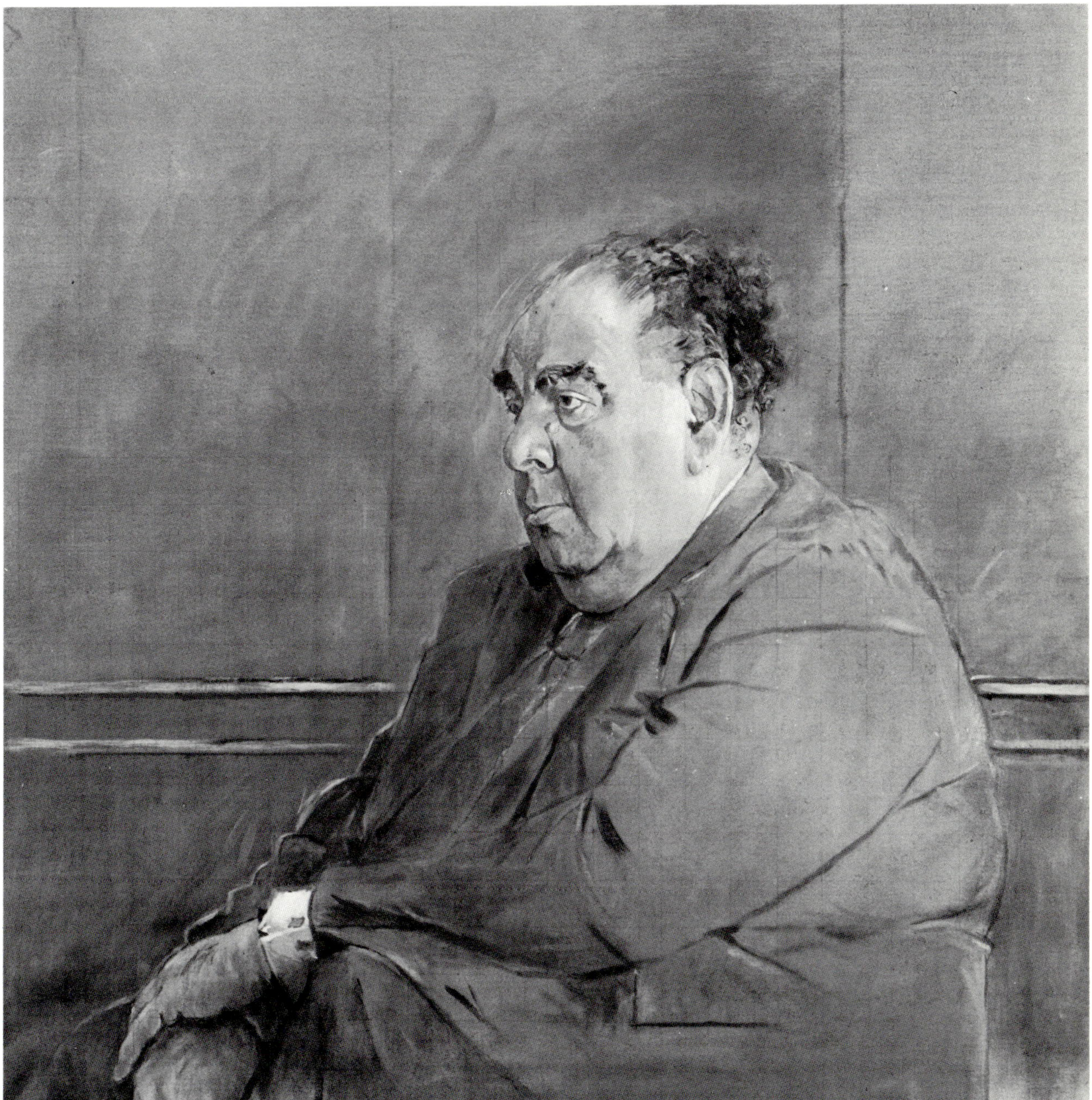

97

Lady Marion Philipps

Farmer, horticulturist and patron of the arts; married to the Lord Lieutenant of Pembrokeshire (Dyfed).

Private commission; the sittings took place in Menton in February and March 1974, and the painting was given to the sitter as a present in 1975.

98
The definitive portrait
Oil on canvas
$20\frac{7}{8} \times 19\frac{3}{4}$ (53 × 50.2)
Signed and dated lower right:
Sutherland/15.III 74

An exceptionally delicately painted portrait, in a high key, and set against a background of leaves. As in the case of the portrait of Lord Clark (No. 76), the inspiration is the tradition of fifteenth-century profile portraiture.

Lent by Lady Marion Philipps

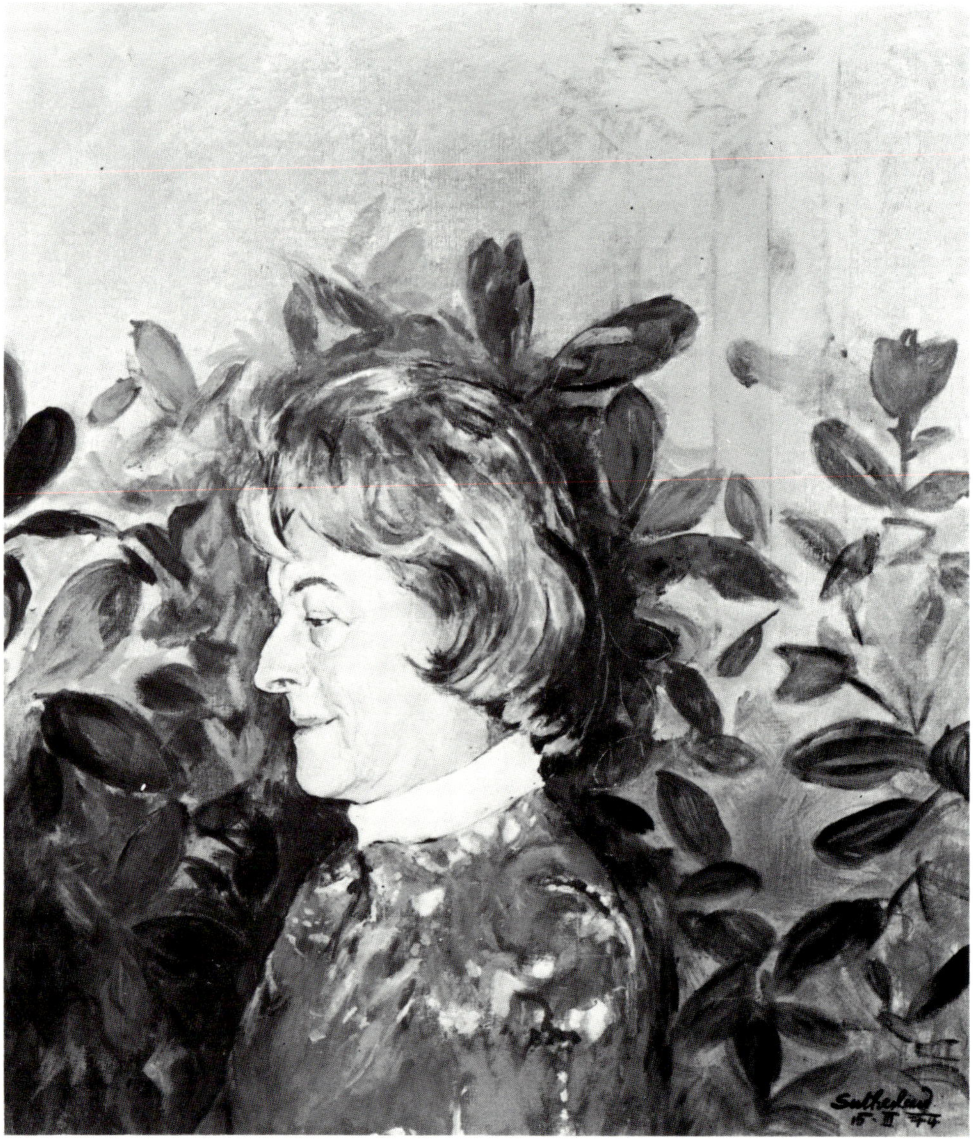

98

Pierre Schlumberger

French; geophysicist, formerly Chairman of Schlumberger Ltd; connoisseur and collector.

The commission was begun in February 1976 and completed in March.

99
The definitive portrait
Oil on canvas
$39\frac{1}{2} \times 38$ (100.3 × 96.5)
Signed and dated lower right:
G.S/1976

A brilliantly conceived, relaxed portrait in which the emphasis is concentrated on the hand holding the cigar and upon the head, characteristic and absolutely like in expression; the sitter is turning towards the spectator, genial and smiling, as though listening to something being said to him. The two elements suggesting the structure of the armchair are totally abstract, and a strip of green on the right, echoing the green coat worn by the sitter, stabilises the composition.

Lent by Monsieur Pierre Schlumberger

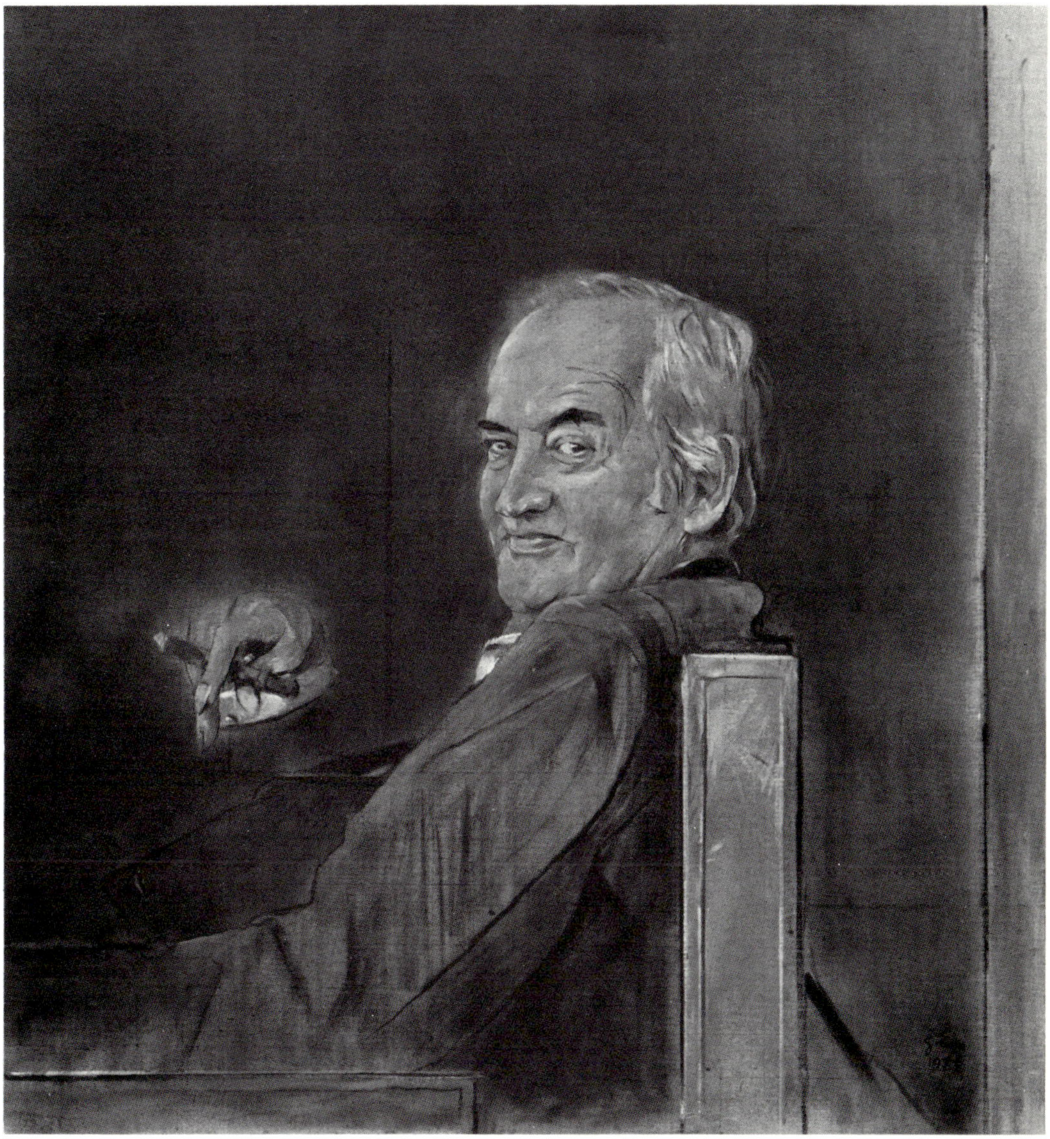

99

Sir Charles Clore

Financier; Chairman and Director of numerous companies engaged in commercial and industrial enterprises.

The commission was begun and completed in 1967. A further oil was executed recently.

100
Head and shoulders facing frontally
Oil on canvas
$18\frac{3}{4} \times 17\frac{3}{4}$ (47.6 × 45)
Executed in 1977

This canvas, based on the sketches made in 1967, but not in the pose of the definitive portrait, was painted for the artist's own satisfaction. It has not been possible, in view of its recent execution, to publish an illustration.

Lent by Mrs Graham Sutherland

Graham Sutherland, O.M.

Painter and printmaker; designer of the great tapestry for Coventry Cathedral.

101
Self-portrait
Oil on canvas
$20\frac{5}{8} \times 19\frac{7}{8}$ (52.5 × 50.5)
Signed and dated lower right: *G.S. 1977*

Graham Sutherland has been very reticent with regard to painting his own portrait. Apart from this recent canvas, there is only one self-portrait in oils extant, a representation of himself at the tables at the Casino in Monte Carlo. It has not been possible to illustrate this recently painted work.

Lent by Mrs Graham Sutherland

List of sitters

List of lenders

Back Cover
Extract from statement by Graham Sutherland published in *Eight European Artists,* photographed and edited by Felix H. Man, London, n.d. (=1954). By courtesy of Graham Sutherland, Felix H. Man and William Heinemann Ltd.